POLISH MIGRATION TO THE UK IN THE 'NEW' EUROPEAN UNION

Studies in Migration and Diaspora

Series Editor:
Anne J. Kershen, Queen Mary College, University of London, UK

Studies in Migration and Diaspora is a series designed to showcase the interdisciplinary and multidisciplinary nature of research in this important field. Volumes in the series cover local, national and global issues and engage with both historical and contemporary events. The books will appeal to scholars, students and all those engaged in the study of migration and diaspora. Amongst the topics covered are minority ethnic relations, transnational movements and the cultural, social and political implications of moving from 'over there', to 'over here'.

Also in the series:

Gendering Migration
Masculinity, Femininity and Ethnicity in Post-War Britain
Edited by Louise Ryan and Wendy Webster
ISBN 978-0-7546-7178-7

Contemporary British Identity
English Language, Migrants and Public Discourse
Christina Julios
ISBN 978-0-7546-7158-9

Migration and Domestic Work
A European Perspective on a Global Theme
Edited by Helma Lutz
ISBN 978-0-7546-4790-4

Negotiating Boundaries in the City
Migration, Ethnicity and Gender in Britain
Joanna Herbert
ISBN 978-0-7546-4677-8

The Cultures of Economic Migration
International Perspectives
Edited by Suman Gupta and Tope Omoniyi
ISBN 978-0-7546-7070-4

Polish Migration to the UK in the 'New' European Union
After 2004

Edited by
KATHY BURRELL
De Montfort University, UK

Routledge
Taylor & Francis Group

LONDON AND NEW YORK

First published 2009 by Ashgate Publishing

2 Park Square, Milton Park, Abingdon, Oxon OX14 4RN
711 Third Avenue, New York, NY 10017, USA

Routledge is an imprint of the Taylor & Francis Group, an informa business

First issued in paperback 2016

British Library Cataloguing in Publication Data
Polish migration to the UK in the 'new' European Union :
    after 2004. - (Studies in migration and diaspora)
    1. Polish people - Great Britain - Social conditions - 21st
    century 2. Alien labor - Great Britain - History - 21st
    century 3. Great Britain - Emigration and immigration -
    History - 21st century 4. Poland - Emigration and
    immigration - History - 21st century
    305.8'9185'041

Library of Congress Cataloging-in-Publication Data
Polish migration to the UK in the 'new' European Union : after 2004 / [edited] by Kathy Burrell.
       p. cm. -- (Studies in migration and diaspora)
    Includes bibliographical references and index.
    ISBN 978-0-7546-7387-3
    1. Poland--Emigration and immigration. 2. Great Britain--Emigration and immigration.
3. Alien labor, Polish--Great Britain. I. Burrell, Kathy.

    JV8195.P645 2009
    304.8'410438--dc22

                                                                    2008050817

ISBN 13: 978-0-7546-7387-3 (hbk)
ISBN 13: 978-1-138-25418-3 (pbk)

Contents

**PART II   EXPERIENCES OF IMMIGRATION
                 AND 'SETTLEMENT'**

List of Figures

List of Tables

Notes on Contributors

Emilia Brinkmeier is a doctoral candidate at the Institute of Social Studies and Centre for Migration Research, University of Warsaw. Her main interests are in the mechanisms and consequences of migration, processes of adaptation of immigrants and ethnic minority identities. She has published several papers on Polish migration in German, Polish and English, including a recent article in the *Journal of Ethnic and Migration Studies*.

Kathy Burrell is a Senior Lecturer in Modern History at De Montfort University, Leicester, UK. Her previous publications include *Moving Lives: Narratives of Nation* and *Migration among Europeans in Post-War Britain* (Ashgate, 2006) and edited with Panikos Panayi, *Histories and Memories: Migrants and their History in Britain* (I.B.Tauris, 2006), and articles in journals such as the *Journal of Material Culture* and *Mobilities*. She is currently researching Polish migration to the UK since the 1950s, concentrating on material culture and changing experiences of mobility.

Ayona Datta is a Lecturer in the Cities Programme, London School of Economics. Her research areas span architecture and urban design, human geography and gender studies. Her current research entitled 'Home-building, Migration and the City' explores how notions of home and the global city are shaped through the building acts of East European migrant workers arriving in London after 2004. She has published in several refereed journals such as *Urban Geography, Gender, Place and Culture, Cultural Geographies, Environment and Planning A, Antipode* and *Transactions of the Institute of British Geographers*.

Tim Elrick is currently completing his PhD on migrant entrepreneurship at the Free University of Berlin. He is a Social and Cultural Geographer and is working on labour migration, social in-/exclusion and social networks. He led the empirical part of the research on Polish and Romanian migration to Western Europe in the EU Marie Curie Excellence Grant project 'Expanding the Knowledge Base of European Labour Migration Policies (Knowmig)' at the University of Edinburgh. His recent publications include articles in *Europe-Asia Studies* and the *Journal of Ethnic and Migration Studies*.

Agnieszka Fihel is a PhD candidate at the Centre for Migration Research, Department of Economic Sciences, University of Warsaw. Her thesis examines women's roles in society, and she has also worked on two projects within the

Centre on migration within the expanded European Union and migration and community settlement.

Aleksandra Galasińska is a Research Fellow in European Studies at the University of Wolverhampton. Her current research interests focus upon the issues of the relationship between language/discourse and society and social identities, and in particular the extent to which communism as well as the economic, political and social transformations in the Central and Eastern Europe have contributed to 'post-communist' identity. Key publications include articles in the *Journal of Ethnic and Migration Studies* and *Narrative Inquiry*.

Paweł Kaczmarczyk is an Assistant Professor at the Faculty of Economic Sciences (Chair of Demography), University of Warsaw. He is the Head of the Central and East European Economic Research Centre (Warsaw University) and Joint Graduate Instruction Centre (Warsaw University and Warsaw School of Economics). His main research interests include the causes and consequences of international labour migration, migration and the labour market, and migration policy with a special emphasis on Central and Eastern Europe. He has published extensively on Polish migration.

Olga Kozłowska is a doctoral student in the History and Governance Research Institute (HAGRI), University of Wolverhampton. In her research she pursues the issue of discursive constructions of migration experiences among recent Polish migrants to the UK, specifically how these individuals deal with the reality of living and working in a host country. She is currently also working as a researcher in HAGRI on the experiences of child forced labourers in occupied Poland. Until recently she had been working in the Centre for Health and Social Care Improvement at the University of Wolverhampton on Polish migrants' mental health.

Ewa Mazierska, is a Reader in Contemporary Cinema at the University of Central Lancashire. Her research interests include European Cinema, including cinemas of Eastern Europe and British Cinema, representation of cities and travel in film, gender, and postmodernism in cinema. She has published extensively in the field, with her most recent book being *Women in Polish Cinema* (Berghahn, 2006).

Marta Rabikowska is a Senior Lecturer in Advertising and Media at the University of East London. Her research in consumption studies is focused on the notion of identity in relation to ethnicity and space. She is currently doing an ethnographic research on consumers' choices and retail space among different ethnic groups in London.

Louise Ryan is a Reader in Migration and Gender and the Co-Director of the Social Policy Research Centre. She has published widely on gender, ethnicity and Irish migration, and has just completed an ESRC funded project on Polish families in London – 'Recent Polish Migrants in London: Networks, Transience and Settlement' (RES-000-22-1552). Her most recent book is the co-edited (with Wendy Webster) volume *Gendering Migration: Masculinity, Femininity and Ethnicity in Post-war Britain* (Ashgate, 2008).

Rosemary Sales is a Professor of Social Policy at Middlesex University, whose interests focus on migration, citizenship and social exclusion. She has been researching Chinese and Polish migration to London, and was a joint grant holder for the 'Recent Polish Migrants in London: Networks, Transience and Settlement' project, funded by the ESRC. She has published extensively on migration, gender and policy.

Bernadetta Siara is a PhD candidate at City University London. She has previously worked on a research project on Polish families in London, and is furthering her research on Polish migration and gender relations during her PhD.

Maruška Svašek is a Lecturer in Social Anthropology at Queen's University Belfast. Her research interests are in emotions, migration, art, material culture and border issues, and she has published widely in these areas.

Mary Tilki is a Principal Lecturer in Health and Social Care at Middlesex University, and has research interests in migration, gender and ethnicity. She has recently researched Polish migrants as part of the ESRC funded project 'Recent Polish Migrants in London: Networks, Transience and Settlement'.

Anne White is a Senior Lecturer in Russian and East European Studies at the University of Bath. Her current research is focusing on social change and social inequality in Russia's regions, particularly on livelihood strategies, and migration and gender issues, principally Polish labour migration to the United Kingdom. She has published widely on Russian internal migration and civil society in Russia.

Acknowledgements

Firstly, I would like to thank the Historical Studies Research Committee at De Montfort University, and Jeff Hill especially, for helping to fund the conference, held in April 2007 at De Montfort, at which many of the chapters in this book were originally presented. I would also like to thank Andrea Jones for her invaluable help with the organization of this conference, and all the original conference participants for their contributions.

I am particularly indebted to Alison Stenning for her support of the book all the way through, and for her careful refereeing of the introductory chapter. I would also like to thank David McEvoy for his comments on Chapter 10. On a personal note I am grateful, as ever, to my parents for their encouragement and interest in the volume.

Finally, I would like to thank Matt for all his help with the technical side of the book, and for his phenomenal support throughout the project.

Series Editor's Preface

The Treaty of Accession[1] which came into operation on 1 May 2004 precipitated an unanticipated and unprecedented influx of immigrants to Britain. Originally the British government 'guesstimated' that the number of entrants would be low. This proved not to be not the case. In early spring 2008 a report published by the IPPR recorded the number of A8 immigrants in Britain as more than 765,000, two-thirds of whom were Polish.[2] In contrast, the report highlighted the fact that, with the economy in downturn, a reverse migration was taking place; some 250,000 short-term migrants had returned home – though this is not to say that there are not others arriving to take their place. Regardless of the variables, there is no doubt that Britain and Poland have experienced unusual, if not unique, flows of migration. It is a phenomenon which demands academic record and analysis.

In putting together this volume Kathy Burrell has set out to satisfy that demand by providing those engaged in studying migration with cutting edge accounts of the Polish migrant experience. The book fulfils the multi-disciplinary requirements of those working in migration and diaspora studies, bringing together cultural studies, economics, geography, health, history, linguistics and political science.

All too often migration studies are macro, or at best meso, focusing on the arrival and settlement of the actors, paying little attention to the places or people left behind. This volume corrects those imbalances. In the section of the book on Poland, we are not only made aware of the economic impact of emigration on the Polish economy and taken on a journey through the history of migration as portrayed in communist and post-communist Polish cinema; we are also presented with illuminating typologies of the emigrants, introduced to their diverse spatial and educational backgrounds, their expectations and the personal and household strategies employed to evaluate and initiate the migration process. The experience of immigration is approached from the grass roots upwards. Contributors provide personal accounts of the difficulties of being Catholic in sectarian Northern Ireland and of the networks that operate across Polish and British borders. In a pair of revealing chapters, readers are introduced to the place of gender in the migration experience. We learn of the idealized – and real – role of the female migrant and

---

1   The Eastern European countries which acceded were: Czech Republic; Estonia; Hungary; Latvia; Lithuania; Poland; Slovakia and Slovenia. At the same time Cyprus and Malta also became members of the EU, their nationals having the same rights as those of the old EU states.

2   Pollard, N. et al. (2008), *Floodgates or Turnstiles? Post-EU Enlargement Migration Flows to (and from) the UK* (London: Institute for Public Policy Research), 5.

of the promotion of Polish masculinity in an alien environment, as well as the way in which materialism is used to recreate home away from home.

It is not only the content of this book which makes it required reading, it is also the contributors: a number of whom are immigrants who have first hand experience of the issues which confront newcomer and outsider. But Burrell has done more than just facilitate the migrant in print; she has also opened the door to young academics, enabling them to publish alongside experts in their fields. By so doing she has put together a book which permits us to fully appreciate the implications of new and previously uncharted patterns of migration in the Europe of the 21st century.

Anne J. Kershen
Queen Mary University of London
2009

Introduction

Migration to the UK from Poland: Continuity and Change in East–West European Mobility

Kathy Burrell

It is almost impossible not to have noticed the profound impact that the 2004 enlargement of the European Union, with the ensuing movements of 'Accession 8' migrants, has had on migration patterns within Europe, and to the United Kingdom and Ireland in particular. From the perspective of the UK, not only have the demographic and geographic characteristics of new incoming migration shifted considerably (although not as much as popularly imagined), but public discourses of migration have similarly altered, leaving behind some of the intensity of hostility directed at 'asylum seekers' (see Kushner 2006), to rest instead on discussions of the new East European migrants, how long they will stay, and what impact they have had on economic growth and public services across the country. Indeed, the recent award of the 2008 Orange Broadband Prize for Women's Literature for *The Road Home*, Rose Tremain's novel about the life of Lev, a male Eastern European migrant in Britain, illustrates how much public interest there has been in this migration.

Among these new A8 immigrants to the UK, those coming from Poland have, arguably, been dominant – the most numerous, and certainly the most visible in the public arena. The Home Office's, admittedly flawed, figures suggest that a minimum of 540,000 Polish citizens have been working in the UK labour market since 2004 – 67 per cent of the total of migrants from the different A8 countries (Home Office 2008: 8).[1] Through a diverse selection of chapters from contributors representing a range of academic disciplines, this book will focus exclusively on these contemporary flows between Poland and the UK, considering a series of issues such as public discourses of emigration in Poland, migration strategies, gender relations, social networks and different political and commercial representations

---

1   As many of the chapters in this volume will also note, these Home Office figures record only registered workers, and so are undoubtedly an underestimation of the real number of new migrants. The Federation of Poles in Great Britain (FPGB) suggests using National Insurance Registration Figures, and quotes Polish Embassy estimates of over 600,000 new Polish migrants in Britain. See the FPGB website <http://www.zpwb.org.uk/4> accessed 5 September 2008.

of Polish populations in the UK. First, however, it is important to provide some historical and geopolitical context for this '2004 phenomenon' – how 'new' is this migration, and what is its wider significance for Europe?

Polish Emigration in Historical Perspective

Emigration from Poland has a long history, and outward migration has been a significant feature of the country's development in the modern era. In the nineteenth century especially, while the land that had formerly been Poland was partitioned under Prussian, Austrian and Russian rule (see Davies 1981), the scale and diversity of emigration was considerable. A growing national consciousness and cultural resistance to partition on the one hand established exile as an integral political tool of opposition, and placed it at the heart of the romantic literature of the era (see, for example, Adam Mickiewicz's epic *Pan Tadeusz* (1834)). Economic instability on the other, led to a steady exodus of Poles from the partitioned lands to the US, this time mainly people with peasant backgrounds hoping to earn enough to return again to buy land (see Thomas and Znaniecki 1918–20), and across Europe, to Germany especially (see Lucassen 2005). At the same time, Jewish emigration from this region rose steadily, triggered by the escalation of violent pogroms in the Russian Empire, but also by the severely limited economic opportunities that a generalized anti-Semitism across the Russian territories had produced. By 1914, over 3.5 million people had left the Polish lands (Iglicka 2001: 13), and this number continued to rise as economic problems beset the newly independent Polish state in the interwar period. While much of this migration proved to be long-term settlement migration, establishing a strong Polish infrastructure in the US especially (Znaniecka Lopata 1994), many of the closer range movements were traditionally cyclical and seasonal in nature, as with much of the shorter distance migration on the continent. Internally, there was also a significant level of population mobility, partly driven by border changes and attempts to repopulate the eastern reaches of the country with ethnically Polish settlers. By the Second World War, Poland had built up a multi-faceted trajectory of mobility, with strong internal and external migratory links, and an enduring tradition of emigration.

As has been widely acknowledged, the outbreak of war in 1939 heralded a dark new era of population movement in Poland; this time, civilian mobility was driven principally by forced and brutal displacement and deportation, with the bulk of the country's armed forces having to re-form outside of Poland, fighting with the Allied war effort (see Lane 2004; Burrell 2006a). At the end of the war it was clear that those who had been displaced, and had survived, faced a choice of returning to a country which was now under Soviet influence, or remaining outside of the country's new borders, joining, and refashioning, the established Polish diaspora. In Britain, the decision to allow Polish soldiers to demob and settle (see Zubryzcki 1956), alongside the policy of bringing in displaced people from the labour camps of Europe to fill labour shortages (Tannahill 1958; Kay and Miles 1992) established, essentially for the first time, a sizeable ethnic Polish 'community' in the country, peaking at over 160,000 (Burrell 2006a: 5). This new refugee population, however, was global in its geographic reach, with wartime Polish emigrants scattered as far apart as the US and Canada, Australia and Kazakhstan. If previous waves had been largely economically motivated, with a substantial part of population mobility being short-term movements, this post-war settlement was palpably different – long-term, and struggling with the political and emotional ramifications of exile (see Jaroszyńska-Kirchmann 2004; Burrell 2006b).

The nature of outward migration changed again with the establishment of the communist regime after the war had ended. While the immediate post-war years witnessed chaotic population movements – expulsions and 'resettlements' of Germans and Ukrainians (Kurcz 2000; Babinski 2000), the repopulation of returnees from Soviet territories, and the 'internal' resettlement of Poles from lost lands in the east (such as Lwów) to newly gained territory in the west (such as Wrocław) – the defining characteristic, at least superficially, of Poland under communism was international immobility. Potential movement outside of the country was highly politicized; while there was relative freedom of travel within the Eastern bloc, and even though Poland was the most liberal communist country on this issue (Cyrus 2006: 33), people could not keep their passports at home for most of the duration of the regime, and 'going west' hinged on governmental permission, secured usually only through invitations, student places and specific job offers (see Burrell 2008a; Burrell 2008b).

Nevertheless, and as Iglicka (2001) chronicles extensively, after 1956, when there was some relaxation in mobility stipulations, there was considerable emigration under communism. Those with German ancestry were able to move to West Germany with *Aussiedler* status, increased anti-Semitism in 1968 especially triggered the emigration of thousands of Jewish Poles (Wolak 2004), people left to join family or get married abroad, and the political upheaval of the 1980s led to large-scale waves of emigration, predominantly permanent movements to the US (see Erdmans 1998). That same decade also saw increased short-term, and usually covert, labour migration to Germany, arguably a direct continuation of previous mobility trends. So while emigration was not officially sanctioned, over two million Polish people left Poland in the 1980s (Iglicka 2001: 24). The UK was not a major recipient of this emigration, but flows of migration were sustained between the two countries, with Sword (1996) suggesting that between several hundred and a few thousand Polish people came to the UK each year after 1956, gaining momentum in the 1980s. With this new migration, the dynamics of the established Polish population altered slightly; although the newcomers did not have an enormous impact on the infrastructure of the 'community', the different historical backgrounds of the migrants and the settled refugees led to some tensions, at least at a local level (see Burrell 2008c).

1989 and 2004: Shifting East–West Geopolitics and Mobility

The fall of communism in 1989 undoubtedly signalled a fundamental change in both Poland's migration profile and the wider balance of movement within Europe. With official barriers to outward migration gone, Poland's population was free again to leave in order to live and work abroad, and, crucially, to return afterwards (see Iglicka 2001: 28). While 1989 clearly marked a new era in Polish emigration, however, much of the post-socialist migration movements appear to be continuations of previously established trends. As Wallace (2002) argues, the post-1989 period witnessed an intensification of short-term, circular, movements – what she terms mobility rather than migration – with Germany remaining as a key destination. This rise in short-term movements was, nevertheless, accompanied by a corresponding fall in permanent emigration (Cyrus 2006: 38), fuelling the feeling that Europe as a whole had become much more fluid, and that the old rules and understandings of migration within the continent were being rewritten.

The liquidity of these post-socialist population movements has received considerable academic attention, with numerous studies addressing the newness of these East–West movements, alongside other changing dynamics such as the development of Southern Europe as a receiving rather than sending region of migration (see for example King 1993a; King 1993b; Wallace and Stola 2001; Górny and Ruspini 2004). Individual ethnographic studies, such as Kopnina's (2005) work on Russian migrants in London and Amsterdam, have further added to the story of Europe, even before 2004, as a continent in the middle of a new era of interior mobility. For Polish migration in particular, great emphasis has been placed on the increasing diversity of destination countries in the sights of Polish migrants. Iglicka (2001: 47) notes that Italy and Greece were already established as places to work in the 1980s, becoming more firmly entrenched as destinations in the 1990s, and Triandafyllidou (2006) especially illuminates the experiences of Poles across Europe, in the UK, Germany, Italy and Greece. Other work focuses on the Polish presence in cities such as Brussels (see Grzymała-Kazłowska 2005), while the gendered nature of Polish migration movements has been studied, illustrating in particular the roles of East European female migrants in sustaining migration networks in Western and Southern Europe, often working in the domestic and care work sectors (see Coyle 2007; Hellermann 2006; Guzik 2005; and more generally Anthias and Lazaridis 2000).

There are two points to make about this apparent explosion in mobility within Europe in the latter stages of the twentieth century. The first is tied closely to Fortier's (2006) assertion that Europe itself can be imagined through its migration flows – that the identity of the continent is, to some extent, represented and reflected in the movement of bodies within it, and the ways in which these bodies are regulated. It is tempting to link the increased freedom of movement of Eastern Europeans with the various commentaries about the 'return to Europe' of former Eastern bloc countries, and the perceived temporal and spatial journeys that these post-socialist states have been embarking on to move back into the European fold

– as if they had not previously been 'properly' European – and reconfigure the geopolitical shape of Europe once again (see Hagen 2003). As Burroway and Verdery argue (1999: 4), the widely accepted concept of post-socialist 'transition' implies, often misleadingly, that these countries are transforming from something old into something new and better, following a linear time-line of progression so that they will eventually come to better match the norms of (Western) European countries.

This is certainly a narrative that many post-socialist countries have themselves embraced; Ziegler (2002: 680) notes that Poland enthusiastically emphasized a 'new' cartographical positioning in Europe after 1989, issuing maps which depicted Poland with close geopolitical ties to Europe, rather than Eastern or even Soviet Europe: 'New maps showed Poland either alone or in a European context, cropped to give the country a more central position on the mental map it wanted to sear into the world's collective consciousness'. Hagen (2003) similarly highlights the increased usage of the terms '*Mitteleuropa*' and more particularly 'Central Europe', as vehicles for redefining the western positioning of several former Eastern bloc countries. In this new 'restored' Europe, the increased movement of Europeans could be regarded as a physical embodiment of the joining of East and West, the connections literally being made by the traversing journeys of Central European migrants. It has to be noted, too, that this geopolitical reimagining of Europe was also accompanied by a significant shrinkage in the practical size of the continent, with the Internet, more accessible travel and the low-cost air travel industry creating, by the end of the century, considerable time–space compression which could only make the migration and transnational projects of would-be migrants easier.

While powerful and beguiling, however, the gap between this rhetoric and the reality of a 'returned' Europe is the second point to address. No amount of European rebranding could disguise the underlying inequalities among European citizens in the new Europe. The divide between East and West was clearly still visible after 1989, not just in the economic upheaval witnessed by the post-socialist countries, but also in the persistence of entrenched, and arguably post-colonial (see Fortier 2006: 318), discourses of the 'backwardness' of Eastern Europe, and in the treatment and experiences of those testing the limits of the new Europe themselves. Equality of mobility was certainly not achieved, and the different national borders continued to act as significant barriers to those moving. It may have been easy to leave countries such as Poland, but entering other countries was still dependent on visa arrangements and the discretion, labour market policies and migrant worker recruitment schemes of national governments – the UK's Seasonal Agricultural Workers Scheme (SAWS), which brought several thousand East European and Baltic migrants to the UK to undertake agricultural work, being a good example (see Taylor and Rogaly 2004: 12; Stenning et al. 2006). Outside of schemes like these, significant obstacles to international travel persisted, not least due to the high costs – often financially prohibitive – that Polish citizens faced in order to go abroad (see Stenning 2005: 124). The actual qualitative experience of travel in Europe for East Europeans, therefore, had not improved as much as imagined, with non EU members still limited in their potential movements and segregated at borders, answering uncomfortable questions about their intentions in the western nations (see Verstraete 2003; Burrell 2008b).

This multi-tiered nature of the new Europe inevitably shaped the work experiences of these post-socialist Polish migrants (see Wallace 2002: 615), and much of the research on Polish migrants in Europe during this period has highlighted the clandestine nature of some working practices, or at least more generally illustrates the vulnerability of the migrants in their chosen countries (see Triandafyllidou 2006). In the UK, Jordan (2002) and Düvell (2004) found that undocumented Polish migrants' social networks were restricted by their legal status and in their sample several respondents had been exploited in their workplaces, although others in their research had legal papers and some were running their own businesses. Migrants' narratives from this era do tend to emphasize the issue of legality, border checks and difficulties accessing mainstream services such as bank accounts (see Coyle 2007: 38). Judged by the migration experiences of its population at any rate, the 'return to Europe' of Poland had not yet been completed by the start of the twenty-first century.

If 1989 was only partly a revolution in East European migration, then perhaps 2004 has delivered a more satisfactory watershed in the continent's migration trajectory. Certainly 2004 has been heralded as a profound moment; as Favell (2008: 702) argues, 'Borders are coming down, and a new European migration system is being established on the continent'. Internal European migrants can now be considered as 'free movers', rather than immigrants (Favell 2008: 703). It must be noted too that 2007 has further cemented these changes, with the year opening with the accession of Romania and Bulgaria to the EU, and closing with the truly historic extension of the Schengen agreement to the former Eastern bloc countries. Europe, now, needs to move away from traditional understandings of migration as being something almost exclusively associated with decades of guest-worker models and post-colonial labour forces, and, as Favell suggests, learn from the US/Mexico scenario, where local economic asymmetry ensures that migration is driven by regional dynamics – although arguably this *is* something the UK is already familiar with because of its long-standing history of Irish immigration. However Europe approaches its new migration system, it is undeniable that the qualitative experiences of travel and migration have for many East Europeans been transformed. Just how far this transformation reaches is open to debate – not all Europeans are 'free movers', not all countries are allowing free settlement, and EU membership still excludes as much as includes (see Jileva 2002). For Polish migration specifically, though, and in particular from the point of view of the UK, 2004 has indeed been a watershed moment in history.

After 2004: Polish Migrants in the United Kingdom

Having been one of the largest immigrant groups in the immediate post-war, pre-commonwealth migration period in the UK, since 2004, Polish nationals have once again become a statistically significant ethnic minority population, and appear to be one of the fastest growing migrant populations in the country. The figures suggested by the Worker Registration Scheme – over 540,000 – are all the more important when they are considered in the context of other historical migration movements to the UK. Counting only first generation migrants, as the WRS has since 2004, the 2001 UK census enumerated 466,000 people born in India, 321,000 born in Pakistan, 255,000 in the Caribbean and 154,000 in Bangladesh (Kyambi 2005: 76–80, 96). While these different populations are much larger when considering second and third generations, this does illustrate that the scale of A8 migration, from Poland especially, marks an important shift in the UK's migration profile. The fact that this migration has occurred over such a short period of time, and has become so visible so quickly – in the press and on local landscapes through shops and businesses – also marks this movement out as new. This migration, furthermore, has been distributed very widely across the UK. Home Office (2008) figures indicate that the Anglia and the Midlands regions have attracted the greatest numbers of A8 migrants, and again, while this does not take into account unregistered migrants, who make up a significant component of London's migrant population in particular, it does underline just what an impact this migration has had on the UK as a whole (see also Stenning and Dawley 2009).[2] It is difficult to think of another migrant group which has established itself so quickly, and so widely, in British history (for more on this see Holmes 1988; Panayi 1994, 1999).

Of course, Polish, and A8, migration to the UK has not been taking place in a vacuum. London, especially, has witnessed phenomenal growth in immigration levels in the last two decades, with the city now almost entirely dependent on immigrant labour to function (see Datta et al. 2006). Other new migrations have been taking place too, from different African nations, from Latin America (McIlwaine 2007), increased flows from China, and highly skilled and young migration flows from France, Australia, New Zealand and South Africa especially (Kyambi 2005). In 2001, the number of people born in France living in the UK was 94,000, while those born in Australia was 106,000 – both populations which had grown considerably in the previous decade (Kyambi 2005: 46, 113). Outside of London there have also been important transformations; the rural labour force (fruit picking for example) is arguably as dependent on foreign labour as the capital. It took the tragedy of the deaths of 23 Chinese migrants working as cockle pickers

---

2   These regions are Post Office categories which do not exactly match the UK Government's defined regions (again see Stenning and Dawley 2009). Anglia, however, can be loosely defined as 'East England' and includes the main urban areas of Norwich, Peterborough, Ipswich, Chelmsford, Cambridge, Northampton and Lincoln.

at Morecambe Bay to draw attention to the presence of this labour force in the UK, but many academic studies have been focusing on the work and lives of these migrant populations outside metropolitan areas (see Taylor and Rogaly 2004).

However, it has been this A8 migration which has attracted the most sustained press interest, locally and nationally. Research by Fomina and Frelak (2008) into the tone of this coverage found it to range widely between depicting the newcomers as good workers who will aid the UK economy, through to reinforcing stereotypical images of Eastern European migrants as a frightening foreign other, bringing odd cultural traits, pushing up crime rates and exhausting local services. While this report does not necessarily accentuate the negative aspects of recent press coverage – claiming for example that 'the language [used in newspapers] should not be considered as deliberately discriminatory against Poles' (Fomina and Frelak 2008: 74) – it is instructive to follow the exchanges which have been made between the *Daily Mail*, and, more recently, *The Times* newspapers, and the Federation of Poles in Great Britain (FPGB) which has lodged formal complaints against both papers' coverage of recent Polish immigration – exchanges which have been brokered by the Press Complaints Commission.[3] For example, in February 2008 the FPGB claimed that the *Daily Mail*'s

> headlines and lead paragraphs contain emotional phrases likely to evolve a resentful response from a reader and the *Mail* has managed consistently to eke out the negative story where possible. We even have an example earlier this month where a *Daily Mail* feature writer was offering £100 'for anonymous horror stories of people who have employed Eastern European staff, only for them to steal from them, disappear, or have lied about their resident status'.[4]

Coupled with other press coverage which notes the hostility directed at new East European migrants, these issues raise important questions about how well received this new migration has really been.[5] The presumed cultural capital that comes with being white and Christian has not prevented discrimination and exploitation – indeed, the work of US ethnic historians should remind us that 'whiteness' is a mutable category, and that newcomers, regardless of their physical colour, are not usually readily accepted as 'white', and all that this label entails (see Ignatieve 1995; Roediger 2005).

---

3   See the Federation of Poles in Great Britain website, where these issues, and the various press releases, have been recorded, most recently in the 'current matters' section: <http://www.zpwb.org.uk/en/Current_Matters> accessed 5 September 2008. This has been documented especially well by the *Guardian*'s Media coverage: <http://www.guardian.co.uk/media/2008/aug/05/dailymail.pressandpublishing1> accessed 5 September 2008.

4   See http://www.zpwb.org.uk/3, accessed 5 September 2008.

5   See for example the *Guardian*'s piece (Jones, 2008) on one man being driven out of his Salford home for having a Polish girlfriend and Slovakian lodger.

This media interest has, not surprisingly, been accompanied by close academic scrutiny too. Four inter-related themes seem to have emerged: first, migration motivations; second, a continued interest in whether these flows constitute temporary or permanent migration; third, experiences of work; and fourth, life beyond the workplace. This first theme covers a vast array of academic research, starting with the careful documentations of change and transition, poverty and loss of political trust in post-socialist Eastern Europe by geographers and anthropologists (for example, Burawoy and Verdery 1999; Lovell 2001; Fodor 2002; Stenning 2005; Buzar 2007). It is this work, and other research like it, which enables the background to emigration in the post-socialist era to be fully understood. The focus on the economically driven nature of this migration has been strong; many researchers have highlighted, for example, the high levels of unemployment in Poland – 20 per cent in 2003 (Drinkwater et al. 2006: 2) – to explain these trends. The role of the UK labour market, in opening its doors to new migrants, has also been widely recognized as the fundamental factor in contemporary migration flows (for example, see Pollard et al. 2008).

Interestingly though, other, non-economic motivations for migration have also been studied – something which White's and Galasińska and Kozłowska's chapters explore in depth in this volume. With young people being identified as the most significant demographic component of this new migration, the aspiration of youth has been closely considered. Fabiszak (2007) sees much of this migration as something akin to 'gap year' travel, and Eade et al. (207: 34) have asserted that many of these younger, often highly skilled migrants, can be termed 'searchers', migrating as much for new experiences and skills, as the economic needs of employment. Datta (2007) has further added to this argument, investigating the growing 'cosmopolitanism' of young London-based Poles.

While there has been broad agreement on what is driving this migration, the issue of whether it will be short or long-term has proved to be more complex. Most assumptions have been that this migration is, and will continue to be, temporary. Certainly earlier work predicted short-term flows (Wallace 2002), and this seems borne out to some extent by the recent Institute for Public Policy Research report *Floodgates or Turnstiles?* (Pollard et al. 2008), which shows that not only are numbers now falling, but that more people are returning to Poland. However, as Ruhs (2005: 25) has noted, this issue is not necessarily so clear cut, and there is strong evidence – also demonstrated in several of the chapters in this volume – to suggest that at least a significant proportion of the new migrants plan to stay for a long time. In their research, Eade et al. (2007) identified a diverse range of migrants with equally varying intentions – 'storks' (circular migrants), 'hamsters' (those working to be able to go back with some savings), the aforementioned 'searchers' and, crucially, 'stayers'. As Spencer et al. (2007: 77) have pointed out, migrants' intentions about their lengths of stay actually change over time; it will take a few more years yet to fully grasp the temporal patterns of this migration.

As indicated, work has also been an important focus in A8 migration research. These newcomers have been depicted largely as economic migrants, so employment has understandably been central to their lives in the UK. One important strand of research has focused on the wider structure of the labour force (Stenning et al. 2006) – perhaps not surprisingly, employers have been found to be in the most advantageous position in this 'new' labour market (see Ruhs 2006: 17), using the new flexible supply of labour to plug shortages relatively cheaply. Studies of migrants' actual experiences of work have been crucial in grounding A8 migration research too. The Joseph Rowntree Foundation *Fair Enough?* report (Anderson et al. 2006), for example, noted that A8 migrants are facing variable conditions in the workplace, that they are more likely to be in temporary jobs, and have working rights that are more weakly protected when compared to UK citizens. More in-depth studies, such as Janta's (2007) research on Polish migrants in the hospitality sector – which demonstrates the coping mechanisms of different workers as they struggle in their jobs – reinforces the sense that working conditions can be very tough. While there is evidence of migrants 'trading up' jobs over time, and it is clear that the employment opportunities of those who were already working in the UK before 2004 vastly improved with EU accession (Anderson et al. 2006), some studies highlight the mismatch between the often highly qualified migrants and their low-skilled jobs (Pollard et al. 2008: 37), an issue which Fihel and Kaczmarczyk explore in this volume.

Finally, the worlds of the migrants outside of the workplace have been addressed too. The Joseph Rowntree Foundation, for example, has focused on 'wellbeing' more generally, highlighting, among other issues, the poor, but improving, housing conditions faced by the new migrants (Spencer et al. 2007: 48). Osipovic (2008) also considers the migrants' vulnerability in their new country, arguing that the legal position of A8 immigrants is actually quite complex, and that many new migrants, despite being EU citizens, remain unaware of their rights, within and without the workplace. Other research paints a more positive picture – of growing interaction with the 'wider society' over time (Spencer et al. 2007: 58), and of strong social networks being established between different migrants themselves – a theme which Ryan et al. consider in this volume (see also Garapich 2008). Although other studies have drawn attention to the antagonism Poles especially seem to show towards other Poles (Garapich 2007), there is still strong evidence to suggest that migrants are making 'homes' in the UK quite successfully (for example Metykova 2007; Parutis 2007; Rabikowska and Burrell, this volume).

Accompanying this work has also been a series of local studies, considering the impact of Polish migration in specific areas. While London has been the focus for many research projects (Ryan et al. and Datta, this volume; Eade et al. 2007), work has been undertaken across the whole country, grounding the impacts and experiences of the new migrants on a local scale. Stenning et al. (2006), for example, have looked in-depth at the A8 immigration dynamics in Newcastle and Peterborough, analysing local labour markets, the various policy responses of the local authorities to the new migration, and the social lives of the migrants as they build social networks in their new environments. It is especially important to note the work on Peterborough, which illustrates how fundamental A8 migrants have become in fuelling the rural Fenland economies (Stenning et al. 2006: 81). Leeds City Council has also funded a substantial study into the local impacts of A8 migrants (see Cook et al. 2008), and most local councils have produced short reports on the affects of immigration in their immediate areas (for example, see Roberts-Thompson 2007 on Leicester).

Outline of the Book

It is clear that a considerable, though far from exhaustive, amount of research has already been undertaken into A8 migration. Some of the most influential work has actually been large survey style reports – perfect for offering important overviews into current trends, but perhaps less able to offer significant depth of analysis or empirical data. The chapters in this volume, therefore, build on the groundwork that these early reports have provided, but offer a range of more detailed perspectives on post-accession migration from Poland to the UK. Importantly for such a timely and significant topic, the contributors to this book are drawn from a wide range of academic disciplines – economics, social geography, sociology, modern languages and area studies, social anthropology, advertising and media studies, history, linguistics and discourse analysis, film studies and urban studies – all taking different approaches to the study of contemporary Polish migration, and all offering highly nuanced insights, sometimes similar, sometimes quite distinct. There are interesting juxtapositions between some of the chapters – a chapter based on statistical analysis, for instance, sharing a section with discourse analysis and film studies contributions – but collectively they are able to shed light on many aspects of this migration, ranging from concrete figures on migration trends, commentary on how Polish migration has changed, through to what it has actually felt like to leave Poland and come to the UK, and what has driven people to do so.

The book is divided into two parts, both of five chapters; the first, 'Contexts, Strategies and Discourses of Emigration', focuses predominantly on Poland as a country of emigration, and the second, 'Experiences of Immigration and "Settlement"', principally concentrates on migrants after their initial migration, as they navigate their new lives in the UK. Clearly this is an imperfect divide – as many of the chapters illustrate, the respective spaces of Poland and the UK cannot be separated so easily, with migrants criss-crossing over transnational borders all the time, continually blurring and reconfiguring the boundaries of their lives in Poland and their lives in the UK. This artificial division does, however, allow both Poland and the UK to be analysed fully, providing a more balanced platform from which to understand contemporary migration trends.

Part I begins with Agnieszka Fihel and Paweł Kaczmarczyk's chapter 'Migration: A Threat or a Chance? Recent Migration of Poles and its Impact on the Polish Labour Market'. This chapter explores in more detail the impact of 2004 on migration movements from Poland, illuminates who is leaving – their age, gender, geographical and educational backgrounds – and where they are going, and assesses the impact of this emigration on the Polish labour market, challenging the notion of 'brain drain' that has gained currency in Polish public discourse. Through a close analysis of the available data on this migration, from Poland and the UK, their chapter demonstrates the diversity of the people who are migrating from Poland, and, more importantly, underlines just how fundamental the changes that 2004 has brought have been for Polish international mobility.

With this basis established, the next two chapters consider different contexts and strategies of emigration through smaller regionalized case-studies. Tim Elrick and Emilia Brinkmeier use their research from two places in rural Poland to show, on a smaller scale, how 2004 has changed outward migration patterns. Here the local contexts are crucial – one area has traditionally sent people predominantly to Germany, the other has more diverse migration links. The response to 2004 has not been even; while the former area has seen a large increase in migration to places such as the UK and Ireland, the latter has not witnessed significant alterations to its established patterns of migration. If 2004 has been pivotal on a macro, national scale, the regional and local dynamics of migration paint a more complex picture. In investigating why this has been the case, Elrick and Brinkmeier unearth interesting developments in migrants' strategies, and in the role of informal and formal agents in promoting and facilitating migration. Anne White's research has a similar starting point, small town Poland, and she too asserts the importance of recognizing the local peculiarities of migration patterns, and the need to understand local migration cultures. To do this, she focuses on the migration strategies of Polish families, as a very specific section of the emigrating population, utilizing the analytical tool of 'livelihoods' to consider why families choose to leave Poland. She demonstrates how 2004 has changed family migration strategies, allowing people to contemplate a more permanent move with their families, rather than leaving them behind, and throughout the chapter illustrates the emotional, human dimension of the migration progress. Both of these chapters offer important insights into daily life in Poland which is often missing from destination-based research.

The remaining chapters in Part I move away from the pragmatism of migration strategies to concentrate instead on discourses of migration. In their chapter 'Discourses of a "Normal Life" among Post-accession Migrants from Poland to Britain', Aleksandra Galasińska and Olga Kozłowska argue that, just as 2004 has eased some of the struggles of migration, so the narratives that migrants construct about their movements have also changed. Using data from interviews and Internet discussion boards – a vital arena for Polish migration research – they focus on one key post-socialist discourse in particular, the desire for 'normality', and show how this plays out in the migrants' stories, delicately probing the hopes and frustrations of their respondents as they justify their decision to leave Poland and move to the UK, searching for a 'normal life'. Again, the personal experiences of migration are animated and explored. Ewa Mazierka's contribution, the final chapter in this part, considers another type of discourse – this time post-war Polish cinema – and brings an important historical and cultural context to the volume. By charting the depiction of emigration in Polish films since the early years of the communist regime, Mazierska demonstrates the politicization of emigration in Poland's recent history. She points to how negatively emigration has been portrayed on the big screen in Poland, despite the long tradition of migration, and shows how even contemporary films do not capture much of the optimism that accompanies migration, especially among the young. Her chapter is invaluable for understanding shifting public discourses on emigration in Poland, and for appreciating the complex relationship that this so-called country of emigration has with its outward flows of people.

Part II moves the focus away from Poland to the UK, and starts with Maruška Svašek's chapter 'Shared History? Polish Migrant Experiences and the Politics of Display in Northern Ireland', which considers the settlement of Polish migrants in Belfast. Two themes stand out as particularly important in this chapter; first, the specificity of local settings in the UK – as well as Poland – which Belfast, as a city with longstanding religious and political divisions, illustrates perfectly. Incoming Poles, predominantly Catholic, find themselves unwittingly emerged in a highly sophisticated local geography of identities, with their religious backgrounds arguably as important as their national ones in positioning them in their destination. Svašek's chapter also demonstrates the politicization of settlement processes, chronicling the participation of recently arrived Poles in a project to aid local understandings of ethnic minority groups, and analysing the negotiations which took place to decide how this new migration should be represented.

London is the setting of the next chapter by Louise Ryan, Rosemary Sales and Mary Tilki, who document recent Polish migration to the capital, concentrating on the different types of social networks that the migrants develop and maintain, within London, but also transnationally, with friends and family in Poland. On the one hand they show how important even 'weak ties' are for securing jobs and accommodation, and demonstrate how migrants' networks can be extended beyond their immediate contacts, but on the other they also explore the vulnerability of migrants when crucial networks are absent, and what happens when certain ties are deemed to constrain rather than help. They also argue that within the Polish population generally there are significant tensions, something that Bernadetta Siara considers in her chapter 'UK Poles and the Negotiation of Gender and Ethnic Identity in Cyberspace', which, like Galasińska and Kozłowska's research, uses the Internet to study contemporary Polish migration. In her contribution she investigates how certain cyberspaces are used as places where new migrants can debate important issues relating to gender and ethnicity, matters that they cannot easily discuss in other arenas. Using data collected from discussion forums she shows how gender roles are being tested and transformed through migration, how these changes are being debated and negotiated from a variety of different viewpoints, and how developments such as mixed ethnicity relationships help position the Polish migrants in their new multicultural environments.

The intersections of gender and ethnicity are considered from a different perspective by Ayona Datta in her study of Polish builders in London. Here the focus is on masculinities, and how the gendered performances of Polish construction workers signifies both their identities as men, but also as Polish nationals, in the close environment of domestic housing construction sites. Their 'way of being men' is markedly different from the gendered norms of the 'English' builders they work with, from the jokes they share on-site, to the socializing they join in with after work. This chapter is a reminder that it is often the workplace which is the key site of social interaction for new migrants, staging their encounters with fellow migrants, but also with the wider population more generally. The final chapter, 'The Material Worlds of Recent Polish Migrants: Transnationalism, Food, Shops and Home', sees Marta Rabikowska and Kathy Burrell move the analysis to another important space in the lives of many Polish migrants: shops selling Polish products. Chronicling the rapid proliferation of these shops, and concentrating especially on the emotional significance of having easily available Polish foodstuffs for the new migrants, they explore how these new shops have changed consumption patterns, investigate how migrants choose between the different types of shops, and analyse the ethnic diversity of many of the shops, and the areas in which they are located. Ultimately, they consider to what extent these shops, along with the food and goods regularly brought back from Poland, help to make the UK feel like 'home'.

Taken together, these chapters mark a real step forward in the analysis of contemporary Polish migration to the UK, the impact of this migration on both countries, and the emotional journeys undertaken by the migrants themselves.

References

Ahmed, S., Fortier, A-M. and Sheller, M. (eds) (2003), *Uprootings/Regroundings: Questions of Home and Migration* (Oxford: Berg).

Anderson, B., Ruhs, M., Rogaly, B. and Spencer, S. (2006), *Fair Enough? Central and East European Migrants in Low-wage Employment in the UK* (York: Joseph Rowntree Foundation).

Anthias, F. and Lazaridis, G. (eds) (2000), *Gender and Migration in Southern Europe: Women on the Move* (Oxford: Berg).

Babinski, G. (2000), 'Ukrainians in Poland after the Second World War', in Hamilton Iglicka (eds).

Burawoy, M. and Verdery, K. (eds) (1999), *Uncertain Transition: Ethnographies of Change in the Postsocialist World* (Lanham, MD: Rowman and Littlefield).

Burrell, K. (2006a), *Moving Lives: Narratives of Nation and Migration among Europeans in Post-war Britain* (Aldershot: Ashgate).

Burrell, K. (2006b), 'Personal, Inherited, Collective: Layering and Communicating the Memory of Forced Polish Migration', *Immigrants and Minorities* 24:2, 144–63.

Burrell, K. (2008a), 'Managing, Learning and Sending: The Material Lives and Journeys of Polish Women in Britain', *Journal of Material Culture* 13:1, 63–83.

Burrell, K. (2008b), 'Materialising the Border: Spaces of Mobility and Material Culture in Migration from Post-Socialist Poland', *Mobilities* 3:3, 331–51.

Burrell, K. (2008c), 'Time Matters: Temporal Contexts of Polish Transnationalism', in Smith and Eade (eds).

Buzar, S. (2007), *Energy Poverty in Eastern Europe: Hidden Geographies of Deprivation* (Aldershot: Ashgate).

Cook, J., Dwyer, P. and Waite, L. (2008), *The Impact of New A8 Migrant Communities in Leeds* (Leeds: Leeds City Council).

Coyle, A. (2007), 'Resistance, Regulation and Rights: The Changing Status of Polish Women's Migration and Work in the 'New' Europe', *European Journal of Women's Studies* 14:1, 37–50.

Cyrus, N. (2006), 'Polish Emigration: Permanent and Temporary Patterns', in Triandafyllidou (ed.).

Datta, A. (2007), 'East European Builders in London: Everyday Cosmopolitanism in Everyday Places of the Global City'. Paper presented at the RGS-IBG Annual Conference, 28 August 2007.

Datta, K., McIlwaine, C., Evans, Y., Herbert, J., May, J. and Wills, J. (2006), *Work and Survival Strategies among Low Paid Migrants in London* (London: Queen Mary, University of London).

Davies, N. (1981), *God's Playground: A History of Poland in Two Volumes* (Oxford: Clarendon).

Drinkwater, S., Eade, J. and Garapich, M. (2006), *Poles Apart? EU Enlargement and the Labour Market Outcomes of Immigrants in the UK. Institute for the Study of Labor* (IZA) (IZA Discussion Paper 2410), <http://ideas.repec.org/p/iza/izadps/dp2410.html>, accessed 23 May 2007.

Düvell, F. (2004), *Polish Undocumented Immigrants, Regular High-skilled Workers and Entrepreneurs in the UK*. Prace Migracyjne Series No. 54 (Warsaw: Institute for Social Studies, University of Warsaw).

Eade, J., Drinkwater, S. and Garapich, M.P. (2007), *Class and Ethnicity: Polish Migrant Workers in London – Full Research Report*. ESRC End of Award Report, RES-000-22-1294 (Swindon: Economic and Social Research Council).

Erdmans, M. (1998), *Opposite Poles: Immigrants and Ethnics in Polish Chicago, 1976–1990* (University Park, PA: Pennsylvania State University Press).

Fabiszak, M. (2007), 'Migration as Schooling, Migration as Holidays'. Paper presented at 'New Europeans under Scrutiny: Workshop on State-of-the-Art Research on Polish Migration to the UK', University of Wolverhampton, 2 February 2007.

Favell, A. (2008), 'The New Face of East West Migration in Europe', *Journal of Ethnic and Migration Studies* 34:5, 701–16.

Fodor, E. (2002), 'Gender and the Experience of Poverty in Eastern Europe and Russia after 1989', *Communist and Post-communist Studies* 35:4, 369–82.

Fomina, J. and Frelak, J. (2008), *Next Stopski London: Public Perceptions of Labour Migration within the EU. The Case of Polish Labour Migrants in the British Press* (Warsaw: Institute of Public Affairs).

Fortier, A. (2006), 'The Politics of Scaling, Timing and Embodying: Rethinking the "New Europe"', *Mobilities* 1:3, 313–31.

Garapich, M. (2007), 'Discursive Hostility and Shame – An Exploration into the Everyday Negotiation of Ethnicity among Polish Migrants in London'. Paper presented at 'Three Years On: EU Accession and East European Migration to the UK and Ireland' Symposium, De Montfort University, Leicester, 20–21 April 2007.

Garapich, M. (2008), 'The Migration Industry and Civil Society: Polish Immigrants in the United Kingdom Before and After EU Enlargement', *Journal of Ethnic and Migration Studies* 34:5, 735–52.

Górny, A. and Ruspini, P. (eds) (2004), *Migration in the New Europe: East-West Revisited* (Basingstoke: Palgrave Macmillan).

Grzymała-Kazłowska, A. (2005), 'From Ethnic Cooperation to In-Group Competition: Undocumented Polish Workers in Brussels', *Journal of Ethnic and Migration Studies* 31:4, 675–97.

Guzik, M. (2005), *Szare Madonny [Everyday Madonnas]* (Krosno: Krośnieńska Oficyna Wydawnicza).

Hagen, J. (2003), 'Redrawing the Imagined Map of Europe: The Rise and Fall of the "Center"', *Political Geography* 22:5, 489–517.

Hamilton, F. and Iglicka, K. (eds) (2000), 'From Homogeneity to Multiculturalism: Minorities Old and New in Poland'. SSEES Occasional Paper No. 45 (London: School of Slavonic and East European Studies, University of London).

Hellerman, C. (2006), 'Migrating Alone: Tackling Social Capital? Women from Eastern Europe in Portugal', *Ethnic and Racial Studies* 29:6, 1135–52.

Holmes, C. (1988), *John Bull's Island: Immigration and British Society, 1871–1971* (Basingstoke: Macmillan).

Home Office UK Border Agency, Department for Work and Pensions, HM Revenue and Customs and Communities and Local Government (2008), *Accession Monitoring Report May 2004–March 2008*.<http://www.ukba.homeoffice. gov.uk/sitecontent/documents/aboutus/reports/accession_monitoring_report/ report15/may04mar08.pdf?view=Binary>, accessed 3 June 2008.

Iglicka, K. (2001), *Poland's Post-war Dynamic of Migration* (Aldershot: Ashgate).

Ignatieve, N. (1995), *How the Irish Became White* (London: Routledge).

Janta, H. (2007), 'The Experience of Polish Migrants Working in the Hospitality Industry in the UK'. Paper presented at 'Three Years On: EU Accession and East European Migration to the UK and Ireland' Symposium, De Montfort University, Leicester, 20–21 April 2007.

Jaroszyńska-Kirchmann, A. (2004), *The Exile Mission: The Polish Political Diaspora and Polish Americans 1939–1956* (Athens, OH: Ohio University Press).

Jileva, E. (2002), 'Visa and Free Movement of Labour: The Uneven Imposition of the EU *acquis* on the Accession States', *Journal of Ethnic and Migration Studies* 28:4, 683–700.

Jones, E. (2008), 'Get them Polish out of your house or I'll burn it down', The *Guardian*, 'G2' supplement, 4 January 2008.

Jordan, B. (2002), 'Polish Migrant Workers in London: Mobility, Labour Markets and the Prospects for Democratic Development'. Paper presented at the 'Beyond Transition: Development Perspectives and Dilemmas' Conference, Warsaw, 12–13 April 2002. <www.case.com.pl/dyn/servFile.php?plik_id=71598>, accessed 28 April 2006.

Kay, D. and Miles, R. (1992), *Refugees or Migrant Workers?: European Volunteer Workers in Britain, 1946–1951* (London: Routledge).

King, R. (ed.) (1993a), *The New Geography of European Migrations* (London: Belhaven Press).

King, R. (ed.) (1993b), *Mass Migrations in Europe: The Legacy and the Future* (London: Belhaven Press).

Kopnina, H. (2005), *East to West Migration: Russian Migrants in Western Europe* (Aldershot: Ashgate).

Kurcz, Z. (2000), 'The German Minority in Poland after 1945', in Hamilton and Iglicka (eds).

Kushner, T. (2006), *Remembering Refugees: Then and Now* (Manchester: Manchester University Press).

Kyambi, S. (2005), *Beyond Black and White: Mapping New Immigrant Communities* (London: Institute for Public Policy Research).

Lane, T. (2004), *Victims of Stalin and Hitler: The Exodus of Poles and Balts to Britain* (Basingstoke: Palgrave Macmillan).

Lovell, D. (2001), 'Trust and the Politics of Postcommunism', *Communist and Post-communist Studies* 34:1, 27–38.

Lucassen, L. (2005), *The Immigrant Threat: The Integration of Old and New Migrants in Western Europe Since 1850* (Urbana, IL: University of Illinois Press).

McIlwaine, C. (2007), *Living in Latin London: How Latin American Migrants Survive in the City* (London: Leverhulme Trust and Queen Mary, University of London).

Metykova, M. (2007), 'Suspended Normalcy: Eastern European Migrants in London and Edinburgh'. Paper presented at 'Normalcy: Opportunity or Standard? The Confrontation of Eastern European and Western Culture in the EU' Symposium, University of East London, 27 April 2007.

Osipovic, D. (2008), 'Polish Migrants as UK Social Citizens: Policy Framework for Social Rights' Take-up and its Links with Migration Time Horizons'. Paper presented at 'Temporary Migration and Community Cohesion: The Nature and

Impact of Migration from East-Central Europe to Western Europe' Workshop, University of Bath, 8 January 2008.

Panayi, P. (1994), *Immigration, Ethnicity and Racism in Britain, 1815–1945* (Manchester: Manchester University Press).

Panayi, P. (1999), *The Impact of Immigration: A Documentary History of the Effects and Experiences of Immigrants in Britain since 1945* (Manchester: Manchester University Press).

Parutis, V. (2007), '"At Home" in Migration: Lithuanian Migrants in the UK'. Paper presented at 'Three Years On: EU Accession and East European Migration to the UK and Ireland' Symposium, De Montfort University, Leicester, 20–21 April 2007.

Pollard, N., Latorre, M. and Sriskandarajah, D. (2008), *Floodgates or Turnstiles? Post-EU Enlargement Migration Flows to (and from) the UK* (London: Institute for Public Policy Research).

Roberts-Thomson, T. (2007), *Report on European Union A8 Migrant Workers in Leicester* (Leicester: Leicester City Council).

Roediger, D. (2005), *Working Toward Whiteness: How America's Immigrants Became White* (New York, NY: Basic Books).

Ruhs, M. (2006), *Greasing the Wheels of the Flexible Labour Market: East European Labour Immigration in the UK.* Centre on Migration, Policy and Society Working Paper No. 38 (Oxford: University of Oxford).

Smith, M. and Eade, J. (eds) (2008), *Transnational Ties: Cities, Migrations, and Identities* (Edison, NJ: Transaction Publishers).

Spencer, S., Ruhs, M., Anderson, B. and Rogaly, B. (2007), *Migrants' Lives Beyond the Workplace: The Experiences of Central and East Europeans in the UK* (York: Joseph Rowntree Foundation).

Stenning, A. (2005), 'Post-socialism and the Changing Geographies of the Everyday in Poland', *Transactions of the Institute of British Geographers* 30:1, 113–27.

Stenning, A., Champion, T., Conway, C., Coombes, M., Dawley, S., Dixon, L., Raybould, S. and Richardson, R. (2006), *Assessing the Local and Regional Impacts of International Migration: Final Report of a Research Project for the Department for Communities and Local Government* (New Horizons Theme 1b: Migration and Demographic Change) (Newcastle: Centre for Urban and Regional Development Studies, Newcastle University).

Stenning, A. and Dawley, S. (2009), 'Poles to Newcastle: Grounding New Migrant Flows in Peripheral Regions', *European Urban and Regional Studies*.

Sword, K. (1996), *Identity in Flux: The Polish Community in Britain.* SSEES Occasional Paper No. 36 (London: School of Slavonic and East European Studies, University of London).

Tannahill, J. (1958), *European Volunteer Workers in Britain* (Manchester: Manchester University Press).

Taylor, B. and Rogaly, B. (2004), *Report on Migrant Working in West Norfolk* (Norwich: Norfolk County Council).

Thomas, W. and Znaniecki, F. (1918–20), *The Polish Peasant in Europe and America* (Chicago IL: University of Chicago Press).

Triandafyllidou, A. (ed.) (2006), *Contemporary Polish Migration in Europe; Complex Patterns of Movement and Settlement* (Lewiston, NY: Edwin Mellen).

Verstraete, G. (2003), 'Technological Frontiers and the Politics of Mobility in the European Union', in Ahmed et al. (eds).

Wallace, C. and Stola, D. (eds) (2001), *Patterns of Migration in Central Europe* (Basingstoke: Palgrave Macmillan).

Wallace, C. (2002), 'Opening and Closing Borders: Migration and Mobility in East-Central Europe', *Journal of Ethnic and Migration Studies* 28:4, 603–25.

Wolak, A. (2004), *Forced Out: The Fate of Polish Jewry in Communist Poland* (Tucson, AZ: Fenestra Books).

Ziegler, D. (2002), 'Post-communist Eastern Europe and the Cartography of Independence', *Political Geography* 21:5, 671–86.

Znaniecka Lopata, H. (1994), *Polish Americans* (New Brunswick, NJ: Transaction Publishers).

Zubryzcki, J. (1956), *Polish Immigrants in Britain: A Study of Adjustment* (The Hague: Martinus Nijhoff).

PART I
Contexts, Strategies and Discourses of Emigration

Chapter 1
Migration: A Threat or a Chance?
Recent Migration of Poles and its Impact
on the Polish Labour Market

Agnieszka Fihel and Paweł Kaczmarczyk

From the nineteenth century onwards, Poland has been an important sending country in the global migration system. Underdeveloped both economically and socially, it has found itself on the periphery of an increasingly dynamic developing western world, perfectly placed as a country of emigration. During the communist period, however, migratory outflows from Poland, though fuelled by a range of political and economic push and pull factors, were seriously limited.[1] It was not until the 1980s that emigration, often undertaken under the cover of tourist movements, took place on a massive scale. This pattern continued after the fall of communism with Polish nationals being allowed to travel to many west European countries through various entry/visa schemes, with others working abroad as undocumented labour. In fact, many Poles devised a strategy of 'commuting' between their usual residence and often irregular work in the West as a viable way of making a living. In a relatively short period of time, communities of undocumented temporary workers from Poland mushroomed in Western European cities such as Berlin, Brussels, London, Rome and Vienna. However, it is the 2004 European Union enlargement that can be identified as the milestone for migration trends in Poland. The accession of Central and Eastern European countries into the European Union and the ensuing, if gradual, opening up of labour markets in the 'old 15', have both tapped into an enormous potential for emigration in Poland.

In the public debate which has taken place in Poland about the different consequences of the county's EU accession, numerous hazards resulting from massive emigration have been identified and discussed. Interestingly, in the very first phase of the debate a positive approach towards this outflow predominated. The migration of Poles was perceived as a welcome 'labour market relief' and, potentially, a source of foreign exchange, largely through remittances. A few years on, however, more recent outflows from Poland are being increasingly described

---

1   These push and pull factors included notorious shortages in the supply of basic goods and the dramatically rising value of the dollar that made foreign employment exceptionally profitable, and, as far as pull factors are concerned, the 'open door' policy for political migrants from Central and Eastern Europe in Western Europe.

as a threat to the Polish economy and society. A long list of ascribed negative aspects includes severe labour force shortages, a 'brain drain' and the social costs of increased mobility. Against this background we would like to pose a few questions. What is the real impact of migration on the Polish labour market? Does the recent outflow of highly skilled workers pose a threat to the Polish economy, or should it instead be perceived as a manifestation of the more beneficial 'brain overflow'? And, lastly, can the outflow of highly skilled people be characterized as brain drain or rather 'brain waste'?

To answer these questions we will look at this most recent phenomenon of Polish mobility and identify its main structural features – scale, duration, destination countries, skills level, and connection to the labour market – in the most important destination countries, and particularly in the United Kingdom. This analysis will be presented in the context of past migration processes and interpreted within the framework of continuity and change with respect to migratory behaviour. In the last part of the chapter we will discuss the impacts of the recent outflow on the Polish economy and society, putting special emphasis on labour market processes.

Migration and Mobility: Methodological Challenges

Despite the rise in documented flows of people around the world, defining and assessing the scale of this international mobility has become more and more difficult. This is mainly caused by two developments. Firstly, there has been an increasing variety of migration behaviours and types of migrants. Due to both enhanced freedom of movement and technological changes, many people leave their home countries with very vague plans on how long they will be away or continue to move between their countries of origin and destination. The duration of 'stay abroad' is constantly redefined and migration, therefore, cannot easily be described by the 'old-fashioned' concepts of short-term and long-term. Nor is it possible to simply collate all these specific categories of migrants and create a single artificial one. Secondly, deficiencies in migration registration methods have led to the omission of return and short-term migrants in official statistics. For example, the Polish population register captures only those migrants who make their stay overseas permanent, which constitutes a relatively marginal proportion of all persons staying abroad.[2] The population census would be the best source of statistical information on Polish emigrants, but unfortunately the last one was conducted in Poland in 2002, prior to EU enlargement.

In this analysis, therefore, we use the Polish Labour Force Survey (LFS), which despite only offering an approximate picture of the scale of short-term and long-term migration and the socio-demographic characteristics of migrants from Poland, is arguably the most useful statistical material available. Inevitably, there

---

2   For example, between 1990 and 2005 around 353,000 people were registered as permanent emigrants from Poland.

are limitations with this data set. The LFS only records adults who at the time of the survey had been living abroad for longer than two months and, at the same time, had at least one household member still living in Poland – this survey, therefore, is not considered to be representative of all persons living abroad.[3] Nevertheless, this source material does shed light on the international mobility of the Polish population. The results of the analysis will be presented separately for two groups of people: those who left Poland in the period 1999–2003 (referred to as pre-accession migrants) and those who left in the period 1 May 2004–31 December 2006 (post-accession migrants). We will also present statistics derived from the Worker Registration Scheme, another data source that provides a relatively precise picture of contemporary labour migration from Poland to the United Kingdom.[4]

1 May 2004: The Outbreak of Mobility

As the different statistical sources illustrate, the 2004 EU enlargement has been the most important emigration stimulus in Poland's contemporary history. According to the estimates recently made by the Central Statistical Office (2008), the number of Polish nationals staying abroad for longer than two months increased from approximately one million at the end of 2004 to 2.3 million three years later (see Table 1.1). Due to the fact that the Polish Central Statistical Office considered several sources of information on migration from Poland, including data originating from the main destination countries and LFS data, these estimates seem to be the most reliable so far.

The Polish LFS data reveals a similar picture. According to the data, since 2004 a rapid increase in the number of Polish nationals staying abroad has been observed

---

3   If, in a household selected for the survey, all members are abroad, there is no family member to report it. Therefore, the LFS indentifies only those migrants who have at least one family member still present in Poland and does not capture other migrants. It is necessary to note that the LFS was primary designed for the purpose of labour market analysis. However, analysis of LFS data and National Census data reveals that the data obtained from the Polish LFS can be used with regard to the structural features of migration but not the scale of mobility.

4   At least if we assume that the number and structure of applicants may serve as an indicator of 'real' migration to the country. As the WRS only documents registered workers it potentially underestimates the real number of workers. However, the German Economic Institute (DIW) made an evaluation of the WRS data and reached a conclusion that it overestimates the scale of inflow. It is due to the fact that each registration represents one job and not necessarily one migrant and that according to the estimates of the Home Office more than 40 per cent of registered migrants were present in the UK prior to the accession and just used the opportunity to legalize their stay abroad (Traser 2005). However, based on the Labor Force Survey data Portes and French (2005) showed that the WRS depicts the migration phenomenon quite precisely, although they do suggest that many of the newcomers left the country after a few months.

Table 1.1 The estimated number of Polish citizens (in thousands) staying abroad for longer than two months by destination country

Destination	May 2002	End of 2004	End of 2006	End of 2007
Total	786	1,000	1,950	2,270
European Union	451	750	1,550	1,860
Austria	11	15	34	39
Belgium	14	13	28	31
France	21	30	49	55
Germany	294	385	450	490
Ireland	2	15	120	200
Italy	39	59	85	87
Netherlands	10	23	55	98
Spain	14	26	44	80
Sweden	6	11	25	27
United Kingdom	24	150	580	690

Source: Central Statistic Office (2008).

(see Figure 1.1): in the middle of 2007 this number was double that of three years before.[5] Not surprisingly, this outflow was closely related to labour emigration, with the share of migrants who work during their stay abroad increasing from 70–80 per cent in the 1990s to 94 per cent in the post-accession period. In addition, in 2004 the increase in the volume of outflow was almost exclusively a result of rising short-term mobility (lasting more than two but less than 12 months): the number of migrants who were staying abroad for less than 12 months more than doubled between 2000 and 2005, and the share of short-term migrants increased from 48 per cent in 1995 to 60 per cent in 2004. Since 2006, however, the proportion of long-term migrants has risen to such an extent that in 2007 the ratio of short-term to long-term migrants became 1:1, a similar situation to the 1990s.[6] At the moment we can only speculate whether this increase in the volume of long-term outflow migration will result in settlement emigration. This, in fact, constitutes one of the most important puzzles and unresolved issues in recent debates on migration from Poland. The sheer increase in scale of the outward

---

5   However, in the last period of analysis, namely the third quarter of 2007, a slight decrease in the number of short-term migrants was observed. This may be a seasonal effect, but also may indicate the first returns to Poland.

6   This was the result of the fact that many migrants prolonged their stay abroad and were recorded in subsequent years as long-term migrants.

Table 1.2　　**Percentage of Polish migrants (aged 15 and over who have been abroad for more than two months) who left in the pre-accession and post-accession periods by destination country**

Destination country	Pre-accession period	Post-accession period
European Union		
No labour market restrictions	12.1	42.4
Ireland	1.4	9.1
Sweden	1.0	1.9
UK	9.7	31.4
Labour market restrictions	62.6	45.3
Austria	2.9	1.5
Belgium	3.4	1.7
France	3.8	3.2
Germany	32.1	18.9
Greece	1.6	1.5
Italy	11.9	8.4
Netherlands	3.0	3.0
Norway	0.5	2.0
Spain	2.6	3.1
Non-EU	25.3	12.3
Other in Europe	1.1	1.5
Canada	1.0	0.8
US	19.3	9.1
Other	3.9	0.9

Notes: The pre-accession period is defined here as 1999–2003 and the post-accession period as 1 May 2004–31 December 2006.

Source: University of Warsaw Centre for Migration Research Migrants' Database, based on the Polish LFS.

mobility of Polish citizens, however, is perhaps the most significant legacy of EU membership for Poland's population structure.

In addition, as the statistical material demonstrates, Polish accession into the EU also brought with it substantial changes in the mobility directions of Polish citizens. Almost all countries of the EU15 (or EEA) experienced an elevated inflow of people from Poland (Grabowska-Lusińska and Okólski 2008), but in most of the post-accession destinations the mass inflow of Polish migrants has been unprecedented. This is particularly true with regard to Ireland and the United Kingdom, but similar trends were also observed in Denmark, Iceland, Norway, Spain and Sweden. The United Kingdom has now, overwhelmingly, taken the position of the main and

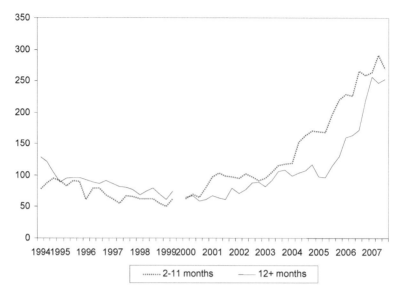

Figure 1.1   The number of Polish migrants (in thousands) staying abroad for longer than two months, by length of stay and quarter of year, 1994–2007

Source: Derived from Kępińska (2007).

dominant destination country, a position which was occupied by Germany prior to the 2004 EU enlargement.[7] The estimates of the Central Statistical Office indicate that 690,000 Polish nationals were staying in the UK at the end of 2007, almost a thirtyfold increase compared to May 2002 (see Table 1.1).

According to the LFS, the United Kingdom together with Ireland and Sweden (the two other countries that did not introduce labour market restrictions) attracted 12 per cent of those who left before 2004 and as many as 42 per cent of post-accession migrants (Table 1.2; Figure 1.2), whereas the respective collective share for the main receiving countries prior to the accession – Germany, the US and Italy – decreased from 63 per cent to 36 per cent. Thus EU membership has clearly had a considerable impact upon the geography of outward migration flows of Polish citizens, as well as the scale.

---

7   At the end of 2006 Germany attracted 450,000 Polish nationals, but these estimates encompass only those migrants who were staying abroad for longer than 2 months, and, thus, it is necessary to add to the number presented above about 250,000–280,000 Polish seasonal workers who each year find legal employment in Germany on the basis of bilateral international agreement. Nevertheless, considering the average length of stay abroad it is justified to say that post the 2004 EU enlargement the United Kingdom became the most important destination country for Polish migrants.

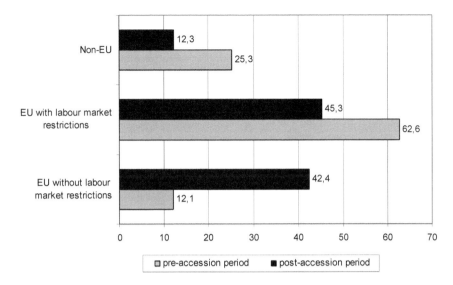

Figure 1.2   Percentage of Polish migrants who left in the pre-accession and post-accession periods, grouped by type of destination country*

Note: *The EU with labour market restrictions category encompasses Ireland, Sweden and the United Kingdom; all other EU countries fall into the without labour market restrictions category. The pre- and post-accession periods are defined here as in Table 1.2.

Source: University of Warsaw Centre for Migration Research Migrants' Database, based on the Polish LFS.

The Socio-demographic Profile of Polish Migrants

The distinctive nature of the socio-demographic profile of migrants is probably one of the most significant features of population movements. According to the LFS, for example, Polish migrants differ substantially from the general population of Poland. With regard to age, labour migration clearly attracts young people of an economically active age, whereas children and older people are under-represented compared to the sending population. The specific selection of migrants is also usually conditioned to a large extent by various determinants in the receiving countries – mainly by the demand for foreign workers, but also by institutional factors such as transitional arrangements for access to the labour market and social security systems. With the opening of the Irish, Swedish and British labour markets to Polish migrants, pull factors started to play a more significant role in migration from Poland, and the incidence of specific groups of people migrating over others became more marked. The different characteristics of both pre-accession and post-accession migrant cohorts can be broken down.

Table 1.3   The education structure of Polish migrants who left in the pre- and post-accession periods, in per cent

Level of education	Pre-accession period	Post-accession period
University degree	14.7	19.8
Secondary	14.0	14.2
Secondary vocational	26.1	28.1
Vocational	34.8	30.9
Primary	9.9	7.0
Unfinished	0.4	0.0
Total	100.0	100.0

Source: University of Warsaw Centre for Migration Research Migrants' Database, based on the Polish LFS.

Firstly, both before and after EU enlargement the outflow from Poland has been disproportionately male with regard to gender makeup. Before 2004, men constituted 57 per cent of migrants, meaning that there were 100 women to 133 men. After 2004, however, this percentage increased to 65 per cent, or 186 men per 100 women. Considering that 47 per cent of the general adult population of Poland is male, this reveals how men are over-represented in out migration compared to women. Secondly, the outflow from Poland has been dominated by young or very young people. Since EU enlargement the age structure of Polish migrants has changed significantly. On average those who are living abroad are now younger than before: the mean age decreased by 1.5 years (from 33.9 to 32.4), and the median age fell by two years (from 30 to 28). The percentage of migrants aged 20–24 has increased from 23 per cent to 24 per cent, of those aged 25–29 from 22 per cent to 28 per cent, and of those aged 30–34 from 12 per cent to 14 per cent. Thirdly, the educational profile of Polish migrants has also shifted. As Table 1.3 illustrates, the pre-accession outflow from Poland was dominated by people with either a secondary vocational or vocational education, who constituted 61 per cent of migrants. After 2004 these categories have remained the most important overall, but the proportion of university graduates has risen significantly. Every fifth post-accession migrant has a tertiary education, which, considering that just 14.3 per cent of the overall population of Poland are university graduates (in 2004) indicates a loss of human capital (the 'brain drain' phenomenon).

Finally, migrants from medium-sized and small towns and villages have been consistently over-represented relative to the resident population, while migrants from large cities have been under-represented. Compared to most EU member countries, a large proportion of Poland's population live in rural areas and small towns. Over the past 15 or so years, the proportion of the total population living in rural areas (38.5 per cent in 2006) has generally been stable, if not increasing. In this context, having a significant percentage of migrants originating from rural areas and small towns (under 20,000 inhabitants) is a natural consequence of the spatial distribution of the Polish population. Generally, however, the proportion of people from rural and small town areas has been 59 per cent of pre-accession and 56 per cent of post-accession migrants, whereas inhabitants from medium (20–100,000 inhabitants) and large (over 100,000 inhabitants) cities constituted, respectively, 21 per cent and 20 per cent of pre-accession, and 20 and 24 per cent of post-accession migrants. This pattern of spatial selectivity among Polish migrants – one of the most important issues with regard to the consequences of labour mobility – is closely related to the structure of local and regional labour markets and work opportunities in the place of residence. Fewer opportunities in smaller towns and rural locales have led to more out migration from these areas.

In spite of the clear heterogeneity of Polish migrants, it is still useful to consider the socio-demographic profiles of pre-accession and post-accession migrants. If pre-accession migrants can be said to adhere to one particular profile, the post-2004 outflow is more differentiated, consisting of both the original 'type' of migrants and the new profile of post-accession flows. The latter consists mainly of young and well educated people originating from medium and large cities, who are predominately male and aged 20–29, with 20 per cent being university graduates. Less than ten per cent of these individuals originated from households dependent on benefits in Poland, such as various welfare benefits or unemployment and disability benefit. On the other hand, the pre-accession migration flows, and also the post-accession flows to Germany, Italy and other traditional destinations, consisted of people who are statistically older, more poorly educated and originating mainly from rural areas and small towns. Moreover, the proportion of migrant households relying on welfare benefits was significantly higher in the pre-accession period than in the case of the post-accession outflow.

The United Kingdom: The Main Destination of Recent Polish Migrants

Contemporary migration from Poland to the United Kingdom dates back to the end of the Second World War when the British government actively recruited foreign workers to meet the needs of rebuilding the country after the war. The Polish Resettlement Act, issued by the British government in 1947, allowed Polish servicemen and women who had fought in Western Europe, and did not want to return to communist Poland, to demobilize in the United Kingdom. At the same time, a number of British work schemes were arranged for displaced persons in central Europe, including people of Polish origin. By 1951 over 160,000 Polish nationals had settled in the United Kingdom and until 1989 several thousand more continued to join family members there, arriving in order to marry, study or escape political persecution (Sword et al. 1989; Górny and Osipovič 2006). According to the British population census, at the beginning of the 1990s almost 74,000 people who had been born in Poland were living in the United Kingdom. By 2001 this number had decreased to 61,000, mainly due to the ageing of the post-war migrant group, but also due to returns to Poland after the fall of the Iron Curtain. During

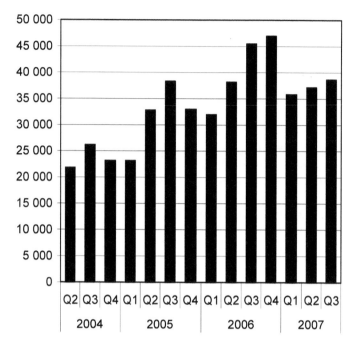

Figure 1.3   The number of approved WRS applications made by Polish citizens by quarter of year

Source: Home Office et al. 2008.

the 1990s, Polish nationals often undertook short-term labour migrations into the United Kingdom. Most migrants worked irregularly, which makes it extremely hard to estimate the true scale of the phenomenon. However, the British Labour Force Survey indicated that by 2003 34,000 Polish citizens (and 21,000 Czechs and Slovaks) were already living in the United Kingdom (Salt 2006). Presumably the real figures were much higher as the British LFS omits long-term migrants, that is those people whose stay was longer than one year at the time the data was collated.

Interestingly, this figure was ignored by the experts from the Home Office (Dustmann et al. 2003) who were responsible for forecasting the post-accession flow from the new member states into the United Kingdom. The results of econometric modelling indicated a small increase in the scale of future inflows: from 5,000 to 13,000 people annually until 2010. This result was reached, among other reasons, due to an assumption that the German labour market would also be opened up to migrants from Poland and other new member states. In fact, the lifting of restrictions on labour migration from these countries by Ireland, Sweden and the United Kingdom and, subsequently, the imposition of transitory limits in the rest of the 'old 15', were crucially important in determining the destinations

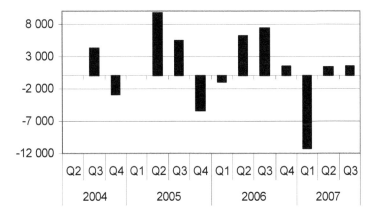

Figure 1.4   Change in number of approved WRS applications made by Polish citizens by quarter of year

Source: Home Office et al. 2008.

and sizes of post-accession flows of migrants. As far as the United Kingdom is concerned, two other pull-factors might have been relevant: first, the expansion of the British economy created a strong demand for labour, and secondly, the relatively low cultural barriers for a great number of migrants already familiar with the English language.

Evidently, the scale of Polish migration to the United Kingdom turned out to be much higher than anticipated by this forecast. The post-accession movement can, in fact, be considered as the second wave of migration from Poland, similar to the first, post-war wave. However, this most recent inflow did not start on 1 May 2004, something which is reflected not only by the above-mentioned British LFS data, but also by the applications made to the Worker Registration Scheme. In the first month after EU enlargement, every fourth application to the WRS was made by a newly arrived migrant, whereas the rest were made by those who had already been living in the United Kingdom (Portes and French 2005). For those who had been in the United Kingdom prior to accession, registration with the WRS was a way of legalizing their work in Britain.

All in all, the date of 1 May 2004 did constitute an important turning point in migration from Poland to the United Kingdom. The significance of this flow becomes indisputable when it is compared with movements from countries which have traditionally provided the pool of foreign labour for the United Kingdom. According to the National Insurance number statistics, since the fiscal year 2004/2005 Poles have been the major immigrant group, outnumbering even citizens of India and Pakistan. In the year 2006/2007 every third National Insurance number was allotted to a citizen of Poland. The total number of insurance numbers issued in the period April 2003 – March 2006 to Polish citizens was as high as

245,000. In the period May 2004 – September 2007 over 470,000 Polish citizens applied to the Worker Registration Scheme, an average of 36,500 per quarter.[8] It might be argued, however, that the number of WRS applications has now reached a threshold: in 2007 it started to level off, and in the second and third quarters of 2007 even decreased by three per cent and then 15 per cent in comparison to the respective periods of 2006 (see Figures 1.3 and 1.4).

The Socio-demographic Profile of Polish Migrants in the UK

As far as socio-demographic features are concerned, Polish migrants targeting the United Kingdom (and Ireland as well) constitute a very distinct group compared to migrants heading to other destinations. First of all, Polish post-accession migrants in the United Kingdom are predominantly very young; among them 72 per cent are aged 20 to 29, whereas only 16 per cent are 35 and above. Furthermore, the median age of those in Britain is just 25, making the population of Polish migrants in the country the youngest among all destinations of Polish citizens (see Figure 1.5). The increasing importance of Ireland and the United Kingdom among the destination countries was the chief reason for the decrease in the mean age of all post-accession migrants from Poland.

Second, of all the destination countries, the UK attracts the largest proportion of Polish university graduates. Figure 1.6 reveals striking differences with regard to the educational selectivity of post-accession migrants. According to the Polish LFS, the percentage of Polish migrants who are highly educated is 24 per cent in the United Kingdom, 22 per cent in Ireland, 19 per cent in the United States, and only eight per cent in Italy and six per cent in Germany (Figure 1.6). The apparent brain drain from Poland, defined as an overrepresentation of highly educated migrants in comparison to the sending population, is not the result of a generally greater propensity to leave Poland by the more highly skilled – this would have resulted in the category of those with university education seeing the biggest rise. Instead, due to the change of main destination countries, specifically the dominance of Ireland and the UK in attracting university graduates, the number of highly skilled migrants (and, thus, their share) has risen. It is also interesting to note that the post-accession flow of highly skilled migrants to the UK and Ireland has consisted mostly of very young people: at the time of EU enlargement 50 per cent of them were aged 25 and under, with a further 25 per cent aged 26–27.[9] This leads to the conclusion that many university graduates going to Ireland and the UK have never searched for employment opportunities in their home country but left Poland straight after finishing their education. This hypothesis was strongly

---

8   This number includes only those labour migrants who arrived after the 2004 EU enlargement, are not self-employed and do not work for a non-British employer.

9   This very young age structure referred also to migrants with secondary and secondary vocational levels of education.

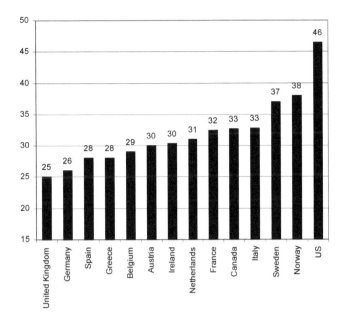

Figure 1.5   **The median age of Polish post-accession migrants by destination country**

Source: University of Warsaw Centre for Migration Research Migrants' Database, based on the Polish LFS.

supported by the findings of in-depth surveys conducted in selected Polish regions in the second half of 2007 (Kaczmarczyk 2008).

Thirdly, in the case of the outflow to the UK, the largest proportion is, as would be expected, accounted for by inhabitants of small towns (41 per cent; Figure 1.7). However, in comparison to flows from Poland to other destinations, the share of those originating from large and medium cities is relatively high.[10] This is in line with the educational structure of the migrants: the higher the proportion of university graduates among migrants, the higher the share of inhabitants of large cities. From a geographical perspective, migrants from Poland to the UK come mostly from the southern region of Poland (see Figure 1.8), which is either underdeveloped (in the case of the South-East) or the most densely populated (the South-Centre and South-West).

To sum up, the socio-demographic profile of Polish migrants differs significantly according to the country of destination. The three EU member states that did not introduce labour market restrictions towards Polish migrants attracted mainly

---

10   In the case of traditional, pre-accession destinations such as Germany, Italy and the US, every second migrant came from rural areas. In the case of Austria, three out of four Polish post-accession migrants recruited from rural areas.

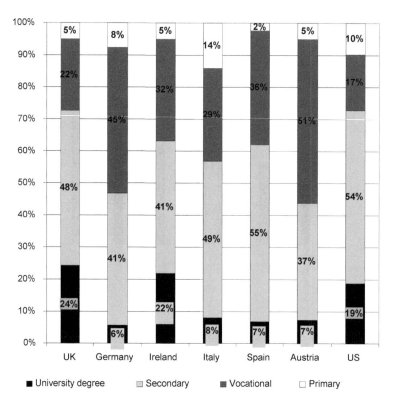

Figure 1.6   Polish post-accession migrants by education level and destination country, in per cent

Source: University of Warsaw Centre for Migration Research Migrants' Database, based on the Polish LFS.

younger and better educated people, a substantial number of whom probably had at least a basic knowledge of English (or other foreign languages). A large number of these people would have begun their occupational lives through undertaking international migration, but this would probably not have taken place if the labour restrictions had been introduced in all EU member states. The pull of Sweden, Ireland and the UK after 1 May 2004, moreover, was so strong that it also changed the directional mobilities of other young migrants who, before this date, had already moved to other destinations.

These particular features – young age and good qualifications – increase the chances of success in the open labour market of any destination country and the UK is the best example of such a lack of labour restrictions. The UK has largely attracted young (aged 20–29) and highly educated migrants, with the proportion of university graduates among the inflow high at slightly less than 30 per cent. This is very similar to the socio-demographic profile of migrants going to Ireland, where

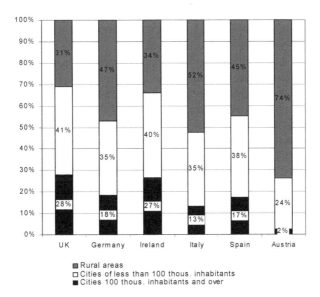

Figure 1.7   Polish post-accession migrants by type of settlement of origin and destination country, in per cent

Source: University of Warsaw Centre for Migration Research Migrants' Database, based on the Polish LFS.

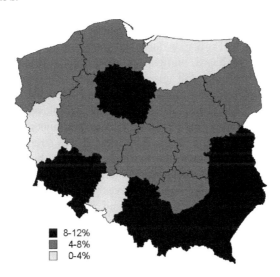

Figure 1.8   Polish post-accession migrants who left for the UK by place of origin in Poland, as percentage of all emigrants to UK

Source: University of Warsaw Centre for Migration Research Migrants' Database, based on the Polish LFS.

the English language has also been a pull factor, and just the opposite of migrants going to Germany and Italy.

This selectivity in the profile of post-accession migrants choosing the UK has been based on the fact that migration is now perceived as a good start to, the continuation of, or simply the attainment of a career. Prior to EU enlargement migration was a necessity for those who could not make a living in their region of origin, and who moved to seek better work opportunities than those available in their home country. In other words, EU enlargement brought an impetus for emigration to a new group of people, mostly those who would not have coped with, or benefited from, the stricter working regulations abroad beforehand.

The Impact of Labour Markets on Recent Poles' Mobility

Economic migration theory suggests that a massive outflow of labour (as in the case of contemporary Poland) should result in a decline in unemployment (the so called 'export of unemployment' hypothesis), an increase in the number of vacancies, rising pressure on wages and, eventually, the immigration of foreign labour (as a consequence of rising demand for labour). As already stated, one of the leading issues in the public debate pre-accession was the potential impact that international migration would have on the level and structure of unemployment, and specifically the prediction that mass migration would have a positive impact on the domestic labour market.

Before we present the arguments for and against this hypothesis, it is important to note that the Polish labour market during the transition period was characterized by severe structural problems, particularly low levels of human capital among the workforce, regional and skill mismatches and low internal mobility. These and other factors (including the impact of business cycles) led to extremely high unemployment rates, a large number of long-term unemployed, particularly high unemployment rates among youth and women, and low labour force participation and employment rates. Prior to 2004, then, Poland was struggling with serious job shortages and unemployment levels which were very high even by Central European standards; in 2002 the unemployment rate was approximately 20 per cent (Kaczmarczyk 2008). By 2003, however, a gradual improvement in the labour market situation was visible and this trend continued in the following years, gaining momentum after EU enlargement. Between the second quarter of 2004 and the first quarter of 2007 the number of unemployed individuals decreased from over three million to 1.5 million people. In 2007 the unemployment rate (according to the Polish LFS) fell below ten per cent. This change in the labour market could therefore easily be ascribed to the massive outflow of labour in the post-accession phase.

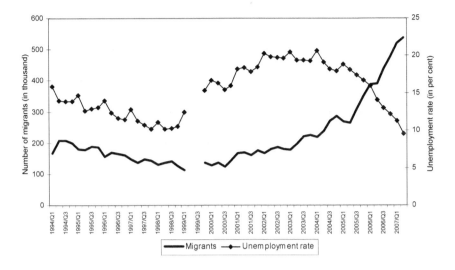

Figure 1.9 Migrants from Poland and the unemployment rate according to LFS, 1994–2007

Source: Kaczmarczyk and Okólski 2008a.

Figure 1.9 reveals a close correlation between unemployment levels and the scale of international migration (according to the Polish LFS data).[11] This data supports the common hypothesis that prior to 2004 unemployment was one of the most important push factors that was causing people to look for jobs abroad. However, since 2004, this tendency has changed completely – the rising intensity of migration was accompanied by declining unemployment. This certainly seems to reinforce the theory that this outflow has led to a decrease in unemployment.

Two other effects appeared as well. Firstly, since 2005 the number of vacancies has been rising rapidly. In the fourth quarter of 2005 a mere two per cent of companies reported hiring difficulties, but in the second quarter of 2007 this had risen to 13 per cent. In a few sectors shortages of workers became particularly severe; for example, in the construction industry over 30 per cent of companies reported hiring difficulties. Labour shortages have been declared by companies to be the most significant barrier to growth for the last two years (Narodowy Bank Polski 2007; World Bank 2007). Secondly, the impact of high unemployment on wages in Poland was particularly noticeable between 2004 and 2006 – during this period growth was limited to only two per cent. However, in 2007 the average monthly salary rose by around nine per cent and in a few sectors the increase was much higher, with agriculture at 11 per cent and construction at 16 per cent (World Bank 2007).

---

11   In fact, the Pearson correlation coefficient for the period 1999 (4th quarter) – 2004 (1st quarter) equalled 0.80 and for the post-accession period was as high as -0.98.

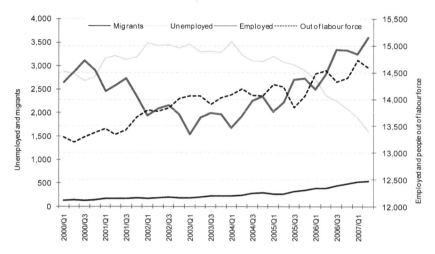

Figure 1.10   Migration and labour market phenomena according to the LFS, 2000–2007

Source: Kaczmarczyk and Okólski 2008b.

All these changes are usually presented as direct consequences of EU enlargement and mass post-accession outflow. It seems to be commonly accepted that migration has brought considerable labour market relief, especially with regard to unemployment, but has also led to severe labour shortages. However, as suggested by a few papers (Kaczmarczyk and Okólski 2008a, 2008b), the currently available statistical evidence does not necessarily support the assumption that recent labour market developments have been influenced primarily by migration. A few points can be made.

Firstly, an analysis of the labour market situation in other CEE countries indicates that most of them are struggling with rising shortages of labour. This situation holds true both in the case of those countries which have suffered a massive outflow of the workforce (Lithuania, Latvia, Poland) as well as those where migration has been of marginal importance (Hungary, the Czech Republic). Therefore, we may conclude that the increasing number of vacancies is not necessarily a result of outflow, but rather the consequence of a favourable economic climate and the resultant process of job creation. Post-accession migration, however, has certainly exacerbated the shortages of skills and workers which is clearly visible in the case of the Polish labour market.

Secondly, as suggested above, the decline in the number of people unemployed may primarily be a consequence of job creation and growth in employment. In Poland the number of people in employment increased from 13.7 million in 2004 to 15.2 million in 2007 (as Figure 1.10 shows).

Thirdly, in addition, if we compare the scale of migration from Poland and the scale of other labour market aggregates such as employment and unemployment (see Figure 1.10), it is clear that the volume of post-accession migration, even if very large in absolute terms, appears rather moderate in relation to the total number of employed and unemployed. Therefore, against this background, it would be reasonable to claim that the outflow of people cannot influence the domestic labour market situation in such a profound way.

Finally, this data also demonstrates another interesting trend related to the economic activity of the population, namely the continually rising number of those who are deemed to be inactive in the Polish labour market. In the context of the 'export of unemployment' hypothesis it has to be noted that the significant reduction in unemployment observed in the last four years may have resulted from a growing number of inactive people who have been discouraged from seeking employment, and not from migration. Obviously, individuals who left the labour force within the domestic labour market can also still become international migrants, but this hypothesis cannot be proven on an aggregate level.[12]

All in all, taken together, these empirical arguments clearly illustrate that the recent changes in the Polish labour market need to be understood as outcomes of the interplay of many different factors – economic fluctuations and business cycles, the restructuring of the economy such as through the privatization of state owned companies and foreign investment – in addition to the international mobility of people. Consequently, it would be hard to ascribe recent developments in the labour markets solely to post-accession outflow, although the immense scale of recent international mobility can definitely heighten the impact of other economic processes.

One other significant factor, furthermore, has almost been absent in the public debate on migration and related phenomena. As recently suggested by Polish researchers (Grabowska-Lusińska and Okólski 2008; Kaczmarczyk and Okólski 2008b), an important aspect of the post-accession outflow is its potential relationship to the so called 'crowding-out phenomenon'. The 'crowding-out' hypothesis argues that a central prerequisite for relatively backward economies to be able to 'catch up' is a massive outflow of the economically redundant population. Such a process was identified, among others, in Southern European countries (Layard et al. 1994). However, during the last few decades emigration from Poland (as well as from other CEE countries) did not produce a 'crowding-out' effect. In fact, until very recently the outflow from Poland had had little impact on its population and economy. This was due partly to the fact that migration was strongly controlled and thus limited in scale, but also, secondly, because of the natural increase in the country's population. During the 1980s and 1990s, despite a sizeable outflow and

---

12   In-depth micro level research reveals that the 'export of unemployment' hypothesis can only be supported to a limited extent. According to the data gathered for four Polish regions, almost half of all those leaving to go abroad had had permanent jobs in Poland before departure. The most striking feature of recent migration is the rising share of young people who are entering the EU labour market without prior experiences of the Polish one (Kaczmarczyk 2008).

the absence of significant immigration, the population of Poland was continuously on the rise.

Post-accession large-scale migration, and its accompanying structural characteristics, offered an opportunity, for the very first time in post-war history, for serious changes in the Polish labour market. From the research which has been undertaken in selected Polish regions it seems that the spectacular increase in the scale of recent mobility can be attributed primarily to the intensified migration activities of relatively young (up to 35 years) and well educated people. They are predominantly choosing the UK and Ireland and their main motivations are not only purely economic factors such as higher wages, but also the chance to improve language skills and the opportunity to work and stay abroad legally. Additionally – and this seems extremely important in the context of the 'crowding-out' hypothesis – they originate, to a relatively large extent, from tiny towns or rural areas. For this group of people, migration is to be perceived, then, not only as an escape from unemployment but also as a chance to improve their position in the Polish labour market by gaining additional skills, professional experience or accumulating the capital needed to start their own businesses (Kaczmarczyk 2008). This kind of strategy can be understood as a consequence of the structural features of the Polish labour market and the new opportunities which have opened up since May 2004. After 1989, the human capital attributes of the younger sections of the population improved significantly, but this was not matched by changes in the labour market. As a consequence, local labour markets in rural areas and tiny towns, not being able to offer good prospects for young and well educated people, became a 'trap' for a relatively large group of people who effectively became economically redundant. Therefore, in this context, the 'crowding-out' theory suggests that there is now an opportunity to propose and introduce reforms which might lead to a significant improvement in the domestic labour market in the long term.

This phenomenon is closely linked to another issue that has been discussed extensively with regard to Polish migration – the mobility of the highly skilled and the ensuing threat of a national brain drain through their migration. The portrayal of a dangerous brain drain, however, is not necessarily straightforward. To start with, during the communist period two large-scale outflows of highly skilled people had already taken place.[13] Various datasets have indicated, however, that the educational profile of migrants changed during the period of transition. Since 1990, the proportion of migrants with the lowest level of education has been increasing

---

13   The two most important episodes are the period 1968–1971 when approximately 13,000 Polish citizens of Jewish ethnicity were expelled, and a large migration in the early 1980s following the introduction of martial law. According to Sakson (2002), of the almost 700,000 emigrants who left Poland between 1981 and 1988, 15 per cent had a higher degree and a further 31 per cent had completed secondary school. At the same time, the proportion of people with a university degree in the total population was around seven per cent, so there was a significant overrepresentation of emigrants with high levels of human capital in relation to the whole population of Poland.

and the share of those with post-secondary education decreasing. For example, in 1988 the percentage of migrants with a university degree was nine per cent whereas the figure for those with just primary education was 37 per cent, while in 2003 it was four per cent and 55 per cent respectively. Various studies conducted both in Poland and in different receiving countries have also showed that the most migrants were typically people with low skills, lower qualifications and a lack of foreign language proficiency (Korczyńska 2003; Kaczmarczyk 2005).

This picture, though, was starting to change in the second half of the 1990s, first as a consequence of increased educational attainment across the population, and second, due to the severe economic crisis and high unemployment figures for the young and highly skilled. According to the 2002 Population Census, the educational structure of the people staying outside Poland for more than two months was far better than that of the whole population (aged 15 and over). The number of migrants with a science degree was double, the number with a professional Master's degree (MA) or equivalent was 36 per cent higher, and those with another type of higher degree was 26 per cent higher than all the other inhabitants of Poland. As already discussed, after 1997 these shifts were accompanied by substantial changes in the choice of receiving countries, especially among the most highly educated. The same conclusions have been drawn from studies carried out in the destination countries, particularly in the UK and Ireland. Data collected through an online survey (December 2006–February 2007) revealed that in one UK sample the share of people with tertiary education was 28.1 per cent (MA or equivalent postgraduate qualification) and 13.7 per cent (undergraduate qualification) (Grabowska-Lusińska and Okólski 2008). Another survey completed with 2,000 Polish migrants in the UK and Ireland in September 2007 had similar findings; this research found that over 22 per cent of the sampled individuals had completed tertiary education and over 90 per cent had at least secondary education (Garapich and Osipovic 2007).

With these issues in mind an important point needs to be made. Typically, a brain drain is treated as an overrepresentation of highly skilled people among emigrants compared to those in the sending population generally. This approach, however, may be misleading in the case of Poland (as well as other CEE countries). Because of how migration outflows have been structured by age, and due to the increasing access to higher education in these countries, statistical data may indicate the existence of the brain drain phenomenon even if it does not take place. In the last 20 years, Poland has experienced a true educational breakthrough. Between 1970 and 2001, the number of university graduates among the Polish population increased from two per cent to 12 per cent; at the end of the 1990s, the number of students was 2.6 times higher than in 1990. Nowadays in Poland there are over 1.8 million students, and data from the Central Statistical Office shows that in the early 2000s the gross enrolment ratio in the 19–24 year old age group was close to 50 per cent, meaning that Poland has almost matched the higher education participation rates of developed countries. In this context, the increase in the share of relatively well educated migrants should be perceived as a natural consequence of educational developments in Poland. Additionally, as suggested above, the outflow of people with a tertiary-level education who often face serious problems in the Polish labour market could be described as a 'brain overflow', rather than a brain drain.

It can be argued, then, that although there is to some extent an educational selectivity among emigrants from Poland, this process has not translated into a mass exodus of highly skilled people, and its scale and significance are actually small when compared to the phenomena of the 1980s. Furthermore, in spite of the fact that Polish migrants do tend to be more highly skilled, they are still predominantly concentrated in the secondary sectors of the receiving economies and take jobs in 'typical' migrant sectors such as construction, agriculture, cleaning and hotels. This is clear from the British WRS data. The largest group of A8 workers who registered with the system between May 2004 and December 2007 (39 per cent) were people hired in 'administration, business and management', with a further 19 per cent working in hospitality and catering, ten per cent in agriculture and seven per cent in manufacturing (Home Office et al. 2008). This category of 'administration, business and management' includes recruitment agencies and it is these particular types of company who are responsible for the majority of the employment. More detailed information on the occupations of A8 applicants illustrates that they mainly undertake simple jobs which do not demand high skill levels. Between May 2004 and December 2007 the dominant occupations were jobs such as 'process operative' (27 per cent of all applicants, almost 200,000 registered workers out of 716,000 in total), 'warehouse operative' (eight per cent), packer (six per cent), kitchen and catering assistant (six per cent), or cleaner and/or domestic staff (six per cent). Only minor changes have been recorded since May 2004. The WRS data, therefore, suggests that the vast majority (80–90 per cent) of migrants from the A8 countries are hired for occupations that need no professional qualifications.

If we consider this data alongside the fact that approximately 25–30 per cent of Polish migrants in the UK hold a university degree, it has to be concluded that all the anticipated positive effects of migration, such as opportunities to improve qualifications or for professional development, are out of reach for the majority of educated migrants. Instead there appears to be a developing phenomenon of 'brain wasting' or deskilling, something which was typical of the migration of the 1980s. Obviously the WRS data has limitations for assessing this trend; it only records legal employment, and also just provides information on migrants' first jobs in the UK. Low-skilled jobs might be a gateway into the UK labour market for A8 migrants, who after spending a few months abroad would be able to move into the primary sector. However, as other studies have demonstrated, this has not necessarily happened and there has not been a remarkable improvement in the migrants' position in the labour market over time. Drinkwater et al. (2006) have shown that the post-enlargement inflow of Poles to the UK is dominated by well educated people (with on average 13.6 years of schooling), but that their position in the labour market is characterized by very low earnings, a very low self-employment rate, and an overrepresentation in the production industries (25 per cent) and retail/hospitality (29 per cent). In another recent paper, Clark and Drinkwater (2008) strongly support this observation and state that the labour market performance of recent A8 migrants is not only worse in comparison to the native population, but that well qualified migrants from CEE experience very low rates of return on their education. All the available research suggests that there has been a clear manifestation of the 'brain waste' phenomenon among post-accession flows of Polish, and other A8 migrants, in the UK.

Conclusions

Migration from Poland, which is recognized as one of the most important migrant sending countries in Europe, has been substantial for some time now. The post-2004 international mobility of Poles, due to its scale and dynamics, has also been heralded as one of the most spectacular population movements in contemporary European history. A particularly large inflow of migrants has been witnessed in the United Kingdom and Ireland. Polish migrants were barely 'visible' in these countries in the pre-accession period, but since 2004, in a very short period of time, they have became one of the most important, and dynamic, immigrant groups. However, a distinct increase in the presence of Poles was noted in almost all countries of the EEA, particularly in countries like Italy, Spain, the Netherlands, Norway, Sweden and even Iceland. Thus, recent migration from Poland should not be seen in terms of a concentration of movement to selected countries such as the UK and Ireland, but rather as a gradual 'spilling over' of mobility to many destinations.

As this chapter has illustrated, an analysis of the available statistical data leads to the conclusion that EU enlargement has triggered a hitherto 'hibernating' migration potential in Poland and other A8 countries. This phenomenon can be attributed to a complex set of factors including institutional factors such as freedom of movement and access to selected labour markets, but also the development of recruitment services and transportation routes. Migration related risk has reduced radically and the structure of migrants has altered significantly. Recent migration from Poland is considerably different structurally from the movements of the 1990s: it has become more regular than irregular or clandestine, more long-term than circular, and more 'individualistic' than related to household or family strategies. These changes are closely related to the shift in migrant profiles. Post-accession migrants from Poland are, on average, younger and better educated than people who left to go abroad in previous decades. This tendency is particularly visible in the 'new' destinations of Polish migrants, such as the UK and Ireland.

Recent migration from Poland has generally been portrayed as either a short-term opportunity for labour market relief, or as a long-term threat to Poland's economic success. We argue, however, that the impact of migration on the Polish labour market has been exaggerated. Even if the outflow from Poland has had a positive impact on the labour market, recent changes in the domestic labour market have had complex causes, and can be attributed to other factors such as an improved economic climate or wider structural changes. Therefore, we argue that it is important to take a slightly different approach towards the analysis of the impact of migration on the labour market. The available micro-data on Polish migration indicates that in the post-accession period there has been a substantially increased propensity to migrate among young and relatively well educated people originating from economically backward regions characterized by very limited employment opportunities. Such a tendency can be understood in terms of brain overflow and may lead to positive changes in the domestic labour market.

Last but not least, we argue that the recent mobility of Poles should not be presented as constituting a brain drain phenomenon. Post-accession international migration from Poland has increasingly become a domain for well educated people but this is to a large extent a consequence of the structure of the wider population. Furthermore, regardless of the fact that Polish migrants, at least to some extent, possess higher levels of human capital, they are still predominantly concentrated in the secondary sectors of the receiving economies, undertaking jobs in 'typical' migrant sectors such as construction, agriculture, cleaning, restaurants and hotels. A far more damaging situation could be developing then, than brain drain – that of brain waste, the employment of migrants from Poland far below their professional skills. This type of migration scenario could easily lead to a depreciation of the migrants' human capital, and could, in the long run, negatively impact upon their determination to improve their skills and qualifications.

References

Central Statistical Office (2008), *Informacja o rozmiarach i kierunkach emigracji z Polski w latach 2004–2007* [*On the Scale and Directions of Emigration from Poland, 2004–2007*], notatka informacyjna [Press Information] (Warszawa: GUS).

Clark, K. and Drinkwater, S. (2008), 'The Labour Market Performance of Recent Migrants', *Oxford Review of Economic Policy* 24:3.

Drinkwater, S., Eade, J. and Garapich, M. (2006), *Poles Apart? EU Enlargement and the Labour Market Outcomes of Immigrants in the UK.* Discussion Paper No. 2410 (Bonn: Institute for the Study of Labor).

Dustmann, C., Casanova, M., Fertig, M., Preston, I. and Schmidt, C.M. (2003), *The Impact of EU Enlargement on Migration Flows.* Home Office Report 25/03 (London: Home Office).

Górny, A. and Osipovič, D. (2006), *Return Migration of Second-Generation British Poles.* University of Warsaw Centre for Migration Research Working Papers No. 6/64 (Warsaw: University of Warsaw Centre for Migration Research).

Grabowska-Lusińska, I. and Okólski, M. (2008), *Migracje z Polski po 1 maja 2004* [*Post-2004 Migration from Poland*] (Warsaw: Scholar).

Home Office UK Border Agency, Department for Work and Pensions, HM Revenue and Customs and Communities and Local Government (2008), *Accession Monitoring Report May 2004–March 2008* (London: Home Office).

Hryniewicz, J., Jałowieckim, B. and Myncem, A. (1992), *Ucieczka mózgów ze szkolnictwa wyższego i nauki. Raport z badań* [*The Brain Flight from Higher Education and Science. A Report from Research*] (Warsaw: Europejski Instytut Rozwoju Regionalnego i Lokalnego).

Hryniewicz, J., Jałowieckim, B. and Myncem, A. (1997), *Ruchliwość pracowników naukowych w latach 1994–1997* [*The Mobility of Science Workers, 1994–1997*] (Warsaw: Europejski Instytut Rozwoju Regionalnego i Lokalnego).

Jałowieckim, B., Hryniewicz, J. and Mync, A. (1994), *Ucieczka mózgów ze szkolnictwa wyższego Polsce w latach 1992–1993* [*The Brain Flight from Higher Education in Poland, 1992–1993*] (Warsaw: Europejski Instytut Rozwoju Regionalnego i Lokalnego).

Kaczmarczyk, P. (2005), *Migracje zarobkowe Polakow w dobie przemian* [*Migration for Work in the Era of Change*] (Warsaw: WUW).

Kaczmarczyk, P. (2008), *Współczesne migracje Polaków – aspekty regionalne i lokalne* [*Recent Mobility of Poles – Regional and Local Aspects*] (Warsaw: WNE UW).

Kaczmarczyk, P. and Okólski, M. (2008a), *Economic Impacts of Migration on Poland and Baltic States* (Oslo: FAFO).

Kaczmarczyk, P. and Okólski, M. (2008b), 'Demographic and Economic Impacts of Migration on Poland', *Oxford Review of Economic Policy* 24:3.

Kępińska, E. (2007), *Recent Trends in International Migration. The 2007 SOPEMI Report for Poland.* University of Warsaw Centre for Migration Research Working Paper No. 29/87 (Warsaw: University of Warsaw Centre for Migration Research).

Korczyńska, J. (2003), *Sezonowe wyjazdy zarobkowe Polaków do Niemiec* [*Polish Seasonal Migration to Germany*] (Warsaw: Scholar).

Layard, R., Blanchard, O.J., Dornbusch, R. and Krugman, P. (1992), *East-West Migration: The Alternatives* (Cambridge, MA: MIT Press).

Narodowy Bank Polski (2007), *Wstępna informacja o kondycji sektora przedsiębiorstw ze szczególnym uwzględnieniem stanu koniunktury w I kw. 2007* [*An Initial Report on The Condition of The Company Sector with a Particular Focus on Market Opportunities in the First Quarter of 2007*] (Warsaw: Narodowy Bank Polski).

Portes, J. and French, S. (2005), *The Impact of Free Movement of Workers from Central and Eastern Europe on the UK Labour Market: Early Evidence. Working Paper No. 18* (London: Department for Work and Pensions).

Sakson, B. (2002), *Wpływ 'niewidzialnych' migracji zagranicznych lat osiemdziesiatych na struktury demograficzne Polski* [*The Impact of 'Invisible' International Migration in the Eighties on Demographic Structures of Poland*] (Warsaw: SGH).

Salt, J. (2006), *International Migration and the United Kingdom – Report of the United Kingdom SOPEMI* (London: Migration Research Unit, Department of Geography, University College London).

Sword, K., Davies, N. and Ciechanowski, J. (1989), *The Formation of Polish Community in Britain: 1939–1950* (London: School of Slavonic and East European Studies, University of London).

Traser, J. (2005), *Report on the Free Movement of Workers in the EU-25. Who's Afraid of EU Enlargement?* (Brussels: ECAS).

World Bank (2007), *Labor Markets in EU8+2: From the Shortage of Jobs to the Shortage of Skilled Workers.* World Bank EU8+2 Regular Economic Report (Warsaw: World Bank).

Chapter 2

Changing Patterns of Polish Labour Migration after the UK's Opening of the Labour Market? Insights from Rural Case-studies in the Opolskie and Świętokrzyskie Voivodships

Tim Elrick and Emilia Brinkmeier

New Opportunities?

The European Union (EU) enlargement in 2004 opened up the possibility for citizens of the accession countries to not only travel freely within the EU but also to legally take up employment opportunities in some of the old EU member states, among the first ones being the United Kingdom.[1] The first preliminary data from these countries, such as the UK Worker Registration Scheme (WRS) (Home Office et al. 2008), suggests that there has been a substantive response to the offers of those member states to access their labour markets.[2] However, it is assumed that not all workers who registered under the WRS migrated to the UK in the year of registration. Many were already resident in the UK beforehand (cf. Association of Labour Providers 2005: 4; Okólski 2007: 12), and the new options offered by the UK (and others) might have changed prevailing, documented and undocumented, migration patterns.

Drawing on findings from case-studies located in two regions of rural Poland, we would like to present insights into continuities and changes in migration patterns prevailing in these regions and their effect on migration to the UK. As we found significant differences in the reaction of the inhabitants of these regions towards the new opportunities offered by the states adopting an 'open labour

---

1 On 1 May 2004 the United Kingdom, Ireland, and Sweden opened their labour markets to the new accession countries, followed by Spain, Portugal, Greece, Finland and Iceland on 1 May 2006, Italy on 31 July 2006, the Netherlands on 1 May 2007, and, most recently, Luxembourg on 1 November 2007.

2 Salt and Millar (2006: 346) assume that the WRS underestimates the number of people who actually take up work as the self-employed do not have to register in this scheme.

market policy' early on, we would like to offer two possible explanations for the different developments. Firstly, we refer to the distinct histories of migration of both communities, and, secondly, we highlight the role of formal and informal agents in shaping migration before and after EU enlargement in 2004. Taking into account that the enlargement and subsequent opening of the labour markets, especially in the old EU member states, gave a new momentum to East–West migration within Europe (cf. Favell 2008) we also evaluate the impact of these new opportunities for the migrants.

Theoretical Clarifications: Migration Patterns and Networks

When looking at different communities within a country of origin, one can observe a significant diversity in the patterns of migration. We argue that these patterns are mainly determined by a community's history of migration and the migration network active in the community in question. Of course, migration patterns are also dependent on the composition of the migrating population, destinations, time patterns, type of job and degree of legality of the migrants' occupations; however, all of these determinants are also consequences of the wider history of migration and the migration network. For clarity, when referring to *old migration patterns* we mean the patterns already present before the EU accession of the new member states, and likewise we mean the patterns which emerged after May 2004 when speaking of *new migration patterns*.

By *history of migration* we understand the length of time a location has been exposed to large-scale migration within the last few decades. Researchers like Kandel and Massey (2002) (for Poland see Kaczmarczyk et al. 2004) have found that people in locations with a longer history of migration are more prone to engage in migration. This might be accredited to the material manifestations of successful migrants, the exchange of migration experiences and the results of migrants' agency in the home region. The *migrating population* may vary according to gender, previous occupation, age and other individual attributes. Of course, different *destinations* (countries as well as locations) determine the migration patterns as well as the *time patterns*. The latter include the duration migrants stay abroad, as well as the repetitiveness of their migrations. The *type of job*, not only differentiated by business sector but also by mode of work (manual vs. cognitive), interplays with the *legality of the occupation* at the destination. Whereas border-crossings in the EU are nowadays captured for Polish people within the framework of free movement, it still remains important whether their job abroad is documented – registered with the authorities and therefore included in the social systems at the destination, as well as in the tax system there – or if their work is undocumented – which means untaxed income, which is far more attractive, but, at the same time, renders their work fraudulent in most destination countries.

Although labour migration is still determined to a great extent by economic factors on the side of the migrants (labour supply) and the destination countries (labour demand) (cf. Massey et al. 1998) more and more scholars recognize that the social *networks* of migrants also play a crucial role. As migration networks (see Elrick and Ciobanu 2009) facilitate the migration process of most migrants in many different stages like decision making, the actual move or the arrival at the destination, it is necessary to differentiate their forms. Networks are sets of social relations which are often comprised of family members and friends, but also by intermediaries like formal and informal labour recruitment agents and community associations (cf. Boyd 1989; Elrick and Lewandowska 2008). Although networks 'revolve around some organizing principle' (Gurak and Caces 1992: 152), they need not always be institutionalized by the *formal ties* of, for example, migrants' organizations or recruitment agencies, but can also consist of looser relations of friends, acquaintances, or even intermediaries (private persons providing jobs) which we refer to as *informal ties* in this text. While it is possible that people decide on their own whether, when and where to migrate (this accounts for all pioneer migrants), the majority of migrants rely on social networks which include members of their origin community. The reason for this is that family and peers become 'role models through their achievements in foreign countries' (Fawcett 1989: 678f) and they are trusted most when it comes to information about migration (cf. Koser and Pinkerton 2002; Fawcett 1989). This means that migrants are not only powerful intermediaries of views, ideas, values and behaviours in the destination country, but are also the principal means of communicating the opportunities of migration destinations and labour market needs to fellow compatriots still in their origin communities (cf. Heering et al. 2004: 325).

The Case-studies: Two Communities in Rural Poland

In this chapter we will consider the impact of EU enlargement in 2004 on patterns of migration at the level of the individual. To do this, we will use data collected from our two case-studies conducted in rural areas in Poland. One gmina, Nowy Korczyn, is located in the eastern part of Poland, in the Kielce district, north-east of Kraków, in the voivodship of Świętokrzyskie.[3] The other, Wilków gmina, is located in Upper Silesia in the south-west of Poland, east of Wrocław, in the voivodship of Opolskie. These two locations were chosen according to their contrasting characteristics, especially in relation to their intensity and history of migration. Based on statistical data, Kaczmarczyk and Łukowski (2004) had already identified these two communities as locations with a high intensity of migration, although their histories of migration differ significantly. While the

---

3 Each community constitutes an administrative unit called gmina. Each gmina consists of several villages. When referring to the community in this article we mean, at the same time, the whole gmina.

Table 2.1   Age and gender structure of sample

Gmina	Narrative interviews	Male	Female	Up to 30 years old	30 to 44 years old	45 years old and over
Wilków	11	4	7	8	0	3
Nowy Korczyn	11	3	8	3	1	7
Total	**22**	**7**	**15**	**11**	**1**	**10**

Upper Silesian region has a long-standing tradition of circulative migration, especially to Germany, migration in the Kielce district only occurred in the form of eclectic long-term migrations to the US over more recent decades.[4]

Both communities are typically agricultural, although only Wilków is an area with high quality soils. In the 1970s and 1980s several kinds of co-operatives existed on which more than half of the inhabitants were employed at that time. Many people also owned (rather small) farms and cultivated land while working at these co-operatives. When the co-operatives collapsed due to the systemic change in 1989 (some before, and the others shortly after) most of the people focused on their own farms and struggled to survive. It was at this point that migration increased vastly in scale and started being perceived as a real alternative. Into the early twenty first century, agriculture is still officially the main source of income, although the revenues, especially in Nowy Korczyn, are very low and therefore scarcely sufficient on their own. Pensions are the second highest official source of income and sometimes one pension has to provide for a whole family. Migration therefore is a viable option to overcome the income shortage.

Our analysis is based on eleven qualitative interviews with key informants (mayors, voivods, priests, school directors), 22 biographical-narrative interviews with migrants, and three discussion groups with community members (migrants and non-migrants) from the chosen communities, all conducted between February and October 2006. For the interviews we only included people with migration experiences, interviewing either actual or returned migrants. To do so, we looked initially for returned migrants in the origin communities by asking key informants to identify them. Secondly, we sought migrants who were on vacation back in their home villages. Finally, we followed actual, current migrants to their new destinations (in the UK, Germany and Italy) after having identified them from households in the original communities. In line with multi-sited fieldwork conventions (Marcus 1998), we then conducted these interviews in Italy, Germany and the UK. As we only interviewed people with migration experiences, our sample is non-representative

---

4   As the Upper Silesia region was formerly part of Germany many people living there have dual citizenship which allows them to cross the border easily.

Table 2.2   Highest education level of sample

Gmina	Primary school	Vocational school	High school	University	Up to 30 y/o and high school or higher	45 or more y/o and high school or higher
Wilków	1	3	4	3	6 (of 8)	1 (of 3)
Nowy Korczyn	4	2	4	1	2 (of 3)	3 (of 7)
Total	**5**	**5**	**8**	**4**	**8 (of 11)**	**4 (of 10)**

Table 2.3   Destinations of interviewed migrants

Gmina	Germany		Italy		UK		US		Austria		Belgium	
	D	U	D	U	D	U	D	U	D	U	D	U
Wilków	–	5	–	–	3	2	–	–	–	1	–	–
Nowy Korczyn	3	1	2*	6*	1	–	3	–	–	1	–	–
Total	**9**		**6**		**6**		**3**		**2**		**1**	

Notes: Multiple answers possible; D – Documented migrant; U – Undocumented migrant.
*Two migrants to Italy who were formerly involved in undocumented migration became documented after a regularisation.

and arguably compromised by our snowball sampling. However, we did aim for a 'high variance' of attributes among our interviewees (Patton 1990). Although this represents a small sample, our interviews also revealed more patterns of other migrants from the same origin, so we were able get a good insight into the two communities. As our interviews followed a narrative approach, most migrants were happy to talk about their life after finishing their education, which in most cases was closely intertwined with several migration experiences at different times during their lifecourse.

The overall age and gender structure of our sample, as shown in Table 2.1, comprised largely of an age range of migrants from 21 years old up to 55 years old, although the sample in Wilków, the gmina in Upper Silesia, was considerably younger (median 24 years old; Nowy Korczyn, the gmina in Świętokrzyskie, had a median age of 48 years old). The different age distributions in our sample (mainly older people in Nowy Korcyzn, mainly younger people in Wilków) does also represent the overall age distribution of the two communities.

The majority of interviewees were married (13) or lived with a partner (four). Almost half of our sample did not have children (nine), whereas the families tended to be bigger in the eastern community. In Wilków there were more better-qualified migrants in the sample than in Nowy Korczyn (see Table 2.2). Both variables once again tend to represent the same variance distributions in the gminas.

As all interview partners were labour migrants, of course, no one was officially unemployed, but all of the migrants in the Upper Silesian community started migrating from an unemployed status whereas the migrants in the Świętokrzyskie voivodship were, and mostly still are, involved in farming. Table 2.3 gives an account of the migration destinations of the interviewed migrants. It can even be seen from our small sample that in the Wilków gmina undocumented work dominates while in the Nowy Korczyn gmina both types are represented.

Migration Patterns Before 2004

To offer an insight into the changes and continuities in these migration patterns, we will start by comparing the trends in the two case-studies places before and after EU accession. We will then analyse the outcomes according to the two main discriminating factors: the histories of migration and migration networks.

Internal migration in the Nowy Korczyn gmina was recorded a relatively long time ago and has changed significantly over time, but it is still situated in a region with historically modest and not very intensive migration flows.[5] Throughout its history the community has experienced several in- and outflows of different internal migrants. The Kielce region generally has experienced significantly less migration since the liberalization of travel regulations in Poland in the 1970s, however, than the Upper Silesian region where our second case study is based.

International migration started from the community, according to our key informants, in the 1980s with modest flows of long-term (and sometimes even settlement) migration to the US. In the 1990s people slowly started to take up opportunities to migrate seasonally for work in the agricultural sector, enabled by bilateral agreements between the Polish and the German as well as the Spanish governments. According to the available statistical data, migration based on the agreement between Poland and Germany – i.e. migration for documented work – has become more intensive since 1998 (Kaczmarczyk et al. 2004). At the same time, the migration of undocumented workers to Italy was also taking place (predominantly women working in the domestic service and domestic elderly care sectors). According to our interview data, since 1999 Italy has become one of the main migration destinations, followed by Germany, due to evolving migrant networks. The destinations, however, have not been limited to these places, and

---

5   The 6,750 inhabitants which make up the wider community of Nowy Korczyn consist of 24 villages ranging from 90 to 1,000 inhabitants. Nowy Korczyn is the biggest village among them.

some men, for example, have found long-term contractual (but also undocumented) work in the construction sector in Norway – a destination which has increased in popularity across Poland within the last few years (Kępińska Dec 2007: 8f).

Looking at the different attributes of the migrants from Nowy Korczyn, it is not possible to determine a dominant migration pattern. An earlier group of migrants, to the US, was comprised of both married and single, men and women. A second group consisted of women aged either 25 to 35 years old or in their late 50s who circulated between Poland and Italy where they worked undocumented in the domestic service and care sectors. The majority of them were formerly unemployed in Poland – this was actually a prerequisite as these types of jobs require longer stays abroad (several months) and therefore do not enable migrants to hold on to a job in Poland at the same time, although some of the elder migrants also earned (insufficient) pensions in Poland. Most of these migrants to Italy were married to farmers and have children. Finally, the majority of migrants have gone to Germany; they are mainly young men working in the agricultural sector, but women also work there too. These migrants are students and farmers, employed and unemployed alike, and include single people and those with families, all working on vegetable farms (picking asparagus, cabbage or cucumbers) each summer while living on site in Germany.

The Wilków community also has a long but much more intense history of migration.[6] Due to the movement of the German–Polish border after World War II many Germans either left or were forced to leave for Germany. In the 1940s and 1950s, for various political and demographic reasons, the Polish state used this region to repatriate Polish citizens who had been forced to leave the formerly Polish regions east of the new Polish–Russian border. In the end, only very few ethnic Germans, i.e. Polish citizens with German roots, remained in the community. The majority of the community's inhabitants, in fact, are Poles from those eastern regions or descendants of them.[7] However, Wilków neighbours other communities where there are more ethnic Germans, many of whom work, largely undocumented, in Germany (as many of them possess German passports). Thus, migration to Germany from the whole region has a long tradition.

According to our interview partners, in 1986/1987 a small, almost unnoticeable, outflow to Germany started after Polish citizens were allowed to travel to Austria and Germany; the majority went to West Berlin. These were short voyages officially called 'tourist trips'. Both employed and unemployed villagers, however, used to travel by buses or private cars to buy goods abroad in order to sell them afterwards in Polish markets. After more and more co-operatives shut down (around 1989) people started looking for jobs abroad more intensively as there were not many other opportunities available in their region of origin, and the money earned from these 'tourist trips' was only sufficient to cater for 'extra'

---

6   Wilków is comprised of 13 villages where the village Wilków is the biggest one among them. The population of the whole community comprises 4,730 villagers.

7   Those people are called Zabużanie in Poland.

needs. Since 1989, new migration strategies have been taken up, including longer stays abroad which still have a circulatory character. Even permanent settlement has been occurring (especially to Germany, using their intense relations in the region to this country), although not many people left for good. According to our data, migration, especially to Germany, further intensified after the Polish economic recession at the end of the 1990s. Both men and women migrated to work (mostly undocumented) in Germany in the agricultural sector, with men also working in construction and women in the domestic service and domestic elderly care sectors. Between 2000 and 2004, migration to Germany intensified again and new destinations have also started to become more noticeable (although not significant), this time to the Netherlands, Belgium and Norway.

In contrast to the Nowy Korczyn community, a dominant migration pattern can be distinguished in Wilków: younger women (in their 20s) and older women (in their 40s and 50s) work undocumented in Germany in the domestic service and care sectors, migrating for short-term periods. After two to three months, the time-span which was initially set by German visa restrictions, women 'swap' with relatives, friends or neighbours, a pattern which continues throughout the whole year (cf. Morokvašić 2004). The younger female generation also has experience of working in documented employment as au pairs – this type of work often seen as an antecedent to undocumented domestic and care employment. Apparently, growing up in a region with a strong and intense history of migration to Germany, particularly recently, as well as the fact that they have many contacts abroad, allows them to take up undocumented work more often and more easily than in the case of women in Nowy Korczyn.

Paradoxically, while the Upper Silesian region has a long history of migration, especially to Germany due to its close historical links and status as previously German territory, migration for documented employment seems to be rather low. On the other hand, the Kielce district, which has little connection with Germany but instead has some ties with the US, has turned out to be an island of high intensity migration for documented work in Germany.

Migration Patterns After 2004

Even though changes in migration patterns from Poland had been expected at the time of EU accession (cf. Sinn et al. 2001; Boeri and Brücker 2000; Bauer and Zimmermann 1999), our data shows mixed findings. While the Nowy Korczyn gmina does not display significant changes in existing migration patterns and types of migrants, the Wilków gmina does.

In Nowy Korczyn we could only observe small adaptations within the old migration patterns. Namely, women migrating to Italy have started to prolong their stay for longer than the usual two to three months. Also, some eclectic evidence of migration to new destination countries appeared for individual cases to Ireland

(Dublin) and to the UK (London and Edinburgh), commencing half a year after accession, with migrants undertaking documented work in these cities.[8]

In contrast, the outflow from Wilków after 2004 rose drastically. Prevailing patterns grew in intensity and new patterns also developed. Evidently, EU accession has not brought a change in the established migration pattern to Germany in Wilków. According to the college (*Gymnasium*) director, about one third of all parents now migrate, with just a fraction of them seeming to do so with documented contracts. He reported that it was particularly visible at school meetings where more and more parents arrived in new or better cars. Germany still remains the dominant destination (in particular to the areas of Frankfurt, Hamburg and Mannheim where strong networks exist) for the parents of the school children with seasonal jobs in the agricultural sector (for men and women) as well as in the domestic service and elderly care sectors (for women). Interestingly, the main patterns of female migration in the domestic services sector have not changed from the existing circular pattern of two to three months abroad, although, now, the freedom of movement, granted by the EU treaty, would allow migrants to stay longer.[9] It seems from our data that this strategy, initially shaped by external factors, has been internalized by the women and fits into their habitual lifecourse well.

However, the main increase in migration is due to the fact that community members from Wilków have started taking up opportunities for documented employment and residence in countries that opened their borders and markets to workers from the accession countries, especially the UK. This has led to a range of new patterns of migration. The majority of the new Polish migrants to the UK, for example, undertake documented work. Individuals, but also young, unmarried couples migrate. Time restrictions governing the former migration patterns (either bilateral agreements or undocumented work) made it difficult to leave as a couple, but now countries with unrestricted labour market access offer the chance to stay longer and it is considered to be worthwhile leaving as a couple. This also happens in the case of families; migration to the UK is attractive as they can jointly go to work there, taking their children with them – this was very difficult in the old migration patterns. However, families also often send only one parent to the UK as the jobs seem to yield more than those in former migration patterns; before, usually both parents migrated in order to sustain the family income, at the cost of leaving their children with their grandparents, other relatives or even neighbours. In comparison to the old migration patterns, migrants to the UK tend to have been unemployed in Poland, but have a higher education and are younger than before

---

8   Even though Polish migration to the UK has a very long tradition we consider migration after EU enlargement as a new migration pattern since this destination seems to be new for many regions and communities in Poland and its composition differs significantly from previous waves (for the struggle between old Polish migrants and new arrivals see Garapich 2008).

9   This also contradicts our findings from Nowy Korczyn, where women engaged in domestic services migration to Italy mostly stay significantly longer than three months.

(cf. Drinkwater et al. 2006). More and more people are also opting for long or at least longer term (two to three years) migration. As many of the young migrants have high expectations about their career and way of life, they leave Poland due to insufficient earning opportunities and/or in search of a different way of living. Some of these motivations may turn them into settlement migrants. The migrants also appreciate the higher standard of living and the protection the social security system in the UK offers. However, it is too early to decide whether the new Polish migrants will stay for good, as the signifiers of settlement are not fixed and many young rural Poles seem to be very attached to their home country.

Possible Explanations: Persistence and Change in Migration Patterns

In this section we will respond to the two questions which have arisen from this research: why has migration to new destination countries increased so drastically in Wilków, but not in Nowy Korczyn? And, why has the overall intensity of migration increased in Wilków – even taking into account migration patterns occurring before May 2004? We suggest two related explanations: one reason might be found in the different migration histories of the two communities, the other reason might be how informal and formal agents shape migrants' opportunities differently.

Answering the first puzzle, we can firstly refer to the long and intense history of migration which plays a significant role in the case of Wilków. Migrants from this locale seem to have a particular, almost professional attitude towards migration. They seem to be more flexible in adapting their migration strategies. This might be attributed to their exposure to migration (cf. Horváth 2008) and the effects of previous migrations in their places of origin (cf. Elrick 2008). As discussed before, Wilków is located in Upper Silesia, a region with a concentrated history of migration; additionally, many community members were internal migrants after World War II or are descendents of them (cf. Mach 1993). As a consequence, migration is deeply rooted in almost all the families of the community and part of almost everyone's life cycle or family history; therefore, it is regarded as something normal to undertake, just as one more option in life. This stronger 'embeddedness in migration' in the Wilków community might be one catalyst for opening up new migration patterns to new destination countries such as the UK.

Unlike Wilków, the other community, Nowy Korczyn, is located in a region with a significantly weaker intensity of migration, and where, in the past, migration played a role only in the lives of people who had been displaced. Therefore, migration still seems to be an extraordinary event in many people's lives and migration experiences are still scarce. In this case, people seem to be less eager to change their strategies in life as migration appears to carry risks and insecurities and bring high costs (cf. Massey et al. 1998).

A second answer to the question, why migration to new countries, of which the UK is the major destination, has appeared much more intensely in one community than in the other might be explained by the different nature of the migration networks existing in the two communities. Firstly and interrelated with the earlier explanation, migration networks have developed differently due to the different histories of migration. In Wilków, where a long history of migration prevails, well established networks exist among migrants themselves and among migrants and migrants-to-be. Secondly, the development of networks in both communities is also related to geographical differences. While the Nowy Korczyn community is dominated by migrant networks which are formed around separate villages, the Wilków community is dominated by several interlinked networks which work between the villages and Germany. As the villages in Wilków were founded as street villages where one village blends into the next, communications and acquaintances are bolstered more by this geographic pattern than in the Nowy Korczyn gmina, where compact villages lie scattered and distant from each other. These geographic patterns are one of the bases for the communication trends now observed in the villages. Thus, while in Wilków migration destinations are dispersed among migrants from all the community villages, in Nowy Korczyn whole villages seem to specialize each in different destinations. For instance, inhabitants (both men and women) of one village go predominantly to Germany, while the members (mostly women) of another village migrate to Italy, and another village specializes in migration to the Netherlands.

Additionally, 'third actors', such as formal and informal agents who provide information on work, travel routes or housing in exchange of monetary or other remuneration, contribute within the migration networks to the shaping different migration patterns (Elrick and Lewandowska 2008). Here we mean *informal agents* as those involved with the private engagement of people, mediating between the labour demand and supply either just in the destination country, or in both the origin and destination countries. *Formal agents*, by contrast, are people or companies who run registered recruitment agencies in the origin or destination countries. Among such informal agents we found former and even current migrants, migrants' family members, friends from the place of origin, acquaintances (i.e. other Poles or relatives of employers) and natives (e.g. nurses or doctors) in the destination country. The informal agents are, therefore, not only co-ethnics but also Italians and Ukrainians in Italy, Germans in Germany and the British in the UK; formal agents, however, are usually only represented by nationals from the destination country. Informal agents seem to provide mainly undocumented work (although there is evidence in our data that they also offer documented jobs), while formal agents mostly provide documented jobs (but sometimes also, of course unofficial, undocumented ones).

Formal agents appeared in the old migration patterns in only a few cases because documented migration to other EU member states before Poland's accession was limited to bilateral agreements; these channelled migrants into work in a few sectors in which the destination countries suffered labour shortages, such as the agricultural sector or the hospital nursing sector for Germany. Far more common were informal agents who played a major part in most old migration patterns, along with usual migrant network contacts. After EU enlargement, however, formal agents seem to have far outnumbered informal agents in the new emerging migrations to countries such as the UK and Ireland. This is substantiated by data provided by the OECD (Organization for Economic Co-operation and Development) in 2006: the number of labour recruitment agencies in Poland for work abroad has risen disproportionally since 2004, and most of them provide work in the UK or Ireland (Kępińska 2006: 38ff). Additionally, a significant increase in labour recruitment agencies can be observed in the UK as well; more than 170 'labour providers' are registered with the Association of Labour Providers, without even including the uncounted non-collectivized agencies throughout the country.[10]

Of course, formal agents have to work within the legal parameters of mediating migrant labour supply and demand. As there were only very limited options for leaving Poland to work abroad before the country joined the EU, formal agents were influential in only a few migration patterns. However, it is striking that there were quite a lot of informal agents at work. Apart from the migrant networks shaped by migrants, their friends and families, which worked on a non-material exchange basis, migration patterns before EU enlargement were influenced mainly by informal agents. This was especially true for migration to work in the domestic service and domestic elderly care sectors, but also in the construction sector and even in the agricultural sector which was actually designed to be organized just by formal mediators through the bilateral agreements. For example, the network supporting migration for agricultural work in Germany from Nowy Korczyn was initially shaped by an informal agent who provided documented jobs. As this informal agent dealt with all the documents and registered the migrants within the bilateral agreements, the relationship between the Polish labour office and the migrants remained more or less virtual.

Looking at the situation after May 2004, the picture regarding agents has changed a lot. In the case of migration to the UK, both formal and informal agents play a role, but informal agents do so to a far lesser extent than in the old migration patterns. According to our data, informal agents, so far, have been active in just two ways, and mostly just in the country of origin. Firstly, they have been influential in the early stages of post-accession migration to the UK, when the migration networks were not yet established and the old networks (from the migrants to the UK in the 1980s) seemed to be inefficient or were unavailable to potential migrants. Secondly, informal agents now mediate between formal agents (labour providing agencies) in the UK, and potential migrants in the origin communities. The strategies of the informal agents in the case of migration after 2004, though, seem to be less developed than in the case of migration before EU enlargement, which might be due to how recently these new destinations have appeared (given that our data was collected in early 2006).

However, aside from some (so far) statistically insignificant individual departures to the new destinations, formal agents seem to have dominated the

---

10   According to <www.labourproviders.org.uk/alp-members.aspx>, accessed 15 April 2008.

post-accession migration patterns from our case study communities, and especially from Wilków. This view is reinforced by the latest statistical data in Poland and the UK. While in the year 2004 there were only 271 recruitment agencies all over Poland, the number rose to 1,097 in the following year. At the same time, the number of people who took up jobs via these agencies in the UK rose from 6,932 in the year 2004 to 17,120 in the year 2005 (Kępińska 2006). Looking closer at the observed regions, we find a proliferation of recruitment agencies in the Opolskie voivodship, where Wilków is part of, from five (2003) to 29 (2004) and 83 (2005), while the increase of these agencies in the Świętokrzyskie voivodship, where Nowy Korczyn is located, has been significantly lower – from three (2003) to five (2004) to 17 (2005) – even though the number of inhabitants in both voivodships is almost the same (Kępińska 2006). The greater intensity of migration in the Silesian region is therefore also bolstered by the high number of agencies.

The question still remains as to why the old migration patterns, especially to Germany, also intensified in Wilków but not in Nowy Korczyn. Our data supports the idea that inhabitants of the Wilków gmina, who already had established trajectories of going abroad, used the new freedom of movement in an enlarged EU much more than the villagers of Nowy Korczyn, who had a much more limited mobility due to a shorter and less intense history of migration.

Hidden versus Visible Migration

The impact of these different pre and post-accession migration patterns on the migrants and their families is quite significant. To mark this difference we want to introduce a new distinction: *hidden* migration versus *visible* migration.

Most old migration patterns were conducted at a time when legal possibilities to migrate were scarce. Even in the few patterns which allowed for regular circular migrations (within the bilateral agreements) many migrants chose not to play according to the established rules and regulations, or at least to not comply to them completely. This situation determined their lives in the country of destination as well as in Poland. One consequence was that migrants mostly had to rely on informal agents. As the informal agents were aware of this, they turned this situation to their advantage and tried to keep the migrants dependent on them (cf. Elrick and Lewandowska 2008), either by demanding more money or using this dependence in other ways (cf. Ruhs and Anderson 2007). This type of mediation takes place in the grey economy, providing a living in the shadows, and has continued for some time after 1989. As the residence of the migrants in their new country and/or their conducted work is of an irregular nature they are not recognized, but often silently accepted, by the authorities. Consequently, migrants like this are usually not included in any other social activities in their new country outside their work. This also has consequences for the enforceability of their work contracts which means that they are dependent on the benevolence of their employers. Low or no payment, long hours or other maltreatments cannot be legally pursued, not to mention the lack of social benefits or any insurance in the event of an accident or illness. Finally, as most jobs offered in these migration patterns take place inside houses – especially domestic services and elderly care – and are jobs in which migrants are also obliged to live in employer provided accommodation, often on site, this migration is not publicly visible. These factors all lead to a predominance of short-term stays among the migrants. Moreover, these kinds of jobs, and the migrants carrying them out, are usually not an issue in public discourse in the country of destination. Due to these reasons we term these patterns *hidden migration.*

Comparing these to the new migration trends, particularly movements to the UK, we argue that these new patterns offer much better opportunities for migrants as they are *visible migration.* An abundance of formal agents provide attractive documented job opportunities for migrants of all educational levels, ranging from food production to jobs in the catering sector to management jobs. Admittedly, not all Polish migrants find jobs matching their qualification levels (cf. Green et al. 2007). However, most of them are covered by the social welfare system and migrants are entitled to claim pensions or medical treatment, although most migrants to the UK at the moment, as our sample also suggests, are young and healthy workers and do not extensively burden the social security funds (cf. Home Office et al. 2008). Since the majority of the migrants work in documented jobs and stay longer-term they seem to be recognized as potential citizens or (even just) inhabitants whose presence may influence the life of the place where they work. Private and public companies are therefore adjusting their product ranges and marketing strategies towards the newcomers, like, for example, real estate agents or banks advertising in Polish or even the National Health Service (NHS) which has printed maternity leaflets in Polish after recognizing that there was a big inflow of Polish migrants, and started a project to evaluate the needs of the Polish migrants and develop a policy to meet them. The documented nature of most jobs allows the migrants to enforce their contracts – the circumstances of their work, labour hours or amount of salary. The latter, at least, covers the national minimum wage, which is not the case with hidden migration. The new liberty of being able to enter and stay in the UK, as well as having regular jobs, allows for a greater public presence of the migrants. They not only have more freedom in their everyday lives, but they use this freedom to cater for the needs of their co-ethnics by founding Polish specialty shops, newspapers and radio stations (cf. Garapich 2008). Finally, Polish migrants to the UK who have families have proven to themselves that they are able to care more for their children there. Our data revealed that many migrants have used the opportunity to bring their whole nuclear family to the UK, planning for mid-term to long-term stays. Even migrating parents who left their children in villages in Poland have profited from these new options as it is easier to stay in touch with their children at home and even bring them over for holiday, or go back and forth as much as they want to. This has resulted in a noticeable improvement in the caring for children still at school in Poland, as the director of a college in Wilków noted. In general, ties to friends and family members can be maintained much more strongly through frequent visits back home or just easier access to telephone and Internet connections. These consequences are all determined by this migrant-friendly type of visible migration, as new migration to the UK has demonstrated.

Conclusion

Even from the limited scope of our case-studies, we can note that the impact of EU enlargement has not been evenly shaped all over Poland. Depending on the history of migration in specific places, as well as evolving migrant networks, migration patterns might be perpetuated or changed. In the case of the Wilków community, old patterns like domestic service and domestic elderly care employment in Germany, shaped mostly by the history of migration, persist and have even increased as border controls have eased after May 2004; it is now much easier to reach the German destinations, although the work remains undocumented. At the same time, the long history of migration and the special conditions in the Silesian region might have also contributed to the emergence of the new migration pattern of 'documented work in the UK', as a massive increase in this particular pattern can be observed.

In Nowy Korczyn, by contrast, a shorter migration history seems to have reinforced and intensified existing migration patterns, especially those leading to agricultural work in Germany and work in the domestic service and elderly care sectors in Italy, with the latter witnessing an increase in numbers and an extended duration of typical stays due to the changed situation for Polish citizens after EU accession.

As Poland's membership of the European Union brought freedom of movement, migrants' strategies in both communities seem to have changed – from more short-term to more long-term migrations, and even settlement, which seems to also be confirmed by recent statistical data on current migration trends from across Poland (Kępińska 2006). While it is too soon to say this has been a significant change, it is nevertheless a noticeable development.

With regard to formal and informal agents other changes can also be noted. In the old migration patterns especially, informal agents played an important role in perpetuating migration, and they continue to do so within certain migration movements. Within the new migration patterns to places such as the UK, however, informal agents only seem to play a minor role – mainly at the beginning of the formation of migrant networks and as mediators between formal agents in the destination country and migrants in their villages in Poland. Formal agents instead seem to dominate the new migration patterns.

As this research was conducted only shortly after these new migration opportunities appeared it is still uncertain whether these preliminary trends will continue. It will be interesting to see whether EU enlargement in the long run leads to a flattening out of the differences in migration patterns all over Poland. What can be stated, though, is that these new post-accession patterns, resting on new freedom of movement and abundant documented work opportunities, foster a type of migration which can be understood as visible migration. This type of migration undoubtedly has a more positive impact on migrants' lives when compared with former patterns of hidden migration which were dependent on clandestine, undocumented work.

Acknowledgements

The research on which this chapter is based was conducted under the European Union Marie Curie Excellence Grant project 'Expanding the knowledge base of European labour migration policies' (KNOWMIG) (MEXT-CT-2003-002668). We are very grateful to all the interview partners who shared their time and life histories with us. We are also indebted to Christina Boswell (University of Edinburgh) for comments on an earlier draft which helped us to improve this chapter.

References

Association of Labour Providers (2005), *The Role of Migration in the UK Labour Market – ALP Response to Government Strategy on Migration.* Association of Labour Providers, <http://www.labourproviders.org.uk/files/P+R%20papers/the_role_of_migration.pdf>, accessed 16 April 2008.

Bauer, T. and Zimmermann, K. (1999), *Assessment of Possible Migration Pressure and its Labour Market Impact Following EU Enlargement to Central and Eastern Europe.* Institute for the Study of Labor (IZA) (IZA Research Report 3), <http://www.iza.org/en/webcontent/publications/reports/report_pdfs/iza_report_03.pdf>, accessed 18 April 2008.

Boeri, T. and Brücker, H. (2000), *The Impact of Eastern Enlargement on Employment and Labour Markets in the EU Member States.* Institut für Arbeitsmarkt- und Berufsforschung (IAB), <http://www.iab.de/de/389/section.aspx/Publikation/k020114f01>, accessed 18 April 2008.

Boyd, M. (1989), 'Family and Personal Networks in International Migration: Recent Developments and New Agendas', *International Migration Review* 23:3, 638–70.

Drinkwater, S., Eade, J. and Garapich, M. (2006), *Poles Apart? EU Enlargement and the Labour Market Outcomes of Immigrants in the UK.* Institute for the Study of Labor (IZA) (IZA Discussion Paper 2410), <http://ideas.repec.org/p/iza/izadps/dp2410.html>, accessed 18 April 2008.

Elrick, T. (2008), 'The Influence of Migration on Origin Communities: Insights from Polish migrations to the West', *Europe Asia Studies* 60:9, 1505–19.

Elrick, T. and Ciobanu, O. (2009), 'Migration Networks and Policy Impacts: Insights from Romanian-Spanish Migrations', *Global Networks* 9:1.

Elrick, T. and Lewandowska, E. (2008), 'Matching and Making Labour Demand and Supply: Agents in Polish Migrant Networks of Domestic Elderly Care in Germany and Italy', *Journal of Ethnic and Migration Studies* 34:5, 717–34.

Favell, A. (2008), 'The New Face of East-West Migration in Europe', *Journal of Ethnic and Migration Studies* 34:5, 701–16.

Fawcett, J. (1989), 'Networks, Linkages and Migration Systems', *International Migration Review* 23:3, 671–80.

Garapich, M. (2008), 'The Migration Industry and Civil Society: Polish Immigrants in the United Kingdom before and after EU Enlargement', *Journal of Ethnic and Migration Studies* 34:5, 735–52.

Green, A.E., Owen, D. and Jones, P. (2007), *The Economic Impact of Migrant Workers in the West Midlands* (Coventry: West Midlands Regional Observatory. Institute for Employment Research at the University of Warwick).

Gurak, D. and Caces, F. (1992), 'Migration Networks and the Shaping of Migration Systems' in Kritz et al. (eds).

Heering, L., van Wissen, L. and van der Erf, R. (2004), 'The Role of Family Networks and Migration Culture in the Continuation of Moroccan Emigration: A Gender Perspective', *Journal of Ethnic and Migration Studies* 30:2, 323–37.

Home Office UK Border Agency, Department for Work and Pensions, HM Revenue and Customs and Communities and Local Government (2008), *Accession Monitoring Report May 2004–March 2008.* <http://www.ukba.homeoffice.gov.uk/sitecontent/documents/aboutus/reports/accession_monitoring_report/report15/may04mar08.pdf?view=Binary>, accessed 13 May 2008.

Horváth, I. (2008), 'The Culture of Migration of the Rural Romanian Young People', *Journal of Ethnic and Migration Studies* 34:5, 771–86.

Kaczmarczyk, P. and Łukowski, W. (eds) (2004), *Polscy pracownicy na rynku Unii Europejskiej* [*Polish Workers in the European Union Market*] (Warsaw: Scholar).

Kandel, W. and Massey, D. (2002), 'The Culture of Mexican Migration: A Theoretical and Empirical Analysis', *Social Forces* 80:3, 981–1004.

Kępińska, E. (2006), *Recent Trends in International Migration. The 2006 SOPEMI Report for Poland.* University of Warsaw Centre for Migration Research Working Paper No. 15/73 (Warsaw: University of Warsaw Centre for Migration Research).

Kępińska, E. (2007), *Recent Trends in International Migration. The 2007 SOPEMI Report for Poland.* University of Warsaw Centre for Migration Research Working Paper No. 29/87 (Warsaw: University of Warsaw Centre for Migration Research).

Koser, K. and Pinkerton, C. (2002), *The Social Networks of Asylum Seekers and the Dissemination of Information about Countries of Asylum* (London: Home Office).

Kritz, M.M., Lim, L.L. and Zlotnik, H. (eds) (1992), *International Migration Systems: A Global Approach* (Oxford: Clarendon Press).

Mach, Z. (1993), *Symbols, Conflict, and Identity: Essays in Political Anthropology* (New York, NY: State University of New York Press).

Marcus, G. (1998), *Ethnography Through Thick and Thin* (Princeton, NJ: Princeton University Press).

Massey, D.S., Arango, J., Hugo, G., Kouaouci, A., Pellegrino, A. and Taylor, J.E. (1998), *Worlds in Motion: Understanding International Migration at the End of the Millennium* (Oxford: Clarendon Press).

Morokvašić, M. (2004), '"Settled in Mobility": Engendering Post-Wall Migration in Europe', *Feminist Review* 77:1, 7–25.

Office of National Statistics (2006), *Labour Market Trends, October 2006* (London: HMSO).

Okólski, M. (2007), *Europe in Movement: Migration from/to Central and Eastern Europe.* University of Warsaw Centre for Migration Research Working Paper No. 22/80 (Warsaw: University of Warsaw Centre for Migration Research).

Patton, M. (1990), *Qualitative Evaluation and Research Methods* 2nd ed. (Newbury Park, CA; London: Sage).

Ruhs, M. and Anderson, B. (2007), *The Origins and Functions of Illegality in Migrant Labour Markets: An Analysis of Migrants, Employers and the State in the UK* (Oxford: COMPAS, University of Oxford).

Salt, J. and Millar, J. (2006), 'Foreign Labour in the United Kingdom: Current Patterns and Trends', in Office of National Statistics (2006).

Sinn, H-W., Flaig, G., Werding, M., Munz, S., Düll, N. and Hofmann, H. (2001), *EU-Erweiterung und Arbeitskräftemigration. Wege zu einer schrittweisen Annäherung der Arbeitsmärkte* [*EU Enlargement and Worker Migration: Ways to a Gradual Convergence of the Job Markets*] (Munich: IFO, Institute for Economic Research) <http://www.cesifo-group.de/link/migration.pdf>, accessed 18 April 2008.

Chapter 3

Family Migration from Small-town Poland: A Livelihood Strategy Approach

Anne White

This chapter explores the phenomenon of migration by whole families from Poland to the West, with a particular focus on migration to Britain since Poland's accession to the European Union. It asks why families migrate, and how they decide how long to stay abroad. I examine the motives of parents who decide from the outset that the entire family will migrate, as well as other cases where the husband migrates first, expecting to return, but the family then decides to reunite abroad. The chapter also considers the situation of lone parents. The second part of the chapter addresses decision making by migrants once they are already abroad. Migrants often find it hard to answer questions about how long they intend to stay abroad, so it is helpful to concentrate instead on exploring the range of factors which shape their decisions about how long to stay.

The research project investigates families from small towns and villages in Poland, with special focus on migration to three locations in the west of England: Bristol, Bath and Trowbridge, a small town near Bath.[1] In Poland, 33 out of 51 interviews took place in Grajewo, a town of 22,000 in Podlasie Region, four hours' bus ride north-east from Warsaw. The evidence from in-depth interviews is

---

1   Anne White's project, 'Migration as a Family Livelihood Strategy in Poland' (September 2006–June 2009) has been funded since January 2008 by the British Academy; Anne White is the sole researcher. The sources are Polish-language media; interviews with key informants such as teachers, recruitment agency directors and job centre officials; an opinion poll in March 2008, commissioned from BD Consulting, Rzeszów, of 1,101 residents of towns and villages across Podkarpackie Region, excluding the city of Rzeszów; participant observation in a Bath parents' and toddlers' group as a volunteer English teacher; and interviews with Polish mothers. By the end of May 2008, 51 such interviews had been conducted in Poland and 11 interviews in England. Polish interviews were in the small towns of Grajewo (33), Ełk (six) and Suwałki (three), in economically depressed north-east Poland, as well as eight in small towns and villages in the much richer Poznań area. The main focus of the research is on working-class families and 58 of the 62 interviews were with women who did not have university degrees. The Polish research mainly studies the migration potential of families. In some cases respondents were already planning or hoping to migrate; in some others, they did not really want to go, but were agonizing about whether they should. Frequently at least one adult member of these families was or had already been a migrant.

complemented by an opinion poll of small-town and rural residents of Podkarpackie Region in March 2008.

The research has been conducted in both Poland and the United Kingdom in an attempt to understand the entire migration process, including the networks and other links between sending and receiving countries and the emerging dual identities of established migrants who nonetheless retain strong ties to their country of origin. Respondents in Poland include people who have not migrated, or not yet migrated, in the belief that, as Byron suggests, 'accounts which include both migrants and their non-migrant counterparts tend to be more informative about the process than those which consider only the migrants' (Byron 1994: 63). Only by exploring a range of opinions in the sending country can one really understand the local migrant culture.

Usually it is the mother who migrates with her children, following shortly after her husband, so my formal interviews are all with women. Where possible these are supplemented by informal conversations with other members of the family. I am particularly interested in migrants without higher education, from working-class backgrounds. This is not the typical profile of a Polish migrant to the United Kingdom. Such 'typical' migrants are childless, young and highly educated (Home Office et al., various; Fihel and Piętka 2007), by contrast with less well-educated Poles who have tended to work in countries such as Germany or Greece, and, if parents, usually migrate on a temporary or seasonal basis without their families. Nonetheless, anecdotal evidence and media reports suggest a rapid expansion in the number of Polish pupils at British schools and the arrival of more and more families. In the second quarter of 2007 Labour Force Survey data suggested an estimated 170,000 Polish-born children (under 19 years old) are resident in the United Kingdom (IPPR 2008). Polish-speaking children now form the largest group of 'non-English speaking newly-arrived migrant schoolchildren' in England (Pollard et al. 2008: 27).

My research suggests that these children come from a range of social backgrounds, including from the types of family who, before 2004, would more likely have sent one parent to work temporarily in continental Europe. It is impossible to speak with certainty about numbers, however, given the usual problems with migration statistics and, more specifically, the absence of systematic research into Polish family migration. The recent 'state of the art' survey of Polish migration research by the Warsaw Centre of Migration Research uncovered no examples of research into contemporary family migration (Kicinger and Weinar 2007) and it seems that Polish local educational departments do not normally gather statistics about child emigrés (Jach 2007; Żytnicki and Sałwacka 2007; my interviews).

I use a livelihood strategy approach to frame my argument. Becoming and being a migrant involves making a string of important decisions. The word 'strategy' may be rather grand for this often haphazard process, but it is appropriate because it emphasizes the agency of labour migrants: they are to some extent more than simply victims of economic circumstances. Of course, some strategies are more active than others. For example, a passive strategy would be to refrain from having additional children, or to cut back on food consumption. By contrast, the decision to migrate implies making a very decisive change. In both cases, however, the individual often has an element of choice between potential strategies. The precise degree of agency can be debated (see Clarke 1999: 2; Burawoy et al. 2000: 62; Wallace 2002); for the purposes of this chapter, the important point is that in small towns and rural areas the range of opportunities can be quite limited, and this helps explain the popularity of migration.

A livelihood strategy approach is also useful for exploring what happens to migrants once they are abroad. Few newly-arrived migrants immediately settle into a completely different and permanent way of life: searching and experimentation continues, with strategies constantly being reshaped in accordance with the migrant's own changing perceptions and the constraints and opportunities present in the receiving community. Since my main interest is in decisions about how long to stay, I am particularly concerned to examine Roberts's suggestion that 'immigrants are potentially exposed to multiple, and often conflicting expectations of the duration of their migration. For instance, expectations that derive from communities of origin may clash with those present in communities of destination' (Roberts 1995: 44).

The term 'livelihood' is preferred to other adjectives commonly placed before 'strategy', such as 'survival', 'coping' and 'household'. In some respects, 'survival' is apt, because of its 'connotation of exceptionality and extremity' (Shevchenko 2002: 844). Shevchenko criticizes the use of the term because she feels that survival strategies are often not responses to exceptional situations, but become 'routine and normative activities' in the post-communist period. It is hard, though, to distinguish between 'routine' and 'exceptional' where flows in and out of poverty are commonplace. Shevchenko's account of her own respondents, in Moscow, implies that they felt their lives were routinely exceptional (Shevchenko 2002: 844). The same can be said for my small-town interviewees in both Russia (White 2004) and Poland. Sudden shocks such as complete stoppages of cash income into households – often combined with the amassing of large debts – constitute crises, with the threat of descent into deep poverty.

Nonetheless, 'survival' can be an unhelpful adjective. Using the term 'survival' in the post-communist context may imply that people have to 'survive' post-communism, whereas they did not have to survive the period before 1989: they merely 'lived'. There are lines of continuity, however, between communist-era and post-communist strategies. Most obviously, migration in Poland is hardly a new phenomenon. Former Solidarity leader and Polish president Lech Wałęsa, for instance, describes in his autobiography how his parents, invited by their relations, went to work illegally in the US in 1973: 'in our family there had always been someone on the other side of the ocean … one or the other went over there so the rest of the family could count on some security' (Wałęsa 1987: 33, cited in Morawska 2001: 59).

'Livelihood' is also to be preferred over 'survival' because it is a wider concept, embracing a range of potential objectives. It is true, for instance, that some Polish migrants use migration simply to make ends meet, to 'cope' in circumstances where other household income has dried up or is insufficient, but in very many cases there is also an aspiration to earn *extra* money on top of what is strictly needed for survival. In other words, migration both solves the original problem of insufficient household income and also offers the opportunity for enrichment (by local standards). 'Accumulation strategies' (Pickup and White 2003: 421) may combine with 'survival strategies' from the outset; in other cases, accumulation sooner or later replaces survival as the objective.

Secondly, 'livelihood' is a useful concept because livelihoods are usually viewed as having both objective and subjective dimensions. As used in anthropological and development studies literature, 'livelihoods' are not just about making money and obtaining other material resources. A livelihood has been defined by Ellis as 'the activities, the assets, and the access that together determine the living gained by the individual or household' (Ellis 2000: 231). Most importantly, constructing one's livelihood entails behaving in ways which are considered appropriate locally. Pine and Bridger argue that 'survival strategies are not necessarily "economically rational" according to models of supply, demand and efficient self-interest. However, in terms of cultural meaning, local knowledge and understanding, and within the context of social relationships and networks, they are often the best and most sensible responses people can make' (Pine and Bridger 1998: 11). For example, since the early twentieth century many Grajewans have migrated to North America; a hairdresser who moved to Grajewo in 2000 stated in her interview that 'when I moved here I was amazed because in almost every family someone had emigrated to the United States'. In Podlasie as a whole, the US remains the favourite destination for permanent settlement, compared with the United Kingdom for Poland as a whole (Rocznik 2007: 448, 453). There is a tradition of migration to 'be with people you know' (do kogoś), even if this means travelling across the ocean, rather than trying one's luck closer to home in Western Europe. Even in 2008, when the dollar was weak, many Grajewans still preferred to try to join relatives in the US. For example, Maria's unemployed husband planned to visit his sister-in-law and work illegally and he had applied and failed six times for an American visa. Maria explained why he did not try to go to a country such as Britain instead:

> I wouldn't send anyone from my family into the unknown, going to someone from an advertisement, there are offers like that, you hear about them on the television, it's absolutely ... from what you hear, things happen, they cheat you, there are cheats everywhere, aren't there? ... If you go abroad, you must go to someone you know.

Livelihoods, therefore, are rooted in a local context, in local structures and constraints. The individual or household making decisions about livelihood strategies has some agency, but is obviously not an entirely free agent. In order to understand these decisions, notably the decision about whether or not to migrate, it is helpful to first consider the range of livelihood options which the potential migrant considers to be available locally. Because the livelihood strategies literature originates in development studies, it lays emphasis on exploring the informal as well as the formal economy, and this is equally appropriate in post-communist societies such as Poland or Russia. For instance, I interviewed women in a small Polish town centred on a salt mine. The salt mine was the only significant employer. However, because salt reserves were becoming exhausted and because global warming was reducing the demand for salt on icy winter roads, the mine was not operating at full strength, particularly during the warmer months. Its employees therefore had free time to engage in seasonal work abroad, such as blueberry picking in Sweden. The mine management colluded in this arrangement, by offering up to three months of unpaid leave.

A qualitative study of migration decisions which focuses on how households and individuals operate within the context of the local environment is an essential supplement to more macrolevel explanations for migration trends. The current wave of migration from Poland to the United Kingdom is clearly connected to the overall economic environment: the facts that average wages are higher in the UK and that entrance to the labour market has in effect become unrestricted. Hence one can helpfully turn to traditional 'cost–benefit' type explanations for individual migrants' behaviour, combined with dual labour market theory and focus on the political dimension (the UK government's decision to open the doors to new member state workers in 2004). However, since some Poles migrate to Britain and others do not, and some regions of Poland send more migrants than do others, there clearly have to be deeper levels of explanation which refer to personal and community choices and expectations.

Migration Motives: Economic Push Factors

This chapter will first explore the issue of why small-town families migrate. It will examine in turn material and non-material motivations. With regard to economic motives, I explore the extent to which migrants are 'forced', as opposed to choosing a better life. With regard to more subjective dimensions, the chapter will look at opinions about the feasibility and desirability of different types of migration. Although decisions about whether one parent or both will migrate have a very personal, individual dimension, local norms – notably with regard to gender roles – play an important role in their shaping. As is conventional in explaining migration motives, both 'push' and 'pull' factors will be considered. Families have reasons to leave Poland, but they also have reasons to come to England. Often these push/pull factors are two sides of one coin: for example, wages are too low in Poland and simultaneously sufficient in Britain.

Labour migration is often distinguished from forced migration, caused by factors such as wars or political persecution. However, where 'push' factors are very strong, there is a sense in which economic migrants are 'forced'. Moreover, migrants themselves often use these terms, making comments in interviews like 'the family was forced to go because of their financial situation', or 'if the situation changes I might be forced to go back to the UK'. Not surprisingly, this is a sentiment often expressed by respondents from poor areas, particularly in the more underdeveloped, eastern part of Poland (often known as 'Poland B'). This may be partly because there is a more limited range of livelihood options in these areas, hence the sense of being 'forced' is more widespread.

Unemployment is a classic 'push' factor and it is true that unemployment was quite high in Poland in May 2004. Although it has dropped rapidly since, there were still places with high unemployment at the time interviews were conducted. For example, two mothers interviewed in Bath in autumn 2006 had home towns where unemployment was 29.9 per cent and 25.6 per cent in February 2007 (GUS 2007a). Respondents did name unemployment as a cause of 'forced' migration, as in the case of a couple from a village in the Sudeten mountains, where local factories had closed. Their first response to the job shortage was to take employment seven kilometres away, in a German-owned factory which paid such high wages that it was worth commuting. When the factory lowered its wages to local levels the couple had to give up: bus tickets were eating up one third of their income. They had four children, so an energetic response to the situation was required, and migration – originally by the father alone – was seen as an appropriate new strategy.

More typically, however, the financial crisis which prompts 'forced' evacuation is not joint unemployment of both spouses. Unemployment of one parent may be enough to trigger the decision, as in the case of a father of two who found himself jobless and with bad debts after being cheated by a business partner. The family was left in such a precarious position that first the husband and then the rest moved to the UK. In another family, both spouses were employed in Poland. The mother had gone to work in Belgium several times and was very keen to stay in Poland in future. However, she expressed the opinion that if either she or her husband became unemployed, migration would be 'forced' upon them. You could not keep a family and pay off a mortgage on one wage.

In many other cases it seems that both spouses were employed, but were driven to emigration by a feeling of insecurity. This was caused by the perceived insufficiency of their wages, often combined with the fact that they had only occasional or part-time jobs, sometimes in the shadow economy. Given the informal character of many Polish employment contracts, this is a widespread problem, as revealed in Internet discussion forums about the desirability of migration (<www.gazeta.pl>; see also discussion in Stenning 2005). Hence, while it is true that jobs are available in the Polish labour market – though more in some locations than in others – it is the insecure nature of that employment which deters some parents from seeking to make a living in their local area. For example, a couple from the north-west of Poland, near but not on the coast, could only find work during the tourist season. With three children, this was not enough. First he migrated, then she joined him. The mother expressed several times the opinion that in her area 'only lucky people get jobs'. As parents, they could not just hope for a gift of fate. More active strategies were needed.

Whether the economic push factors are unemployment, underemployment or low wages, a common motivation for migration is the sense that local options have been exhausted. The bag of local livelihoods has been dipped into, but now it is empty. Sometimes the final strategy adopted in Poland had proved a particularly hard choice to follow and this also contributed to the sense of coming to 'the end' of Polish options. One couple, for example, adopted the risky although culturally appropriate strategy of running their own bar. The wife attributed their decision to migrate to disillusionment when they realized they could not make the business succeed: 'the main thing was that we'd had enough of running our own business where there were non-stop problems with everything ... I couldn't do anything with it, that really made me fed up, I'd had enough'. Their street was full of bars, but in her opinion no other type of business was even worth attempting, given the local economy. (She herself had tried to run a flower shop before the bar, but this had not succeeded.)

Another couple, with a child and no home of their own, went to care for an elderly stranger, thus addressing both financial and accommodation problems. When this last ditch solution did not work out, they migrated to the UK. In another case, a family applied for social security, but they were so humiliated by their neighbours as a consequence that they felt they had to leave their home: they took the dramatic and unusual step of selling their flat, in other words completely cutting their moorings. As these cases illustrate, desperate potential migrants sometimes try out strategies which are unusual or do not conform to local norms. The uncomfortable situation thus created is in itself a reason to depart.

In such situations a person without dependants could at least practise self-denial, a common and obvious minimalist survival strategy for poor people everywhere. However, it is hard to pursue this policy if you are a parent. When illustrating the family's financial plight, one woman stressed, for example, that sometimes they could not afford the price of the bus ticket for their eldest son to go to school, and that they could not buy the children fruit and sweets. It is not just the fact that large families have low *per capita* income which is a factor prompting migration, but additionally the fact that parents feel compelled to spend more on their children than on themselves. The supposition that you should buy fruit for your child, for example, is an example of a contemporary norm. More important still is adequate housing. Clearly the aspiration to buy or build a house is a very widespread motivation for migration from contemporary Poland, but for families the need for adequate housing is especially acute. In my small-town and rural sample, however, even extended households which seemed to have a relatively lucrative range of livelihood strategies were not able to secure housing on the basis of what was earned in Poland.

Lone parents constitute a special case, since their income is often particularly low and they do not possess the double networks which couples enjoy. Hence the sense of being 'forced' is particularly keen. On the other hand, social disapproval of mothers who leave their children behind in Poland constitutes a pull in the opposite direction. In general, there seems to be agreement that traditional gender role stereotypes remain strong in Poland, although there is also evidence of urban/ rural divides, with rural women being more conventional about matters such as division of household labour (Wachowiak 2002). My interviewees often felt strongly that women should be with their children and that mothers were the chief parents. In my Podkarpackie opinion poll, 85.2 per cent agreed that women with small children should not migrate, leaving their husbands and children, and 63.8 per cent agreed that, even if children were older, it was better for the father to migrate than for the mother. The media on both sides of the political spectrum, particularly the conservative media, run stories about the sorry plight of children abandoned by migrating mothers, children who in some cases end up in children's homes (e.g. Hugo-Bader 2007; Przybyła 2007; Wasek 2007).

My married interviewees, however, were not judgmental about the behaviour of lone parents. For example, one woman still in Poland and not intending to migrate, despite expressing strongly essentialist views about women as mothers and emphasizing that children 'need' a mother, then began to think about actual instances of migration and to make excuses for single mother migrants. Considering who in the local community was, as she put it, 'forced' into emigration, she immediately picked on lone mothers who did not 'have a job, a home, or a bank account'. Another woman who was toying with the idea of migration, perhaps initially her own rather than her husband's, suggested that 'people justify lone mothers, saying, yes, she did leave her child but everyone knows she had to do it, what else could she do?' An extra reason for justifying the behaviour of lone mothers (also used by lone mothers themselves) is that migration is intended to be for settlement, rather than simply earning some extra money. In such cases, where mothers invite their children to come and live with them as soon as they are properly established abroad, they behave like surrogate men, the husbands in families based around married couples. The Podkarpackie sample were asked whether they felt that lone mothers should risk emigration, if they planned, eventually, to reunite with their children abroad: 55.1 per cent agreed that this was 'often a sensible way out of a difficult situation'.[2]

---

2 Responses for men and women were nearly identical; older respondents were somewhat less enthusiastic than younger, with a decline in enthusiasm (and increase in 'don't knows') above the age of 35: 63.5 per cent of 18–35 year olds agreed, compared with 53.2 per cent aged 36–91.

Non-economic Migration Motives and the Rationale for Whole Family Migration

It seems from evidence presented in the preceding paragraphs that families often migrate because they have a sense of having been forced to do so. Often they found themselves in a crisis situation in which they had exhausted local livelihood options. However, it is important to remember that this is how 'it seems' from the migrants' stories. Given the dramatic quality of the migration decision, it is not surprising if it is presented in migrant narratives as being sudden, a response to a single situation. By the same token, women interviewed in Poland, considering situations in which they might potentially migrate, are naturally inclined to identify an abrupt change in circumstances. It is important, however, to remember Halfacree and Boyle's observation that 'the migration decision is situated within the migrant's entire biography' (Halfacree and Boyle 1993: 337).

Interviews also reveal a range of subsidiary motivations, including pull factors, indicating that the strategy is about more than sheer survival. By migrating, Polish families, like migrants everywhere, see themselves as choosing a better life. For example, the same woman who claimed to have emigrated because of the failure of her florist shop and bar also asserted: 'I simply wanted to see if it was possible to live a different way. And to give my children the chance of a slightly better life, since I couldn't ensure them any real future in Poland'.

In several cases the couple wanted to have another child, but did not think this would be affordable if they stayed in Poland. This was chiefly because the mother would have to give up her job, and they could not afford to live just on the husband's Polish salary. Moreover, the mothers were concerned about their job prospects if they tried to return to the Polish labour market later on in life: after the age of thirty the options were very limited for women in their localities. In fact, employment statistics, based on Labour Force Survey data, suggest that women constitute around 70 per cent of economically inactive 35–44 year olds (GUS 2007b: 156), and my interviews in small towns suggested that the situation is particularly difficult in such places.

In other families, the desire to have more time to spend with one's children was an important consideration. A recurring theme was the need, in Poland, to 'work non-stop', and this was seen as leading to neglecting one's children. It was understandable that women who had migrated slightly after their husbands felt this particularly acutely, since the period while he was abroad but she was still in Poland with the children had been particularly exhausting. Hence, although when they arrived in Britain some mothers continued to work long hours, others deliberately cut down their work commitments. These were typically women who expected to stay in the United Kingdom, with low aspirations about family income and no commitment to send remittances back to Poland.

In other respects, too, mothers saw emigration as improving their children's quality of life. For example, one lone mother still in Poland, who was actively researching the possibility of emigration from her small town, expressed her sympathy for local children and young people. They were 'frustrated' because there was nowhere to go, 'no McDonalds, no swimming pool', no afterschool activities unless both parents worked for the only high paying local employer and had only one child. If she got a good job in Britain she would collect her daughter and give her a better life abroad. Parents interviewed in the United Kingdom often stressed that despite the hardships they had encountered as migrants, it was worth it for the sake of giving their children a better start in life. Small towns and villages simply had too little to offer and, since these particular children would in many cases not aspire to university education in Poland, the chance of their being able to make a future in a prosperous Polish city seemed rather remote.

Although interviewees can be reluctant to express selfish motivations, in Poland some mothers' voices nonetheless warmed as they described how they too would like to broaden their horizons. 'I'd like to move around a bit in Europe ... it would be great ... have a change of scenery, something interesting ... earn enough to have a good holiday,' said a cleaner. 'You could have a look at those different countries, have something – how to put it – something to remember, that you'd have memories of later ...' suggested a hospital worker. In other words, and not surprisingly, mothers shared the curiosity and sense of adventure of other young Poles. This motivating factor is often noted in the case of childless migrants. No doubt enjoying travel is much higher up their list of priorities than it is for small-town mothers. All the same, it is important to see the similarities between the two groups, similarities which are masked by the mothers' tendency in migration narratives to construct themselves as responsible mothers, rather than hedonistic individuals.

Mothers are not a separate species: they share some common characteristics with other young migrants, and these include (1) a propensity to take risks and (2) a determination to reunite with their partners. Both characteristics are part of a 'culture of migration' and should be explored within the context of local norms as well as personal characteristics.

One interviewee who was planning to emigrate to the United Kingdom finished off her interview with the statement: 'I have to give it a go – I'm a brave person'. In both countries, respondents echoed her sentiment: migration 'was worth trying'. Migration is never an easy decision for parents, as these women often stressed, but nonetheless it was worth taking a risk. Given the novelty of Polish family migration to Britain, it is indeed a risk. Most of the women interviewed in the UK were pioneers, the first families they knew to emigrate together. Why, therefore, were mothers prepared to take such a risk? Non-migrants often claim that parents who migrate with their children are 'brave', braver than they themselves would be. In other words, it is the personal bravery of individuals which is the most important factor. However, it also seems that local migration cultures are changing, so that brave individuals will migrate without fear of being foolhardy. Except in some locations with a strong migration tradition to other countries (such as the Grajewo–US link), there is an overall perception in post-accession Poland that Britain is an obvious and feasible migration destination. Mothers, as already argued, are not separate from the rest of society and they too are affected by this sense of feasibility. Migration to the UK is almost becoming 'the norm' in the sense of the most commonplace form of behaviour. In regions with a lot of emigration to the UK, it is not surprising that family migration is also becoming more acceptable. In Podkarpackie, where a third of respondents had had close family members in Britain over the past year, 39.1 per cent also felt that 'a lot' of families were migrating to Western Europe from their particular locality. There was 76.4 per cent support for the idea that 'if one spouse has the offer of a good job, or has already found good work in Western Europe, it's worth giving emigration a try'.

On the other hand, parents in Poland expressed very different opinions about whether it was worth taking the risk of their children not integrating. In one case a husband and wife expressed contradictory points of view to different interlocutors. In this case of diverging opinions, the husband was enthusiastic about migrating, which promised him an interesting career development, whereas the wife was studying to improve her qualifications and find a better local job in Poland. He felt the children would adapt, she was more pessimistic, citing their strong emotional ties to their friends at school. In other cases, too, parents' feelings about the feasibility of uprooting their children seemed closely linked to their overall level of enthusiasm for the move. The importance of assessments based on such subjective factors is understandable: it can be difficult for parents to find out in advance how different life in England will be and, however well they know their own children, it is still hard to imagine how they will react in such a new situation. Excessive optimism about children's easy adaptation may be engendered for some potential parents by publications such as the magazine *Praca i życie za granicą* ['Working and Living Abroad'], which paint a rosy picture of life abroad. For example, a July 2007 edition carried a story titled 'Marysia and Basia's fairytale'. The happy Marysia, from a small town near Kielce, was living near Chester with her nine-year-old daughter 'who managed to adapt within the space of a year; she goes to school and the teachers praise her progress in English' ('Bajka').

Couples who migrate with their children are rejecting a 1990s norm: generally, labour migration to other European countries, from small towns and villages, was by one parent alone. Several factors are at play. Women frequently expressed their concern that so many Polish families fall apart as the consequence of migration. This is a phenomenon often covered by the media and sensitively documented in Guzik's portrait of women care workers in Italy (Guzik 2005). It includes both divorce and also situations in which two parents migrate together and become estranged from their children. My interviewees also cited the examples of friends and relatives, and sometimes themselves: usually these stories were about couples breaking up. In one instance, for example, a mother had split up with her children's father after he emigrated. She felt reluctant to settle with him abroad, returned to Poland and established a new relationship. When her second husband decided to work in England, they resolved that the whole family would migrate together. In other words, family migration can be a form of learning from experience, one's own or other peoples. The old model of one parent migration is being rejected because it is perceived as dangerous. Moreover, one parent migration is simply not congenial. When asked why they migrated to be with their husbands, women said that they wanted to be together, that they were missing each other too much. Childless young Poles often invite their boy- and girlfriends to join them abroad, and this could be seen as the pattern of behaviour to be emulated, rather than the more self-sacrificing model offered by the parents of the 1990s – in some cases the respondent's own parents. This illustrates once again how doing what coincides with one's own selfish wishes has come to be seen as a respectable motivation.

It is true that interviews reveal plenty of cases where the husband had gone abroad planning to work alone and then return. However, the significant fact is that in many cases the couple soon began to question whether this migration strategy was really working. On one level, this was presented by interviewees as an issue about material resources. The problem was not the actual job performed by the husband, which was often the same as he had done in Poland (driving or building), and paid well, comparatively to his wage in Poland. The difficulties arose rather from the fact that migration by one family member creates dual location livelihoods, where each spouse has a role to play in contributing to the well-being of the other and of the household as a unit (Sørensen and Olwig 2002). However, this arrangement can in practice prove to be dysfunctional. The husband does not make money as quickly as he had been expecting to do. It can seem too expensive and complicated to continue to maintain two households, leading to a feeling that, as one mother said, 'it was *easier* to live here [in England]'. The prospect of his remaining away for a still longer period, of unpredictable duration, also becomes intolerable for emotional reasons, and this too is the time when worries about marriage break-up become even more acute. Hence the two motives to reunite are mutually reinforcing.

In other cases, family reunification was 'planned' from the start. According to this model, the husband stays on his own in Britain only for as long as it takes to find himself a job and suitable accommodation for the family. However, it is perhaps false to draw too definite a distinction between couples who decide from the beginning to reunite and cases where the husband's migration is originally seen as solitary and temporary. In practice, it seems, many couples adopt the line that they may 'possibly' or 'probably' reunite abroad: it is recognized that the husband's first journey is not necessarily going to prove successful.

An additional element of uncertainty derives from the fact that it is not clear from the beginning whether the wife will wish to relocate. Much hangs on the 'inspection visit' which seems for most couples to be a key part of the reunification process. Sometimes this is actually just a holiday: the wife comes to visit her husband, likes Britain and decides spontaneously that the whole family should move. In other cases, the couple has already nearly decided to uproot the whole family, but before the final decision is taken the wife – and in some cases also children – come over to inspect. Once again, the two types of decision are perhaps not completely different in practice: the wife may come for a 'holiday', for example, but there must always be an element of inspection about such visits.

It is the flexibility of the livelihood strategies which is notable in many cases, a flexibility which partly derives from objective factors such the free travel of labour between Poland and Britain, relatively cheap air and coach tickets, etc. Again, this helps explain the attitude that 'it's worth giving it a go': one can go, but also return. Another factor in some cases is that small-town England is not necessarily that different from small-town Poland. One woman, for example, said how comfortable she felt in Bath: as in her own home town, she could go everywhere on foot, unlike in a big city. Another explained how she had expected Trowbridge to be a larger town, replete with racial tensions and muggings, but discovered from her holiday visit that it would be an easy place to bring her children. 'I found out that it was exactly the same as Poland, if anything the place was smaller, just a large village. You can feel safe here'. The extended family was important for almost all interviewees and could constitute a safety net. Often they had migrated to join siblings, and local networks of siblings and cousins could develop very quickly.

If migration plans can to some extent be open-ended, this again suggests that there may not be such a gulf between the small-town parents and the better educated, childless Polish migrants whose experimental attitude to migration is often commented upon. Eade at al. (2006: 11) suggest that many Poles in London pursue a strategy of deliberate open-endedness, a strategy which they label 'intentional unpredictability'. On the other hand, perhaps one should not exaggerate the amount of agency possessed by small-town migrants. Some families do have limited freedom of manoeuvre about when to reunify. The very poor households experience a period of still greater hardship while the husband spends the first months alone abroad, especially if the wife gives up her job in preparation for the departure. Moreover, as already suggested, she now experiences all the stresses of coping with the children and managing the household on her own. In such cases, the family is under pressure to reunite as quickly as possible. In other situations, especially where there are many or older children, it may very difficult to decide to move, especially if the children are unhappy with the decision. No doubt women who have migrated successfully may tend to downplay these difficult moments retrospectively, but they were very much to the fore in my discussions with women in Poland who were either considering family migration or not ruling it out as an option in the future.

Duration of Stay and Integration

Mothers already in England expressed very different views about how long they would stay. They often asserted early in the interview either that they intended to save up enough money to return quite soon or else that they would return only in the indefinite future. However, despite such indications that they were 'hamsters' or 'stayers' (Eade et al. 2006: 10–11), in the course of conversation, the mothers often began to consider the various options and even appeared to contradict their original assertions about how long they planned to stay in the UK. In other words, their livelihood strategies were not set in stone, but seemed to be rather flexible: there was an element of 'searching', to use Eade et al.'s terminology.

Nonetheless, although parents were in a sense searchers, they were also buffeted by outside factors and they were not really free agents, choosing their own livelihood trajectory. 'Push' and 'pull' are concepts often used to explain decisions to migrate, but, as Russell King suggests (King 2000: 14–15), duration of stay in the receiving country and the timing of the decision to return are also determined by push and pull factors. The migrant, once arrived, feels pushed and pulled back home for emotional reasons but also by factors such as poor housing in the UK, or falling unemployment in Poland. Sometimes the factors which pulled him or her to Britain in the first place may still seem stronger than the pressures to go back, sometimes the pressures to go back become overwhelming.

Parents are no exception, but they experience these factors differently from other migrants. Although it might seem that employment should be a major determining factor, this was not true for the interviewees. This was partly for 'objective' reasons. As already suggested, they were generally satisfied with the nature of their jobs in Britain, having no aspirations to do anything other than manual labour. Moreover, they were pessimistic about employment prospects in their home towns, tending to see recent improvements in the Polish economy as being confined to the cities. On the other hand, compared with childless migrants, for whom employment may be a central part of their existence, parents are likely to consider factors linked to their children as being at least of equal importance, and probably of more. The mothers interviewed bore the main responsibility for their children's welfare, so it was not surprising if factors such as education and homemaking, seemed – in their accounts – to particularly influence parental decisions about whether to return to Poland.

Some parents expressed disappointment with the standard in British schools, and this could potentially influence a decision to return. However, it also made it harder to go back, since children might not be able to study with their peer group but would have to repeat a year in the Polish school, in order to catch up. Ages at which schools are changed are different in Poland and England, further decreasing flexibility for moving back and forward between systems. Furthermore, children at secondary school in particular get 'sucked into the system' and it becomes hard to leave in the middle of studying for GCSEs or A levels. Overall, parents in the UK were very aware of the differences between British and Polish education: 'two separate worlds' in the words of one mother. It seems that some Polish migrants with very young children intend to return to Poland before their children reach school age and in Poland I was told stories of returnees who had done precisely this. In other words, to have a child starting school can be perceived as a kind of point of no return, the end of temporariness and flexibility for young parents.

Generally, those interviewees' children who had been at school more than a few months were integrating and doing well. Parents sometimes seemed rather surprised at just how well, reinforcing the impression that they had found it hard to know in advance of moving to England how their children would fare. Where children were settling comfortably this was a reason for parents to remain. However, secondary school age children – unsurprisingly – sometimes found it harder to integrate, especially if they were in classes with other Polish children. Sometimes, according to the mothers, non-Polish students assumed that they were self-sufficient within their Polish friendship groups, and did not try to befriend them. Hence this age group, which for academic reasons had more cause to stay than younger children, also experienced stronger 'pulls' back towards Poland. Bafekr's study of Polish children in Brussels found a similar distinction between less well-adjusted older and better-adjusted younger children (Bafekr, 1999: 296).

It seems that many new migrants define their planned length of stay as the time it will take to save for a house back home. Once they are abroad, that period can often lengthen. However, although time is measured with reference to savings for the Polish home, there are also aspects of home occupation in England which determine migrants' perceptions of time. Life is measured in rent agreements, six months or a year at a time. Often it is unclear whether a lease will be extended: 'perhaps, and perhaps not. That's really stressful, there's no security,' said one mother. Of course this is a stressful situation for anyone, but worse when there are children who have already been uprooted, often more than once, and given that it is often hard for families – who have to be choosier than other migrants – to find suitable accommodation. They want more space and a garden: these may be luxuries to childless people, but are regarded as essentials for young children.

Having a house or at least land in Poland gives you a place to return and therefore implies that there will be a *time* to return. By contrast, selling your house symbolizes the cutting of ties with Poland and locating the family's future in the UK. My interviews suggest that there are families – including, perhaps surprisingly, some very poor ones – who strive to keep and improve housing in both countries, enabling them to straddle England and Poland and keep their options entirely open. However, often there is little choice but to give up housing in Poland. For example, a flat rented from the local authority in Poland may have to be returned. Hence the family is forced to stop being temporary migrants.

Conclusion

The story of Lech Wałęsa's family, where there was always 'someone on the other side of the ocean', reminds us that dual location livelihoods are nothing new in Poland and that, particularly in some families and regions, migration has seemed an obvious livelihood strategy for many decades. Temporary migration of parents without children became even more widespread in the 1990s, as economic reforms created widespread material hardship for many sections of the population.

Poland's entry into the European Union and the opening of the British labour market to Polish citizens has made it feasible for whole families to relocate to the United Kingdom and it seems that tens of thousands have already done so.

This chapter has explored some reasons behind this latest wave of migration. The 'feasibility' offered by changed immigration rules is only a small part of the story. Discussions with Polish parents in both Poland and England suggest that typical economic 'push' factors remain important, and that, despite Poland's excellent macroeconomic indicators, many small-town households are still poor, debt-ridden and pessimistic about their prospects. In other words, the stimuli to parental migration are still the same as they were in the 1990s.

However, by exploring non-material factors it is possible to explain why livelihood strategies have changed and increasingly involve migration by children as well as their parents. Poles in Poland are much better informed today about life in the United Kingdom. Consequently, small-town and rural parents can feel both that their new way of life in Britain might not represent an enormous break from their way of life in Poland, and that their children would probably have better opportunities. Mothers hope not to have to work such long hours and to have time to spend with their children. Moreover, migration in whole families is a rejection of the 1990s model, which is seen as promoting family break-up. Even where families do stay together, the emotional sacrifices implied by migration of parents alone are viewed as unacceptable. Parents do not hesitate to articulate the view that families want to be together.

Hence it would seem that parents share some characteristics with other migrants to the United Kingdom, notably a willingness to experiment with migration to Britain. This is not surprising given that migration decisions are made in the context of a specific migration culture in the local community. Livelihoods are grounded in local norms and expectations. Nonetheless, families often do find it harder than other potential migrants to uproot themselves, often, it seems, because of anxieties about how children will adapt to life abroad.

Once they are in England, worries about children's adaptation can persist for parents of older children, and this can be a factor 'pulling' them back towards Poland. On the other hand, many children, especially younger ones, seem to adapt quickly, and this can be a powerful reason for parents to stay. Parents, like other migrants, experience conflicting emotions about living abroad, pushes and pulls in both directions which, for other migrants, make it desirable to maintain open-ended strategies. However, parents have quite limited agency in this respect. Rigidities in the education system and the perception that Polish and British systems are very different mean that their children become locked into the British system and it becomes difficult to envisage a return to Poland. Furthermore, the need to make a 'proper home' for their children in England means that parents may have to postpone or abandon plans to acquire better housing in Poland. It is too early to draw definite conclusions about whether Polish families will settle permanently in Britain, but there are plenty of reasons for them to do so.

The case of Polish family migration illustrates the helpfulness of a livelihood strategy approach. It would not be easy to explain why families come to England, and stay, only with reference to the income and employment of specific migrant parents. Only by considering the non-material aspects of livelihoods, and their location within specific local cultures, is it possible to understand this shift in Polish migration patterns.

References

Bafekr, S. (1999), 'Schools and their Undocumented Polish and "Romany Gypsy" Pupils', *International Journal of Educational Research* 31, 295–302.

'Bajka o Marysi i Basi' (2007), *Praca i życie za granicą [Working and Living Abroad]*, 5–18 July, 4.

Byron, M. (1994), *Post-War Caribbean Migration to Britain: The Unfinished Cycle* (Aldershot: Avebury).

Eade, J., Drinkwater, S. and Garapich, M.P. (2006), *Class and Ethnicity – Polish Migrants in London*. Centre for Research on Nationalism, Ethnicity and Multiculturalism, University of Surrey <http://www.surrey.ac.uk/Arts/ CRONEM/polish/POLISH_FINAL_RESEARCH_REPORT_WEB.pdf>, accessed 1 April 2007.

Ellis, F. (2000), *Rural Livelihoods and Diversity in Developing Countries* (Oxford: Oxford University Press).

Fihel, A. and Piętka, E. (2007), *Funkcjonowanie polskich migrantów na brytyjskim rynku pracy [Polish migrants and how they function on the British labour market]*. University of Warsaw Centre for Migration Research Working Paper No. 23/81 (Warsaw: University of Warsaw Centre for Migration Research).

Ghosh, B. (ed.) (2000), *Return Migration: Journey of Hope or Despair?* (Geneva: International Organization for Migration and United Nations).

GUS (Główny Urząd Statystyczny, Central Statistical Office) (2007a), *stopa_ bezrobocia_02_07 [unemployment rates]* <http://www.stat.gov.pl/dane_spol- gosp/praca_ludnosc/index.htm>, accessed 1 April 2007.

GUS (Główny Urząd Statystyczny, Central Statistical Office) (2007b), *Kobiety w Polsce; [Women in Poland]*, <http://www.stat.gov.pl/gus/45_3816_PLK_ HTML.htm>, accessed 1 April 2008.

Guzik, M. (2005), *Szare Madonny [Everyday Madonnas]* (Krosno: Krośnieńska Oficyna Wydawnicza).

Halfacree, K. and Boyle, P. (1993), 'The Challenge Facing Migration Research: the Case for a Biographical Approach', *Progress in Human Geography* 17:3, 333–48.

Home Office UK Border Agency, Department for Work and Pensions, HM Revenue and Customs and Communities and Local Government, *Accession Monitoring Report* (various issues). <http://www.ind.homeoffice.gov.uk/aboutus/reports/ accession_monitoring_report>.

Hugo-Bader, J. (16 October 2007), 'Syndrom F92', *Gazeta Wyborcza* <http://www. gazetawyborcza.pl/1,78488,4576942.html>, accessed 10 December 2007.

IPPR (27 February 2008), E-mail communication regarding unpublished IPPR research from Dr Dhananjayan Sriskandarajah, Director of Research Strategy, Institute for Public Policy Research (London).

Jach, M. (2007), 'Emigrują także dzieci' ['Children emigrate too'), Express Ilustrowany, 31 August 2007, <http://www.wiadomosci24.pl/artykul/emigruja_takze_dzieci_40878.html>, accessed 10 December 2007.

King, R. (2000), 'Generalizations from the History of Return Migration', in Ghosh, B. (ed.).

Morawska, E. (2001), 'Structuring Migration: the Case of Polish Income-seeking Travelers to the West', *Theory and Society* 30:1, 47–80.

Pickup, F. and White, A. (2003), 'Livelihoods in Postcommunist Russia: Urban/ Rural Comparisons', *Work, Employment and Society* 17:3, 419–34.

Pine, F. and Bridger, S. (eds) (1998), *Surviving Post-Socialism: Local Strategies and Regional Responses* (London: Routledge).

Pollard, N., Latorre, M. and Sriskandarajah, D. (2008), *Floodgates or Turnstiles? Post-EU Enlargement Migration Flows to (and from) the UK* (London: Institute for Public Policy Research).

Portes, R. (ed.) (1995), *The Economic Sociology of Immigration: Essays on Networks, Ethnicity and Entrepreneurship* (New York, NY: Russell Sage Foundation).

Przybyła, M. (2007), 'Mama za granicą, dziecko w bidulu', *Praca i nauka za granicą* ('Living and Studying Abroad'), 23 March, p. 12.

Roberts, B. (1995), 'Socially Expected Durations and the Economic Adjustment of Immigrants' in Portes, R. (ed.).

Rocznik Demograficzny (Demographic Yearbook of Poland) 2007 (2007), (Warsaw, Główny Urząd Statystyczny) <http://www.stat.gov.pl/cps/rde/xbcr/gus/PUBL_PUBL_Rocznik_Demograficzny_2007.pdf>, accessed 14 April 2008.

Shevchenko, O. (2002), '"Between the Holes": Emerging Identities and Hybrid Patterns of Consumption in Post-Socialist Russia', *Europe-Asia Studies* 54:6, 841–66.

Sørensen, N. and Olwig, K. (eds) (2002), *Work and Migration: Life and Livelihoods in a Globalizing World* (London: Routledge).

Stenning, A. (2005), 'Re-Placing Work: Economic Transformations and the Shape of a Community in Post-Socialist Poland', *Work, Employment and Society* 19:2, 235–59.

Wachowiak, A. (ed.) (2002), *Przemiany orientacji życiowych kobiet zamężnych* [*Married Women: Changing Attitudes to Life*] (Poznań: Wydawnictwo Fundacji Humaniora).

Wałęsa, L. (1987), *A Way of Hope* (New York, NY: Henry Holt & Company), cited in Morawska (2001).

Wallace, C. (2002), 'Household strategies: their conceptual relevance and analytical scope in social research', *Sociology* 36:2, 275–92.

Wasek, A. (9 February 2007), 'Siemiatyckie Eldorado?' *Nasz Dziennik*, <http://www.naszdziennik.pl/index.php?dat=20070209&typ=my&id=my11.txt>, accessed 10 December 2007.

White, A. (2004), *Small-town Russia: Postcommunist Livelihoods and Identities: a Portrait of the Intelligentsia in Achit, Bednodemyanovsk and Zubtsov, 1999–2000* (London and New York, NY: RoutledgeCurzon).

www.gazeta.pl (various years), 'Przystanek Polska' and other discussion forums.

Żytnicki, P. and Sałwacka, M. (2007), 'Mama i tata za granicą, a dziecko u koleżanki' [*Mum and Dad are abroad, and their child is with Mum's friend*], *Gazeta Zielona Góra*, 4 December 2007, <http://miasta.gazeta.pl/zielonagora/1,35182,4730852.html>, accessed 10 December 2007.

Chapter 4

Discourses of a 'Normal Life' among Post-accession Migrants from Poland to Britain

Aleksandra Galasińska and Olga Kozłowska

This chapter focuses on the construction of the idea of a 'normal life' in the discourses of Polish post-2004 migrants. We are particularly concerned with discursive strategies adopted by migrants which aim to justify their decision to live and work in Britain, one of the first countries from the 'Europe 15' to open its labour market to 'new' Europeans. While earlier migrants usually repeated the historically grounded patterns of clandestine economic migration from Poland, typically based on existing networks of fellow Poles (see Morawska 2001; Triandafyllidou 2006), post-2004 arrivals gradually changed these patterns, moving, travelling and looking for jobs more independently. Having had the opportunity to travel, work and live as they please, as well as being treated more equitably alongside other EU member nationals in the country of destination, Poles in the UK have, correspondingly, steadily transformed their migration stories (see Galasińska and Kozłowska 2006; Galasińska 2009). Most notably, the notion of 'normality' has become more and more salient in their narratives of migration.

This discourse of normality, of longing for 'a normal life', has already been observed and explored within studies on post-communist societies (Kennedy 1994; Eglitis 2002; Rausing 2002). 'Normality', as described by Eglitis (2002), is the aspiration of ambitious post-communist societies. Kennedy (1994) takes a different view, defining this desire for normality as the sign of an exhausted society which no longer wishes to be put through experiments and yearns for a successful future – by implication, a society whose members just want to be treated in a 'normal way'. Such societies, it is argued, long to have an unproblematic identity, 'despite the unprecedented transformation they are living through and the "aberration" of history that led to it' (Kennedy 1994: 4). Members of post-communist societies, therefore, not only wish to create a normal reality but they want to *be* normal; 'They wish to be who they "really" are, or who they ought to be. In short, they want to be something inconsistent with the system they recently overturned and the social relations it produced' (Kennedy 1994: 4). Rausing see this in a similar way, also stressing the geo-political implications of this concept of 'normal' in the context of post-communist transformation, which he argues is 'associated with the solid ordinary comforts of northern Europe' (Rausing 2002: 132).

These studies do have some limitations for the study of migrants' stories, however, because they are restricted to the discourses which circulate within the country's borders. In this study we go beyond these positions and move away from the physical space of Poland, instead focusing on text and talk produced by Poles living abroad. It is important to note that these migration discourses have been constructed at a time of lively nationwide discussion about the quality of people leaving Poland and their success in Britain. This discussion has taken place in the media (television, newspapers, Internet) and takes the form of public (politicians talking about the Polish migrants) and private debates (Internet forums). It has been argued, on the one hand, that too many young people are leaving the country, with some commentators bemoaning the problems of 'brain drain' and a diminishing skilled workforce, as well as the potential financial difficulties this migration will create in the future (a decreased budget and a gap in future pension funds). Others, however, have suggested that Poland will benefit from this emigration due to falling unemployment figures and the potential new skills and experiences of returnees in the future. The patriotism of the migrants has also been called into question, alongside their spirit, moral fibre and reputation. In some quarters they have been called traitors, lazybones, wasters, but in other discussions they have been praised for their bravery and entrepreneurship. Importantly, these debates are echoed in the narratives of Polish migrants talking about their experience of living in Britain, and in the way they spontaneously justify their decision to migrate/stay abroad by offering arguments about the need to migrate for the sake of having 'a normal life' (see Galasińska 2009).

In this analysis we regard this concept of normality as a lived category – one used when constructing the lived experience of social reality and social practices. Even if people do not directly speak about some phenomena as normal, they still construct it within this dimension. To borrow the words of Berger and Luckmann (1966), we aim to understand the reality of everyday life, and more precisely, the foundations of knowledge (common sense) guiding conduct in everyday life – something they argue 'originates in [people's] thoughts and actions, and is maintained as real by these' (Berger and Luckmann 1966: 33). We assert, however, that what for Berger and Luckmann is a matter of thoughts, for discourse analysts is a matter of discourse.

Discursive Approaches to Migrants' Accounts

Our study is anchored in discourse analysis. We see discourse as 'language use conceived as social practice' and a 'way of signifying experience from a particular perspective' (Fairclough 1992: 73). Discourse as language use involves texts, discourse practices and socio-cultural practices. Being a form of social practice 'within a socio-cultural context' (Galasiński 2004: 19), discourse is communicative activity, and this activity is performed by individuals who act not as individuals but as members of social groups, organizations, institutions and cultures (Galasiński

2004). Being a way of signifying experience, 'discourse is a coordinated pattern of words, deeds, values, beliefs, symbols, tools, objects, times, and places in the here and now as a performance that is recognizable as just such a coordination' (Gee 2005: 19).

Discourse analysts therefore deal with 'a view of language at the level of text and a view of language in use' (Paltridge 2006: 9). Firstly, this means that discourse analysis is a textually oriented analysis (Fairclough 1992). Its focus is on the content and the form of discourse – that is the lexico-grammatical resources of language (Galasiński 2004). Secondly, the interest of discourse analysis is in 'how, through the use of language, people achieve certain communicative goals, perform certain communicative acts, participate in certain communicative events and present themselves to others' and what 'ideas and beliefs they communicate as they use language' (Paltridge 2006: 9). In short, an analysis of discourse should be both linguistically and socially oriented (Fairclough 2003; Cameron and Kulick 2003). Therefore, discourse analysis is 'an approach to the analysis of language that looks at patterns of language across texts as well as the social and cultural contexts in which the texts occur' (Paltridge 2006: 1); it offers 'some kind of explanation of why a text is as it is and what it is aiming to do' but also it looks at 'the relationship between discourse and society and aims to describe, interpret and explain the relationship' (Rogers 2004: 2).

We also acknowledge the centrality of narrative as a mode of organizing discourse, human knowledge and interaction (Bruner 1991), and we recognize the model of narrative structure (developed by Labov 1972) and its influence for the analysis of interview narratives. As Bruner observes (1991: 4), 'we organize our experience and our memory of human happenings mainly in the form of narrative – stories, excuses, myths, reasons for doing and not doing and so on'. Similarly, Georgakopoulou and Gautsos (2004: 42) write about narrative discourse as 'exhibiting an unquestionable primacy in our everyday social lives' as 'narratives do not only permeate our lives in their different shapes but also form a constitutive element of them, a fundamental principle of organizing and making sense of our experience'. It involves meaning making, ordering and structuring of the experience (Georgakopolou 2006). We seem to see our world in narrative form (MacIntyre 1981; Carr 1986; Georgakopolou 2006). An emerging definition of 'a narrative' is a construction in talk that includes sequences or consequences (Taylor 2006).

Complementary to other methodological approaches adopted in earlier studies on contemporary Polish migrants to the UK (see for example Burrell 2007; Eade et al. 2007; Garapich 2007a, 2007b; Ryan et al. 2007a, 2007b), we explore migration by analysing interviewee's accounts by using discourse and narrative analysis. As we have shown elsewhere (Galasińska and Kozłowska 2006; Galasińska and Kozłowska 2009), contemporary migrants tend to construct migration as an action which is easy to take, does not need long consideration, long-term preparations nor involves a difficult crossing. It is also a temporary event or an event with an open outcome. Both the decision and journey are presented as relatively straightforward steps and the passage between old and new countries is blurred. Migration is seen to take place in a dynamic, flexible and open space, with the living space of migrants simply extended rather than replaced, giving the impression that people can choose when and where to live, rather than just having to grab any opportunity to migrate as it was in the case of previous economic migrants from Poland during the time of travel and work restrictions.

In addition, the linguistic form of interviews like this usually mirrors the content. When recent migrants are interviewed, for example, they tend to use a non-narrative mode of discourse and therefore present the event of migration as something not worth dwelling on but rather as something that is normal/common. To describe their experience they produce narratives that are concise and which are delivered as informative answers to the interviewer's questions, with short sentences, even sometimes with verbs omitted. The language that is used is not emotionally charged, and is rather colloquial, often including proverbs. It is low in 'tellability' and narrativity. Furthermore, these narratives are sometimes based on argumentative discourses, in which elements of 'for and against' migration arguments are included and internally debated. Significantly, these observations reinforce Papastergiadis' (2000) and McHugh's (2000) assertions that contemporary migration has no single origin and no simple end; 'It is an ongoing process and need to be seen as an open voyage' (Papastergiadis 2000: 4) and it 'is about people dislodged from place, people in motion, people with attachments and connections in multiple places, people living in the moment while looking backward from where they came and forward to an uncertain future' (McHugh 2000: 83).

This study brings together two different projects – one based on analysed interview data and the other on Internet forums – which are both concerned with the discourses of recent Polish migrants, and in particular those issues related to the notion of 'normality'. Firstly, the interview data comes from a study of the lived experience of economic migration from Poland to Britain and was collected a few months after Poland joined the EU in May 2004. Twenty-two in-depth interviews were conducted with highly educated young people who left Poland to take advantage of labour market opportunities in the new enlarged Europe. This target group was chosen as young people have dominated the make-up of Polish migrants in the UK (Osipovic 2007; Pollard et al. 2008). They have also been hit the hardest by unemployment or temporary and low value work in their home country, quite often being denied prospects and stability in their lives during the transformation process in Poland (see Mariański 1995; Stenning 2005). Interviewees came from different parts of Poland and had settled in the West Midlands region, mainly Birmingham and Wolverhampton. Interviews were conducted in Polish and were later partially translated into English. The original flow of narratives is preserved in all of these examples, so what might be regarded as incomprehensive or unclear text it is in fact a lived, unedited talk.

As this chapter will demonstrate, within the particular socio-historical context of this migration very specific ideas about 'normality' arise and take shape. The main focus of this study has been an exploration of the complexities of young migrants' constructions of the 'normal' West and the normality of migrating to the West (see also Kozłowska 2009). This research has focused particularly on young people who have been underemployed in their new host environment, and whose narratives should explain why young Polish people have been willing to take jobs below their qualifications once arrived in the UK. The study's findings indicate that often the migrants justify their decision to migrate by talking about heading for a 'better world' and about participating in an 'ordinary' practice. Both of these perceived qualities highlight the fact that the West is still mythologized as a symbol of prosperity, wealth and a comfortable lifestyle by Poles (see Duvell 2006; Sowiński 2006; Galasińska 2009) but also that contemporary economic migrants move countries in a different socio-economic context to their predecessors.

The other project from which this chapter draws is based on Internet data which was collected from an Internet discussion forum attached to the influential Polish daily *Gazeta Wyborcza*. In order to pinpoint a particular type of discussion, we chose highly commented-upon articles written about the success and a potential return of Polish post-2004 transnational income seekers in the UK, published between 2005 and 2007. The chosen articles (listed at the end of the chapter) were different in style, with the first one written in an informative manner, offering 'objective' information about highly qualified office workers and professionals from Poland, successfully employed in the UK, and quoting statistical data, showing diagrams and avoiding commentary from the editors. The other, by contrast, showed mediated versions of new migrants' personal stories since their arrival in the UK, focusing on their successful social, economic and emotional adaptation to their new, chosen domicile. Together the articles attracted several hundred comments on a readers' forum.

In this chapter we focus on the different personal stories which were presented on the forum as a means of illustrating the discussants' points of view. Choosing this type of data to analyse has important methodological implications. On the one hand it avoids the co-authoring and co-construction of stories elicited by the researcher during interviews, and the asymmetrical power relations which can be played out during an interview process. On the other hand, however, there are limitations too. We do not know much about the profile of the participants – their age, and gender for example – as the forum is anonymous and it is open to anyone (with an Internet connection and knowledge of the Polish language). But it is obvious that these new information technologies enable post-accession migrants to participate actively in an ongoing dialogue with those who stayed in the home country.

Some of the findings from this project have already been disseminated elsewhere (Galasińska 2009), with the linguistic characteristics of these narratives especially being discussed. It was found that the forum contributions tended to be short and compact in form, most probably due to the particular constraints of forum usage, where a long post could easily be ignored or perceived as boring and time consuming by both discussants and readers. Other observations included the exclusive use of the first person singular, in contrast to other social actors such as those who had stayed in Poland and other less successful Polish migrants; the repetitive use of the extreme case formulation *never*, linked with descriptions about manual work or working below one's qualifications; detailed descriptions of getting and performing satisfying, well-paid jobs, usually narrated with market-oriented vocabulary; the dynamically stretched spatial, as well as temporal, nature of the narratives; and finally a tendency towards genderless tellership.

All these factors support the view of post-enlargement migration as an individual, agency-oriented and open-ended process. However, Galasińska (2009) also observed the co-tellership of what appeared, at first glance, as exclusively personal stories, pointing to elements of a generational experience in the data presented. Furthermore, it is also apparent that these personal narratives of post-enlargement migration are used as an argumentative tool against the historically bounded hegemonic discourses of Polish economic migration, contextualized in the era of closed borders pre-1989.

Taken together, these two complementary sets of data allow for an in-depth understanding of post-accession migrants' discourses. They throw light both on discourses of normality, and on the specificities of the social, political, economic and historical contexts of post-accession Polish migration.

Discussions of Work and Life

As stated above, the salient topic of the dialogues in the analysed data focused on the issue of having a 'normal' life and succeeding abroad. In the following discussion we show, firstly, how the interviewees and forum participants talk about everyday practices at work in both countries, and secondly, how they debate and describe life in Britain in general.

To Work Normally

It is generally agreed that economic migrants change countries in order to get better paid jobs or to escape unemployment (Massey et al. 1998). This has certainly been identified as a key factor in contemporary Polish migration (Drinkwater et al. 2006), and so in this section we illustrate the different ways in which the Polish migrants talk about these issues, and how they emphasize other important factors related to work abroad in their narratives.

In the following two examples our respondents talk about problems with employment in Poland. In Example 1, 'Patrycja' discusses the pride that prevented her from applying for a contract extension, while in Example 2, Wojtek focuses on the difficulty of accessing the potential posts.

Example 1: Patrycja, female, 1979 (manual job, working below qualifications)

I: And were you offered a job there [in office where she had her apprenticeship]?

Patrycja: The situation was unclear. Maybe they would like me to stay but they did not offer me anything. It was me who was supposed to ask them to let me stay. So I gave up because my salary was very poor then, maybe they would pay me more later but even if they had I wouldn't accept the job because of my boss. I experienced tough moments when it was difficult to communicate with him. *And I decided that if it is me who should ask for a job then I should withdraw.* And during the first week *here*, on the second day, I got a job.

Example 2: Wojtek, male, 1972 (manual job, working below qualifications)

I: And how was it with work in Poland?

Wojtek: Well very hard. I had never worked professionally, *because I have never had any connections*, neither in the local authority offices, nor in police. I lived in a quite small town so I knew people who graduated from trade schools and they worked in the local authority offices. And I couldn't find a job. I applied everywhere and I was getting various jobs only on the black market. If there was an opportunity to get a job offered by an employment office in a warehouse then mostly these were jobs within a programme of public works that meant that after three months when the subsidies ran out *they were replacing the employees on their own.* And I came here, *all the time I have worked in the same place*, and I have a reputation, from what they say, maybe I will boast a little bit, but as the best employee. I do my best, I do a little bit more than the norm is, I do what I can do. I have already got a contract, for four years, after a few months, and they have no intention of firing me.

For Patrycja, not only is the possibility of getting a job important, but so is the way of acquiring it. In fact, the latter issue seemed to become more important for her. Significantly, she compares how it was in Poland with how it is in Britain and the language used to construct these procedures in both countries is different. In relation to work in Poland, she does not generalize but talks directly about her workplace. In contrast, when talking about getting a job in Britain she uses the general spatial reference 'here'. This strategy creates an illusion of the general ease in obtaining a position. Interestingly, Patrycja does not mention any difference in the type of post she had in Poland and has in Britain, even though her present job is a manual one and not clerical as it was in Poland. For her, pride played a vital role getting employment in a 'normal' way. She did not want to ask her boss for a place after her apprenticeship, she wanted to be offered a position. It is interesting to see that Patrycja does not mention how she got her job in Britain. It just happened.

The difficulty of getting a job is presented by Wojtek as a problem created by employers. He constructs them as active protagonists contributing to the chaos (or even being the main cause of it) and absurdity of the Polish employment market. In this extract the Polish employers seem to act in an arbitrary manner, which is indicated by the expression '*wymieniali sobie*'/'were replacing the employees on their own', that in Polish suggests carelessness about others, lawlessness and attention only to one's own interests. On the other hand, in his narrative there is an impersonal construction of employment procedures in Poland. In the first part of the narrative he talks about 'connections', and his lack of them, as a reason for not having a professional job. Everything except non-professional work seems to be located in a static space that is beyond his reach. This is a system that is omnipresent and one that Wojtek cannot enter or confront. Wojtek's 'bottom-up' perspective of the Polish reality of the workplace is supported by several sociological and anthropological studies which cite the importance of connections and the prevalence of dishonest employment procedures (i.e. Miszalska 1996; Dunn 1999; Łaciak 2005), rooted in ubiquitous informal networks from communist times (see Ledeneva 1998; Wedel 1986, 1992; Kula 2006; Burrell 2008).

In a similar vein, the forum's participants also aired their opinions on the Polish workplace by comparing the Polish and British realities of work.

Example 3: Forum discussant

I am pretty happy with a middle management job, without the prospect of becoming a chairman, but *in a serious and well managed company* in the UK instead and *somehow I don't miss the mess and corrupted arrangements* which I left in one country on the continent...

Example 4: Forum discussant

If I work here in an international company, with professionals from all over the world, I earn several times more than an average British salary, I can easily say that I am, as all my colleagues at work are, a member of the real middle class here and not one which is rising now, if I get promotion every year, I get a pay rise and bonuses and I can pick and choose any job offer if I would like to change my job, *if I achieved that without connections, protection, corruption, bribery and so on*, then what are these closed doors preventing me from having a good night's sleep? Is there the average Pole in Poland, from a middle class or the almost middle class which is rising now or any other class, able to put his foot in the door? Let's see it clearly, honestly and without a false patriotic bias, which prevents us from seeing things in Poland differently, in contrast to Britain.

In contrast to Patrycja and Wojtek's voices, both examples from the forum show a professional '*I*' connected to vocabulary relating to middle management and professional occupations. However, the distancing strategies, through the discussion of particular negative social practices in the home country, remain the same as this person also criticizes Polish practices. Thus both groups, interviewees and the forum participants, share a common social practice – they criticize the reality of working life in Poland and compare it to a friendlier, if not idealized, view of the same in Britain. One of the clearest implications of these constructions of working life in Britain is the perceived 'normality' of latter. This in turn influences the discursive practices used (juxtaposing both countries) and thus it is not a coincidence that all such stories resemble each other. Being repeated by many tellers in the same or similar canonical form, they become a new grand narrative – a blueprint for all stories – which, as Andrews put it, 'offer[s] a way of identifying what is assumed to be a normative experience' (Andrews 2004: 2). It could also be argued that the narratives presented here reflect a generational experience (the majority of migrants are young), which has become a generational memory of migration during the transformation process (see also Galasińska 2009). Young migrants' stories have become culturally embedded in the broader context of post-communist transformation, and in particular EU extension.

We would also like to highlight one more interesting aspect of the narrative in Example 4, namely the issue of time management. In the previous extracts the awful situation in Poland was presented as static, lacking any signs of improvement. The discussant from Example 4 makes it more dynamic and open-ended, pointing at the transformational characteristic of the process of class development in the country. Here is a hint of why reality in Poland, still entangled in the process of transformation, cannot be seen as 'normal', but rather it is in the state of becoming (Bauman 1992; Buchowski 2001). With this hint an element of hope is introduced, which is picked up by those interviewees and forum participants who talk about a potential return to Poland.

Normal Life in Britain, or To Earn 'Enough'

We move now from the narratives where people talk about differences in work practices in Poland and the UK to discourses where they talk about their gratitude for work, mainly for financial reasons, but also related to this idea of a 'normal' life.

Example 5: **Forum discussant**

I have good advice for migrants: learn English thoroughly, invest in yourself, stop looking back at those who lost their chance and stayed in The People's Republic of Poland [the official name of Poland before transformation] and start to live *normally* on the Isles.

Example 6: Forum discussant

The difference is as follows – in Poland this little money is not enough to rent an awful bed-sit, in England for the same amount one can live *normally*, that means one can eat normally, buy clothes, have fun, get a car and accommodation, and not peanuts.

Both of these examples are linked with the adverb 'normally', but they are quite different in style. While the first one, Example 5, is direct but general 'advice' for migrants, the second one, Example 6, offers an explanation of what normal life in Britain means. This contains everyday human activities related to food, clothing, entertainment, housing and transport. Interestingly, this example mirrors the ones from the previous section, offering again a comparison with life in Poland, constructed once more in negative terms.

There is also another interesting aspect, universal across our data, which we would like to focus on. The discussant from Example 6 writes about 'little money' that can ensure people get all the necessities of a real, 'normal' life. This topos of having 'enough', of making ends meet with even modest pay, can be seen as a definition of 'normality' across the sample. Consider the following examples from the forum:

Example 7: Forum discussant

Sorry, but Poles do not go abroad because there is better pay over there. They go because there is a *better life*. And if they earn, *there will be enough* to send to Poland.

Example 8: Forum discussant

Even if someone works for a minimal wage over there, maybe someone is even poor, but *life is much easier* than in Poland. After deducting the cost of living, there *is always something for smaller or bigger pleasures*, one can save a bit.

Example 9: Forum discussant

One *can save* without significant effort 400–500GBP after a month working in a low paid job. Without living with parents, without extra hours.

All three forum participants expressed opinions about the direct correlation between modest earnings and decent living conditions. In Example 7 an explicit view on this matter is presented: pay is not necessarily better, but it is 'enough'. However, by mentioning remittances, this person also refers to the differences between pay in both counties. A hedging or mitigating tactic in the use of the word 'maybe' is adopted by the discussant in Example 8, and this frames the issue of migration as more complicated than a straightforward, black and white picture. Relative poverty might be compensated for by having fun in life. The spectrum of vocabulary relating to earnings being modest but 'enough' (smaller pleasures, save a bit) is completed by an exemplifying number in Example 9.

Once again, in all the analysed examples, there is a juxtaposition of both the sending and receiving country. This stretched spatial quality of the migrants' discourses on the Internet forum is achieved *inter alia* by mentioning Poland either directly or indirectly (such as a description of living and working conditions there as in Example 9). There is a significant difference though between the examined examples from the forum in this section and the interviewees' accounts that will follow. As we explained earlier, when migrants discussed working practices in both countries they usually used the first person singular and offered examples from their own lives. In contrast, discussions of general living conditions in relation to work were usually depersonalized on the forum, where the narrative mode disappeared from the discourse of everyday life. In the extracts from interviews relating to general conditions, however, our informants again used more personalized narratives.

Consider the following examples in which migrants were asked directly to talk about work, but where issues related to life more generally were always 'nearby', going hand in hand with the former.

Example 10: Wojtek, male, 1972 [manual job, working below qualifications]

I: And what does good work mean to you?

Wojtek: Good work it is: … it is such work that *I can live by*, and: work at which I'm confident that I have it the next day. Like the one I have now that I go the next day to work and I know that I have that work. … *Well and: of course also relations at this work* how they respect you and: …

Example 11: Jola, female, 1968 [manual job, working below qualifications]

I: And what does good work mean to you?

Jola: Good work? … Most of all work giving satisfaction, work that I feel good at, *well and work for money that is enough for my needs. And because I don't have outrageous needs, so …*

I: So what are the needs?

J: What are the needs? These are such needs, I don't know, the needs of everyday life, it doesn't have to be, of everyday life, one knows, the normal needs. But … what I think about in the nearest future, I think about buying a car, not a new one of course, *because I can't afford such a car*, but a few years old, not too old. Well for slowly saving for a house, I don't know, buying a good camera. These are such ... mine ...

Wojtek does not simply state that his wish is to earn enough. Enough is constructed as defraying the most basic needs, enough just to survive. It can be food, accommodation, clothes, stationery for children and having things that are of rather low quality just to maintain living and social duties without any luxury. This is implied with the expression '*utrzymać się*'/'live by' that in Polish has minimalist connotations. The other components of the 'good job' description (the certainty of the post, good relations at work) have the same importance for Wojtek as his wages. Moreover, his explanations are rooted strongly in his previous experience of working in Poland where he had problems with providing for his family because he worked illegally for a minimal salary and without any certainty of obtaining work regularly. What is more, Wojtek was treated badly at work as nobody appreciated his work. Thus his past experience, and not just general ideas about work, were guiding him throughout his narrative. But despite making his own experience an anchor for the characterization of the meaning of 'good work' he also implies that it has a wider application. Thus instead of only talking about himself, he transfers to the impersonal 'you' in the last phrase, describing the general principle of how it should be.

Jola also focuses on needs as a determinant of salary level. But this time it is not dignity but moderation that guides her. From among three elements determining good work for Jola, she chooses work satisfaction as the most important one; this is stressed with the expression 'most of all'. And this element is not only constructed as universal, it is also left without any further explanations. But it seems to be a slogan that she repeats. Then there is the second element where Jola shifts to a more personal perspective. She emphasizes that it is *she* who should feel good at work, thus distancing herself from the opinion of others commenting on her work. And she continues with this personal perspective when talking about the third element, earnings and spending. The way she talks about earnings suggests that it is important for her to specify a level of desired salary. It should be an amount of money that 'is enough' (in Polish '*starczać*'/'being enough' implies scant) for 'needs' (and not for extravagance or indulgence). Further on in her interview, when Jola answered a question about ideas about her future, she talked about her spending plans. She mentioned the purchase of 'some little house' and she added 'not too big, not too expensive' and 'some little car' (in Polish both expressions are mollifications of their basics forms).

Talking about money seems to be an important theme for the interviewees. There are two things that indicate this. First, whatever problems it can cause, money is taken up and discussed. Therefore, talking about money is included into the discourse on good work. When talking about good work, one has to talk about money. Second, it is clearly never easy to position oneself in this subject. Any attitude taken, the desire to just earn, or to earn a lot, has to be made reasonable.

These two 'musts' determine the significance of the financial element of the definition of 'good work'.

From the analyses in this section a few conclusions can be derived. Narratives on normal work are created in contrast to an experienced or observed situation in Poland but they are also rooted in the context of migration. First, the way the respondents talk about earnings indicates that it is important for them to take a position on the topic and that it has to be done with frugality. Second, they show that they do not want to have a job that would just be an obligation for them. Thus they position themselves within a group of people who care about what they do. In this section we also portrayed the respondents' detailed images of what a 'normal job market' and 'normal work' should be – the rules that a good job market should operate within and certain features that good work should have. The narratives here were constructed through explicit or implicit critiques of the situation in Poland, with the migrants depicting their migration as motivated not only by economic reasons but also by particular values that they felt were lacking in Poland. What they aimed for was normality.

Conclusions

Narratives on 'normal work' created by the migrants have a special status; they have a significant role to play in the particular story of each interviewee. These narratives not only offer a space to present the values which are important for people in their lives (and thus create an image of a person) but also the values which are important for them in their migration (and thus create an image of a migrant – willing to grow rich quickly or simply looking for a normal life). These strands also conform to, and are shaped by, the discourse of normal work – what can be and should be said about 'normal work' in the context of migration. From the perspective of this research, it is important to note that not only are similar elements pin-pointed as significant for the meaning of 'normal work' in the different accounts, but that they are also constructed in a similar way by the different interviewees. This shows that the same issues are challenging for a particular group of people – the post-accession migrants. Lived definitions of 'good work', definitions that emerged from both focused and spontaneous narratives, are drawn on accessible discourses of good work that are negotiated according to the interviewees' and discussants needs, in this case the need to protect a self-image as a migrant. As a result, these narratives do not just reflect accessible discourses on normal work, but they also represent discourses on migration practices that are accepted in a particular society. It appears that the respondents struggle especially with the image of a migrant as a person who wants to earn a lot quickly, no matter what s/he does for a living. The different ideologies of migration play their role here, where migration is justified by a range of reasons which reach beyond purely economic concerns.

We would also like to return to the topic of moderation, which is a concept which has been important in communist and post-communist Poland, and seems to be closely connected to the discourses of the interviewed migrants. The ethos valued by communist propaganda was marked with a strong anti-materialistic tendency (Miszalska 1998; Inglehart 1988), aiming to promote post-materialistic values and an aversion towards growing rich and also towards rich people. Emotion was valued over pragmatism, and people who could afford commodities (such as a car, a summer house and holidays abroad) were perceived as having excessive needs. However, those who could only provide for their own basic needs were still frustrated with their position. Morawska (1999) observes the same phenomenon in the reality of the post-communist era, where the displayed ownership of middle class status symbol objects has tended to evoke appreciation but also envy among those who cannot afford to 'keep up'. This social phenomenon has been called 'envious egalitarianism' (Nowak 1979; Machonin 1997).

Commenting on an advert slogan from 1992, 'Give yourself a little bit of luxury', Bralczyk (2006) has argued that, at that time, putting together the expressions 'a little bit' and 'luxury' was significant. Just after the communist system, and its related norms of social morality, collapsed, people were not prepared for 'luxury' in its full bloom; embracing excessive luxury would have been inconsistent with the prevailing belief in modesty and moderation as desired values, something Rausing (2002) has observed while investigating consumption of western goods in post-communist Estonia.

It is also worth referring to public evaluations of the 'illegal' economic activities performed by ordinary people in the early years of post-communist transformation. Individuals grabbing money (speculators, middlemen, dishonest salespersons, corrupt government officials) were deemed to be morally reprehensible and unacceptable. But illegal activities were also performed by people 'who were not seeking to get rich, but – who, like almost everyone, were trying to "work the system" to obtain scarce but necessary goods and services and no one "profited" in a big way from them' (Millar and Wolchik 1994: 22), just as in communist times (Kula 2006). These issues have also been considered by Sztompka (2000), who has talked about 'primitive egalitarianism', and the notion that 'all the people have the same size of stomach so they should obtain the same amount of commodities'. This slogan was popular during communism and is perceived to be an underlying cause of some of this dislike of extraordinary successes and profits – an active dislike which Sztompka has observed continued well into the nineties (see also Buchowski 2001). A further interpretation of this discourse of normality, built on narratives of a good labour market and good work, therefore may be possible; these narratives in fact represent a discourse of social justice. Thus, when the interviewees were constructing accounts of good/normal earnings they were not only portraying themselves as people aiming for a basic standard of living and moderation in consumption, but also people looking for a just life that they felt was missing in Poland.

Ultimately, one issue has emerged as dominant in this research; both groups of researched post-enlargement migrants used linguistic resources rooted and embedded in the same discourse of 'normality', which connects closely to conceptualizations of moderation which were prevalent in Poland before 1989. It is one more example that post-communist transformations, although translocal in this case, can only be fully understood in their historical context.

Internet Sources

Andrzejczak, A. 'Polscy emigranci-wrócą czy nie wrócą?' ['*Polish migrants- will they return or not?*'], *Gazeta Wyborcza* [website], (31 January 2008) <http://forum.gazeta.pl/forum/72,2.html?f=23&w=75212435&v=2&s=0> – 138 forum entries.

'Jeśli funt spadnie ponizej 3,50 to wracamy' ['*If sterling will be below 3,50 (PLN) we will come back*'] *Alert24.pl* [website], (11 January 2008) <http://www.alert24.pl/alert24/1,84880,4828738.html> – 128 forum entries.

Nowak, W. 'Z Polska na czysto' ['*In Clean with Poland*'] *Gazeta Wyborcza* [website], (5 September 2005) <http://forum.gazeta.pl/forum/72,2.html?f=52 1&w=28636640&s=0> – 245 forum entries.

'Polacy pracują w Anglii też w białych kołnierzykach' ['*Poles work also as whitecollars in the UK*'], *Gazeta Wyborcza* [website], (29 July 2005) < http://forum.gazeta.pl/forum/72,2.html?f=23&w=27078484&a=27078484> – 93 forum entries.

References

Andrews, M. (2004), 'Counter-narratives and the Power to Oppose', in Bamberg and Andrews (eds).

Baethge, M., Adamski, W. W. and Greskovits, B. (eds) (1997), *Social Structures in the Making* (Warsaw: IFiS Publishers).

Bamberg, M. and Andrews, M. (eds) (2004), *Considering Counter-Narratives: Narrating, Resisting, Making Sense* (Amsterdam: John Benjamins).

Bauman, Z. (1992), 'The Polish Predicament: A Model in Search of Class Interests', *Telos* 25:2, 113–30.

Berger, P. and Luckmann, T. (1966), *The Social Construction of Reality: A Treatise in the Sociology of Knowledge* (Middlesex: Penguin).

Bralczyk, J. (2006), *Polak potrafi. Przysłowia, hasła i inne polskie zdania osobne* [*A Pole can do it. Proverbs, slogans and other Polish sentences*] (Warsaw: Świat Książki).

Bruner, J. (1991), 'The Narrative Construction of Reality', *Critical Inquiry* 18:2, 1–21.

Buchowski, M. (2001), *Rethinking Transformation: An Anthropological Perspective on Postsocialism* (Poznań: Wydawnictwo Humaniora).

Burawoy, M. and Verdery, K. (eds) (1999), *Uncertain Transition: Ethnographies of Change in the Postsocialist World* (Lanham: Rowman and Littlefield).

Burrell, K. (2007), 'Putting 2004 in Context: Polish Migration to Britain before and after EU Accession'. Paper presented at 'New Europeans under Scrutiny: Workshop on State-of-the-Art Research on Polish Migration to the UK', University of Wolverhampton, 2 February 2007.

Burrell, K. (2008), 'Managing, Learning and Sending: The Material Lives and Journeys of Polish Women in Britain', *Journal of Material Culture* 13:1, 63–83.

Cameron, D. and Kulick, D. (2003), *Language and Sexuality* (Cambridge: Cambridge University Press).

Carr, D. (1986), *Time, Narrative, and History* (Bloomington & Indianapolis: Indiana University Press).

Collins, J., Baynham, M. and Slembrouck, S. (eds) (2009), *Globalization and Language Contact: Spatiotemporal Scales, Migration Flows, and Communicative Practices* (London: Continuum).

Drinkwater, S., Eade, J. and Garapich, M.P. (2006), *Poles Apart? EU Enlargement and the Labour Market Outcomes of Immigrants in the UK*. Institute for the Study of Labor (IZA) (IZA Discussion Paper 2410), <http://ideas.repec.org/p/iza/izadps/dp2410.html>, accessed 15 October 2007.

Dunn, E. (1999), 'Slick Salesmen and Simple People. Negotiated Capitalism in a Privatised Polish Firm', in Burawoy and Verdery (eds).

Duvell, F. (2006), 'Polish Immigrants in the United Kingdom', in Triandafyllidou (ed.).

Eade, J., Drinkwater, S. and Garapich, M.P. (2007), *Class and Ethnicity: Polish Migrant Workers in London – Full Research Report*. ESRC End of Award Report, RES-000-22-1294 (Swindon: Economic and Social Research Council).

Eglitis, D. (2002), *Imagining the Nation: History, Modernity, and Revolution in Latvia* (Pennsylvania State University, PA: Penn State Press).

Fairclough, N. (1992), *Discourse and Social Change* (Cambridge: Polity Press).

Fairclough, N. (2003), *Analyzing Discourse: Textual Analysis for Social Research* (London: Routledge).

Galasińska, A. (2009), 'Small stories fight back: Narratives of Polish economic migration on an internet forum', in Galasińska and Krzyżanowski (eds).

Galasińska, A. and Kozłowska, O. (2006), '"Either" or "Both" – The Changing Concept of Living Space among Polish Post-communist Immigrants to the UK'. Paper presented at 'Seminar on Language, Migration and Re-theorization of the Sociolinguistic Space', University of Leeds, 15–16 June 2006.

Galasińska, A. and Kozłowska, O. (2009), '"Either" or "Both" – The Changing Concept of Living Space among Polish Post-communist Immigrants to the UK', in Collins et al. (eds).

Galasińska, A. and Krzyżanowski, M. (eds) (2009), *Discourse and Transformation in Central and Eastern Europe* (Basingstoke: Palgrave).

Galasiński, D. (2004), *Men and the Language of Emotions* (Basingstoke: Palgrave).

Garapich, M. (2007a), 'Discursive Hostility and Shame – An Exploration into the Everyday Negotiation of Ethnicity among Polish Migrants in London'. Paper presented at 'Three Years On: EU Accession and East European Migration to the UK and Ireland' Symposium, De Montfort University, Leicester, 20–21 April 2007.

Garapich, M. (2007b), 'The Builder, the Fighter and the Conman: Class, Shame and Identity among Polish migrants in London'. Paper presented at 'New Europeans under Scrutiny: Workshop on State-of-the-Art Research on Polish Migration to the UK', University of Wolverhampton, 2 February 2007.

Gee, J. (2005), *An Introduction to Discourse Analysis: Theory and Method* (London: Routledge).

Georgakopoulou, A. (2006), 'The Other Side of the Story: Towards a Narrative Analysis of Narrative-in-interaction', *Discourse Studies* 8:2, 265–87.

Georgakopoulou, A. and Goutsos, D. (2004), *Discourse Analysis: An Introduction* 2nd Edition (Edinburgh: Edinburgh University Press).

Kennedy, M. (ed.) (1994), *Envisioning Eastern Europe: Postcommunist Cultural Studies* (Ann Arbor, MI: University of Michigan Press).

Kennedy, M. (1994), 'An Introduction to East European Ideology and Identity in Transformation', in Kennedy (ed.).

Kott, S., Kula, M. and Lindenberg, T. (eds) (2006), *Socialism w Życiu Powszednim* [*Socialism in everyday life*] (Warsaw, Potsdam: Wydawnictwo TRIO & Zentrum fur Zeithistorische Forschung).

Kozłowska, O. (2009), *Looking for Normality. Lived Experience of Economic Migration of Migrants from Post-communist Poland to Britain.* Unpublished PhD Thesis (University of Wolverhampton).

Kula, M. (2006), 'Życie codzienne w komunizmie' [*Everyday life in communism*], in Kott et al. (eds).

Labov, W. (1972), *Language in the Inner City* (Philadelphia, PA: University of Pennsylvania Press).

Łaciak, B. (2005) *Obyczajowosc polska czasu transformacji* [*Polish rituals in the time of transformation*] (Warsaw: Trio).

Ledeneva, A. (1998), *Russia's Economy of Favours: Blat, Networking and Informal Exchange* (Cambridge: Cambridge University Press).

Machonin, P. (1997), 'Social Structure of Communist Societies "Après la lute"', in Baethge et al. (eds).

McHugh, K. (2000), 'Inside, Outside, Upside Down, Backward, Forward, Round and Round: A Case for Ethnographic Studies in Migration', *Progress in Human Geography* 24:1, 71–89.

MacIntyre, A. (1981), *After Virtue* (New York, NY: University of Notre Dame Press).

Mandel, R. and Humphrey, C. (eds) (2002), *Markets and Moralities* (Oxford: Berg).

Mariański, J. (1995), 'Młodzież miedzy tradycja a ponowoczesnością' [*Youth between Tradition and Postmodernity*] (Lublin: KUL).

Massey, D.S., Arango, J., Hugo, G., Kouaouci, A., Pellegrino, A. and Taylor, J.E. (1998), *Worlds in Motion: Understanding International Migration at the End of Millennium* (Oxford: Oxford University Press).

Millar, J. and Wolchik, S. (eds) (1994), *The Social Legacy of Communism* (Cambridge: Woodrow Wilson Centre Press and Cambridge University Press).

Millar, J. and Wolchik, S. (1994), 'Introduction: The Social Legacies and the Aftermath of Communism', in Millar and Wolchik (eds).

Miszalska, A. (1996), *Reakcje społeczne na przemiany ustrojowe* [*Social reaction on political system change*] (Łódź: Wydawnictwo UL).

Miszalska, A. (1998), 'Homo sovieticus w świecie kapitalizmu' ['Homo Sovieticus in the Capitalist World'], Kultura i Społeczeństwo 44:4, 69–88.

Morawska, E. (1999), 'The Malleable *Homo Sovieticus*: Transnational Entrepreneurs in Post-communist East Central Europe', *Communist and Post-Communist Studies* 32:4, 359–78.

Morawska, E. (2001), 'Structuring Migration: The Case of Polish Income-Seeking Travellers to the West', *Theory and Society* 30:1, 47–80.

Nowak, S. (1979), 'System wartości społeczeństwa polskiego' ['*The System of Values of the Polish society*'], *Studia Socjologiczne* 4, 155–73.

Osipovic, D. (2007), 'Household and Family Situation of Recent Polish Migrants in the UK: What it Reveals about the Dynamics of Settlement?'. Paper presented at 'New Europeans under Scrutiny: Workshop on State-of-the-Art Research on Polish Migration to the UK', University of Wolverhampton, 2 February 2007.

Paltridge, B. (2006), *Discourse Analysis: An Introduction* (London: Continuum).

Papestergiadis, N. (2000), *The Turbulence of Migration* (Cambridge: Polity Press).

Pollard, N., Latorre, M. and Sriskandarajah, D. (2008), *Floodgates or Turnstiles? Post-EU Enlargement Migration Flows to (and from) the UK* (London: Institute for Public Policy Research).

Rausing, S. (2002), 'Re-constructing the "Normal"', in Mandel and Humphrey (eds).

Rogers, R. (ed.) (2004), *An Introduction to Critical Discourse Analysis in Education* (Mahwah, NJ: Laurence Erlbaum).

Rogers, R. (2004), 'Setting an Agenda for Critical Discourse Analysis in Education', in Rogers (ed.).

Ryan, L., Sales, R. and Tilki, M. (2007a), 'Recent Polish migrants in London: Gender and Social Networks'. Paper presented at 'Three Years On: EU Accession and East European Migration to the UK and Ireland' Symposium, De Montfort University, Leicester, 20–21 April 2007.

Ryan, L., Sales, R., Tilki, M., and Siara, B. (2007b), 'The Experiences of Recent Polish Migrants in London: Social Networks and Social Support'. Paper presented at 'New Europeans under Scrutiny: Workshop on State-of-the-Art Research on Polish Migration to the UK', University of Wolverhampton, 2 February 2007.

Sowiński, P. (2006), 'Turystyka Zagraniczna a Czarny Rynek w Polsce (1956-1989)' ['*Travelling abroad and the black market in Poland (1956-1989)*'], in Kott et al. (eds).

Stenning, A. (2005), 'Re-Placing Work: Economic Transformations and the Shape of a Community in Post-Socialist Poland', *Work, Employment and Society* 19:2, 235–59.

Sztompka, P. (2000), *Civilisational Competence: A Prerequisite of Post-communist Transition.* <http://www.ces.uj.edu.pl/sztompka/competence.doc>, accessed 5 October 2007.

Taylor, S. (2006), 'Narrative as Construction and Discursive Resource', *Narrative Inquiry* 16:1, 94–109.

Triandafyllidou, A. (ed.) (2006), *Contemporary Polish Migration in Europe; Complex Patterns of Movement and Settlement* (Lewiston, NY: Edwin Mellen).

Triandafyllidou, A. (2006), 'Poles in Europe: Migration in the New Europe', in Triandafyllidou (ed.).

Wedel, J. (1986), *The Private Poland: An Anthropological Look at Everyday Life* (New York, NY: Facts and File).

Wedel, J. (ed.) (1992), *Unplanned Society: Poland During and After Communism* (New York, NY: Columbia University Press).

Chapter 5

In Search of Freedom, Bread and Self-fulfilment: A Short History of Polish Emigrants in Fictional Film

Ewa Mazierska

Poles can be described as a nation of emigrants, in a double sense. Not only are a significant proportion of Poles living abroad, some estimates reaching as many as ten million people, but many of the greatest Polish works of art were created by emigrants, including the 'Polish Bible', *Pan Tadeusz* (1834) by Adam Mickiewicz and the 'Polish anti-Bible' – in the sense that it uses similar language to that of Mickiewicz but instead takes the form of a parody – Witold Gombrowicz's *Trans-Atlantyk* (1951). Similarly, the most famous Polish director, Roman Polanski, is an émigré. Consequently, the topic of emigration and the perspective of emigration play a major role in Polish cultural discourses. In this chapter I am interested in one such discourse: fictional film. My principal interest here is how emigration and Polish emigrants are represented in post-war Polish cinema.

This is not an easy issue to address, not least because conceptualizations of an 'emigrant', as well as its many synonyms, are not fixed. They have changed significantly over the last few decades, the era of postmodernity, which has seen the phenomena of increased mobility, real and virtual, thanks to the development of new technologies such as the Internet and mobile phones, and, with that, more fluidity in people's identities. Let us begin, however, with quotations from the work of three eminent Polish writers all associated with modernist rather than postmodernist literature:

> *Kto pożegna swój kraj, jego krajobrazy i obyczaje, zostaje rzucony na ziemię niczyją podobną do pustyni, jak ta, którą eremici wybierali, żeby tam się modlić i rozmyślać. Wtedy jedynym sposobem przeciwko utracie orientacji jest ustanowić na nowo swoje własne północ, wschód, zachód i południe, i w tej nowej przestrzeni umieścić swój Witebsk czy Dublin podniesione, by tak rzec do drugiej potęgi. Co zostało utracone, zostaje odzyskane na wyższym poziomie jako obecne i żywe.*
>
> [The person who leaves his country, its landscapes and traditions, is thrown into a desert-like land where the Eremites chose to pray and meditate. In such a situation the only way not to lose a sense of direction is to re-establish one's

own north, east, west and south, and in this new place situate one's own Witebsk or Dublin, raised to the second power, so to speak. Thus what was lost becomes regained on a higher level, to be present and alive.] (Miłosz 1992)

A po co tobie Polakiem być?! ... Takiż to rozkoszny był dotąd los Polaków? Nie obrzydłaż tobie polskość twoja? Nie dość odwiecznego Umęczenia, Udręczenia? ... Nie chcesz czym Innym, czym Nowym stać się? Chceszże any wszyscy Chłopcy wasi tylko za Ojcami wszystko w kółko powtarzali? Oj, wypuścić Chłopaków z ojcowskiej klatki, a niech po bezdrożach polatają, niechże i do Nieznanego zajrzą!'

[Why do you want to be a Pole? ... Has Polish fate been so blissful? Are you not fed up with your Polishness? Don't you have enough of this eternal suffering? ... Don't you want to be something Else, something New? Do you want all your Boys to repeat over and over again what their Fathers told them? Let the Boys of their Father's cages go, so that they can ramble through the wilderness and peep into the Unknown.] (Gombrowicz 1953)

Typowym środowiskiem Polaków za granicą jest to, które do przesady kocha Polskę i w tym duchu stara się wychować swoje dzieci. Ale tylko na zewnątrz. Wewnątrz każdy ma swoje myśli, których nie ujawnia czy też nie potrafi ich przed nikim ujawnić.

[Poles abroad typically surround themselves with Poles who love Poland in an exaggerated way and want to bring up their children in this spirit. But this is a superficial impression. Inside everybody has their own opinions [about Poland] which they do not or cannot reveal.] (Mrożek 2006)

It is not difficult to see from these quotations that Polish emigrants, not unlike emigrants of different nationalities (see, for example, Naficy 1999), define themselves in relation to their motherland. Either they attempt somehow to reconstruct Poland abroad, through real or symbolic means – preserving one's language, education, religion – or they try to break their link with the past and acquire a new identity. Whatever strategy they choose, it is suggested that they will suffer trauma, either in the form of the pain of being uprooted or due to their desperate effort to grow new roots.

However, it has been suggested that contemporary Polish emigrants suffer less than migrants used to, or at least that their problems and dilemmas are of a different kind. As if confirming this new understanding and effort to divorce trauma from the concept of emigrant, Stanisław Barańczak, a renowned Polish poet and translator who spent a large proportion of his life in the US, has asked not to be referred to as an emigrant, thus emphasizing his lack of identification with the 'martyrological ethos' of former Polish exiles, which drew heavily on

Polish romantic tradition (see Barańczak 1992).[1] A similarly postmodern attitude is expressed in the novels and public pronouncements of Manuela Gretkowska, one of the most popular writers of the post-communist period, who in books such as *My zdies emigranty* (1991) and *Tarot paryski* (1993) describes the experiences of young Poles living abroad, for whom the problem of roots is either marginal or plainly irrelevant.

The problem of the new emigrants or exiles is further complicated by the fact that emigration has become a metaphor of the postmodern condition. Zygmunt Bauman, one of the leading authors searching for signs of new identities for Westerners and himself a Polish emigrant, almost equates 'contemporary wo/man' or 'postmodern wo/man' with a person who betrays the habits, tastes and views typical of an emigrant (see Bauman 1996). Such an outlook leads to a blurring of the divisions between emigrants and non-emigrants, as well as further stripping the emigrants of the trauma which was previously ascribed to them. As Eva Hoffman observes, 'Exile used to be thought of as a difficult condition. It involves dislocation, disorientation, self-division. But today, at least within the framework of postmodern theory, we have come to value exactly those qualities of experience that exile demands – uncertainty, displacement, the fragmented identity. Within this conceptual framework, exile becomes, well, sexy, glamorous, interesting. Nomadism and diasporism have become fashionable terms in intellectual discourse' (Hoffman 1999: 44).

Whilst accepting that this universalization and glamourizing of the emigrant condition takes place in some intellectual debates about the contemporary world, I will attempt to establish whether it has affected the screen portrait of the Polish emigrant. In my discussion, which will be organized chronologically, I will privilege Polish films, not least because Polish emigrants are rarely featured in the films produced in other countries. However, I will also refer to some films made by Polish émigré directors, Roman Polanski and Jerzy Skolimowski, and when discussing films made after 2004, I will also take into account Ken Loach's *It's a Free World* (2007) which tells stories of a wider spectrum of migrants, searching for peace and employment in the UK (or something like that).

The Communist Period

As one might guess, in Poland emigration was a taboo subject during the communist period. This resulted from the gap between official ideology, which proclaimed the superiority of the socialist East over the capitalist West, and the reality of the majority of citizens wanting to move to the West or transform Poland into a Western-type democracy. To support the notion that socialism was best, the

---

1 The romantic model is associated with Hotel Lambert of the so called 'Great Emigration' of the nineteenth century and Kultura Institute in Maisons-Laffitte in France, founded in 1946 by Jerzy Giedroyc.

State introduced a policy of limited access to documents allowing travel. Passports were kept in special 'passport offices' and were only made available to citizens in certain cases and on certain conditions, for example to go on a trip organized by an official travel office, or to perform an important function by taking part in a sporting competition. Not everybody had the same right to a passport: people whose relatives had fled to the West were often banned from travelling abroad. Of course, it was easier to travel from Poland to other socialist countries than to the West, due to the assumption that hardly anybody would leave Poland (regarded by many Poles as superior over other countries in the Eastern bloc) in order to live in Bulgaria or East Germany. It should be added, though, that emigration policy was not uniform after 1945. Travel abroad was most restricted during the first decades after the victory of socialism. In the 1970s, for example, when I was a teenager, and in the 1980s, when I was a student, it was quite easy to travel to the West and a large proportion of my college colleagues ended up living abroad, principally in Germany and the US.

Because of the censorship surrounding emigration, up to the late 1970s not many films tackled this issue. When they confront it at all, it is done in a rather oblique fashion; we do not see the life of an emigrant and rarely do we learn whether they were a political exile or an economic migrant. We usually only meet such a person when they pay a short visit to Poland, therefore the image of their life and persona is built up from their descriptions, dialogues and behaviour when amongst 'native' Poles. Sometimes they are not shown at all, but only talked about. Moreover, emigration is rarely placed at the centre of the film discourse, which adds to the difficulty of drawing clear conclusions about the lives of Polish emigrants. The lack of a deeper insight into the lives of emigrants can be attributed to economic and political factors. In order to show emigrants as emigrants, so to speak, the filmmakers would have to shoot abroad, for which there was not enough resources in communist Poland. Moreover, such a representation would run the risk of demonstrating that Poland was not the paradise that socialist ideologues claimed it to be.

Nevertheless, from a number of films with this motif it is possible to identify recurrent features of a Polish emigrant. One is detachment from country and family, if not a plain betrayal. We find such an image of an emigrant, for example, in *Szyfry* [*Ciphers*] (1966) by Wojciech Has, where Tadeusz (Jan Kreczmar), a man who has lived abroad for over twenty years, returns home and finds everything there unfamiliar, even bizarre. The whole Polish reality is such an enigma for him that it needs to be deciphered. Although the film's author (whom I regard as the most politically and artistically independent Polish filmmaker of the post-war period) does not accuse his protagonist of betraying his country and family, one can derive such an impression from the narrative. In particular, Has focuses on the damage Tadeusz's emigration inflicts on his son Maciek (Zbigniew Cybulski) who, because of his father's absence, is unable to recover from the nightmares of war.

In *Życie rodzinne* [*Family Life*] (1970), the emigrant is only talked about. This time it is the mother of Wit (Daniel Olbrychski), the main protagonist, who left her husband and children to lead an easy life in the West. Again, although the author does not say so explicitly, he suggests that the mother's departure destroyed Wit's family and that this woman was very selfish, if not an outright whore. After her escape the father became an alcoholic, the daughter went mad and even went to jail for some time, and the son left home, to live a 'normal' life in an industrial town. A not dissimilar image of emigration is offered in other films by Zanussi, principally *Kontrakt* [*Contract*] (1980), where among the guests at a wedding we find an utterly snobbish French ballet diva (Leslie Caron), who was married to the brother of the groom's father. Although her Polish husband is not present at the wedding because by the time of the wedding he is dead, her appearance and behaviour reflects badly on the Polish emigrant, connoting superficiality and excess. This impression is reinforced by the behaviour of another couple at the wedding, a Swedish middle-aged man (Peter Bonke) and his Polish girlfriend (Beata Tyszkiewicz). Her character can be described as an emigrant in waiting – she would do anything to escape to the luxuries of the West, as, we can guess, did Wit's mother in *Family Life*.

The motif of escaping Poland through marriage is also present in the films of Stanisław Bareja, principally *Żona dla Australijczyka* [*Wife for an Australian*] (1963). The story concerns an Australian of Polish origin, Robert (Wiesław Gołas), who visits Poland to find a wife. He finds a pretty girl named Hanka (Elżbieta Czyżewska), working as a singer and dancer in a 'Mazowsze' folk group. The man makes some blunders with the girl and even imprisons her. However, in the end the couple meet on the ship 'Batory' on which Robert returns to Australia. Although it is not spelt out clearly, we might guess that Hanka will use this foreign trip to leave Poland for good and to settle in a more prosperous country. A somewhat similar scenario is offered in another comedy from the 1960s, *Jadą goście jadą* [*The Guests Are Coming*] (1962), directed by Gerard Zalewski, Jan Rutkiewicz, and Romuald Drobaczyński. This time three ex-patriots from the United States pay a short visit to Poland. One comes to see his grandfather before he dies, another to collect soil from some famous battlefields in order to sell it at a profit to other Polish Americans, and the third comes to find a wife.

The motif of Polish emigrants looking for a wife in Poland or of Polish women going abroad to find a husband recurs in the films of the following decades. In my opinion, its persistence testifies to two issues. The first is the relatively low assimilation and low material status of Polish emigrants. They cannot afford a 'proper' American or Australian wife, because even after living in the host countries for thirty or more years, they feel foreign and worry that they can be rejected by the natives. It is worth noting that the emigrants from *Wife for an Australian* and *The Guests Are Coming* come across as simple men as a result of being descendants of earlier Polish economic migrants who were usually poor and uneducated. The search for a Polish wife might be read as a substitute for seeking one's true country and, again, an indicator of their distance from the cultures and countries where they live. The second issue is the high price Polish women have to pay in order to move to the West. This price is their personal freedom; marriage for Polish female migrants is arguably a mild or polite form of prostitution. The authors of the aforementioned films also allude to the fact that in the countries where Polish emigrants live, money is the highest value: everything can be bought for money and sold with profit, including one's own country, as conveyed by the motif of collecting Polish soil in order to sell it.

These various motifs coalesce in *Bilet powrotny* [*Returned Ticket*] (1978), directed by Ewa and Czesław Petelscy. Among the films about emigration made during the communist period Petelscy's movie is exceptional in showing emigrants *as emigrants*, portraying their everyday lives outside Poland, as opposed to only showing them visiting their country of birth. The film is also unusual in being based on an authentic story of a Polish peasant widow who emigrated to Canada to work on her uncle's farm in order to earn enough money to buy a house in town for herself and her son. In Canada, Antonina (Anna Seniuk) first helps her uncle (Henryk Bąk) and then marries a neighbouring farmer (Leszek Herdegen) who is French. However, the marriage ends in disaster when Antonina's husband tries to strangle her and commits suicide upon learning that the woman wants to leave him, taking with her their money. Not only does Antonina end up partly paralysed as a result of this attack but her Polish dream is not fulfilled because her irresponsible son has wasted the dollars she sent him.

Antonina's story can be regarded as paradigmatic for the 'modernist reading' of the figure of a Polish emigrant, as idealized by Miłosz and ridiculed by Gombrowicz. The heroine is presented as somebody who, whilst living in Canada, identifies herself entirely with Poland. On emigration she continues Polish traditions and plans to return to Poland when her 'economic objectives' are fulfilled. It must be added that in her indulgence in Polishness she is not alone. *Returned Ticket* was set and shot in the state of Ontario, in Barry's Bay, the region of the oldest Polish or, more precisely, Kaszubian emigration (see Suder 2003), as marked by Polish shops, restaurants, signposts, even Polish names of villages. At the same time, when Antonina eventually returns to Poland, not unlike the character in Has' *Ciphers*, she finds her country foreign and deeply disappointing.

Although Petelscy's film is based on the premise that capitalist Canada is a richer country than socialist Poland, it plays down their economic contrast by focusing on the similarities between the Polish and Canadian countryside. The fields and cows Antonina tends in Poland and Canada are quite similar. Moreover, the protagonist's lack of interest in consumer goods allows the directors to shift our attention away from those aspects of life in Canada which ordinary Poles at the time found extremely appealing, such as colourful shops. At the same time, their film offers a very critical image of the West and, consequently, can be read as pro-Polish and pro-socialist propaganda. This is because in Canada money rules, to the detriment of human morality and happiness. Antonina's emigration destroys her health, her moral values, her spirit and her bond with Poland, ultimately ruining her. It also does not do her son any good; on the contrary, it precipitates his downfall. Hence, if there is a lesson to be learnt from *Returned Ticket*, it is that it is better to stay in Poland, even at the price of leading a modest life than to seek uncertain fortune abroad.

Roman Polanski's *The Tenant* (1976) is set in Paris and features as the main character a man called Trelkovsky. The nationality of Trelkovsky is in fact never spelt out, but his name, which sounds Polish, and the fact that he is played by Polanski himself allows us to regard him as a Polish emigrant. If we are not sure of his status, it is because he behaves as if he has left his Polish past behind and in his actions he is guided by a desire to be regarded as a proper Frenchman, not just a 'French citizen'. He tries to integrate with his surroundings: goes to a café for his breakfast, visits his work mates at home, takes the depressed friend of a woman who previously lived in his rented flat to a bar and does a lot of walking. However, his efforts to be a proper Frenchman, or a cosmopolitan flâneur, are thwarted because wherever he goes, he experiences hostility and aggression. For example, a stranger in a bar buys everybody a drink except him and his companion. The reason is their sadness, differentiating them from the merry crowd in the pub. He is also ostracized and harassed in the tenement block where he lives. Trelkovsky's landlord, Monsieur Zy, and his neighbours impose on him such a strict code of conduct that he is forced to live a solitary existence. Trelkovsky is asked not to invite any guests and to detach himself from the only person in the apartment block who has shown him sympathy and solidarity and who, like him, is not French. The bigotry of the wider population of Paris is conveyed by the recurrent motif of enquiries about the origin of Trelkovsky's name. Although nobody tells him directly that being foreign reduces him to the position of a second-class citizen, on each occasion he feels compelled to defend his right to live in France. Paris itself, although shot in colour, is grey or nocturnal, therefore unwelcoming and mysterious. Moreover, it is 'under construction', an example being the refurbishment of the metro station. Trelkovsky often walks along the walls that render passers-by entrapped and ghettoized. Even the Seine, usually represented in films as a friendly place, here is a site of alienation. Trelkovsky walks on its banks with nobody in sight, as if confronted by his own complete solitude and nothingness (see Mazierska 2007: 74).

The solitude, aggression and alienation Polanski's character suffers on a daily basis leads him to schizophrenia. He appropriates the personality of Simone Choule, a woman who lived in his apartment there before him and committed suicide. The more sick Trelkovsky gets, the more violent he becomes. He attacks a child playing in the park and tries to strangle a woman who accidentally injures him when he threw himself under her car. His violence is represented as an act of self-defence; he attacks people because he is convinced that they are attacking him or would do so if he does not assault them first. Like Simone Choule, Trelkovsky also commits suicide – to the real or imagined enjoyment of the French people living in his block.

At the moment of his death, Trelkovsky is deprived of everything of value: his Polish past, his French hopes, even his personal identity. It could be suggested that even the most sophisticated creators of socialist propaganda would not invent such a bleak scenario for a Polish emigrant. *The Tenant* can also be regarded as a film ultimately about an emigrant as a figure of modernity: neither here, nor there, he ends as nobody.

The First Solidarity and Martial Law Films

In the 1980s, following first the victory of Solidarity and then the introduction of martial law, emigration became a nationwide and highly politicized issue. In this period over one million Poles left their country, many times more than in the whole period between the end of the Second World War and 1980. The largest group of emigrants was constituted by those who left Poland before martial law was announced in December 1981 and decided not to return, taking advantage of the chance to settle in Western countries. The second important group was made up of Solidarity activists who left during military rule, encouraged by the government which wanted to get rid of a substantial part of the political opposition (see Stola 2002). Obviously, during this period it was next to impossible to present mass migration on screen, as it would be tantamount to admitting that the political and economic situation in Poland had deteriorated significantly. However, films tackling the 'Solidarity' emigration burst onto the film scene shortly after communism collapsed. Most notably, two main films on this subject, *Ostatni prom* [*The Last Ferry*] by Waldemar Krzystek and *300 mil do nieba* [*300 Miles to Heaven*] by Maciej Dejczer, were both shot and had their premieres in 1989, the year of Polish transformation from communism to post-communism. In these and some other films depicting this period, emigrants and would-be emigrants are practically forced to leave Poland because by staying there they risk political persecution, fear and poverty. Moreover, emigration is shown as something virtually everybody wants to do, and the more it becomes a forbidden fruit, the more tempting it becomes.

This idea is openly expressed in *The Last Ferry* by the captain of a Polish ship who in theory is taking passengers for a holiday cruise to various ports on the Baltic coast, but whose ship is in practice used as a vessel of escape from Poland. He says to an official from the Secret Service that if his passengers continue to ask for asylum in Sweden or Germany, by the time of his retirement there will be nobody left in Poland. Indeed, almost everyone on the ferry, upon learning that it will not go to Hamburg after all but return to the Polish port of Świnoujście (which follows the announcement of martial law), jump into the freezing waters of the Baltic, risking their lives, in order to be taken by German fishing boats to Western ports. Those who not do so are a couple who are expecting a child, frightened that it might lead to a miscarriage, and a secondary school teacher and Solidarity activist Marek (Krzysztof Kolberger) on a mission to smuggle abroad some important Solidarity documents. He decides to return to Poland because he wants to carry on as a mentor of his young students. I argue that by including this character, who gives up an apparently better life abroad, Krzystek, perhaps unwittingly, subscribes to the opinion, communicated in the previous films, that leaving one's country equals betrayal. In order to make Poland a better place, one from which it is unnecessary to escape, one has to stay and act, if not using legal means, then illegally. Interestingly, in Dejczer's films those most critical about emigration are the young: Marek's pupils. They regard emigrants as rats who are escaping a sinking ship. In line with this attitude, they greet Marek upon his arrival back in Poland as a hero.

A somewhat different attitude to the morality of emigration is offered in *300 Miles to Heaven*. Dejczer, who based his film on a true story, casts as the main characters two boys, Jędrek and Grześ, who run away from home and go to Denmark hidden under a lorry. Their escape is represented as a heroic and patriotic act. They leave home to help their parents who have problems with the authorities due to being openly anti-communist (the father was expelled from school for teaching an unofficial version of Polish history) and, consequently, are poor. Equally, their parents, despite great sadness about their separation, in a telephone conversation which follows the court decision depriving them of their parenting rights, ask them never to return home. Obviously, this request underscores the oppressive nature of life in late communist Poland.

The films of Krzystek and Dejczer, as well as some others referring to this period and depicting attempts to emigrate from Poland such as *Kobieta samotna* [*A Women on Her Own*] (1981), directed by Agnieszka Holland and *Stan wewnętrzny* [*Inner State*] (1983), directed by Krzysztof Tchórzewski, convey a sense of finality and tragedy, typical for a modernist approach to emigration. The very titles of some of the films, such as *The Last Ferry* and *300 Miles to Heaven*, signal this finality. Emigration equals the ultimate loss of one's country and family. Another feature is emphasizing the gulf, both geographical and political/economic, between Poland and the host country. Poland is represented as oppressive and grim, the West as colourful and free. In *300 Miles to Heaven* the difference is encapsulated by the colourful clothes the boys receive in the refugee camp upon their arrival in Denmark, and the difference in manners between Polish and Danish policemen and other officials. Polish ones are callous and they treat children as criminals; the Danish, by contrast, are gentle and friendly. Moreover, although Jędrek and Grześ do not work and their only money is what they receive from officials running the asylum camp, they save enough to send to their parents. Similarly, in *The Last Ferry* the crew of the German fishing boat that rescues Poles who jump from the ferry are presented as very friendly and mild-mannered. One gets the impression that beyond the Iron Curtain there is a paradise where angels wait for the Poles to arrive. Yet, this image is sustained largely by the fact that the films finish before this assumption is tested

A somewhat different image of the emigrants and the host country is offered by the émigré director, Jerzy Skolimowski. His *Moonlighting* (1982), set in London during December 1981, the month when martial law was announced in Poland, presents a group of Polish workers who came to London to work illegally, renovating the house of some rich Polish man. They live in appalling conditions, work very hard to save for their families, as well as being alienated and isolated due to not knowing the language, having no work permits and not being able to communicate with their families back in Poland due to the military restrictions. They are more like prisoners, locked in the house in which they work and devoid of any agency, being subjugated and exploited by their Polish leader, Nowak (Jeremy Irons), who is himself exploited by his Polish boss. Another factor in their sense of alienation is the attitude of British people to them. Although London in *Moonlighting* is full of posters proclaiming the solidarity of English people with Poles suffering as a result of the military coup, the real British people in contact with real Poles come across as hostile, hypocritical and bigoted. Their only advantage is their ability to return home, when their job is finished. Thus, in *Moonlighting*, Skolimowski initiates a series of films in which emigration is presented not as final, but as a temporary affair: a means to finance a particular project. Such experience, although unpleasant in the extreme, does not have the drama of leaving one's country for good. Another reason why it lacks drama is that it is private, as opposed to political – they are not political dissidents, and their stay in London does not put their families in jeopardy. Moreover, Skolimowski's Poles, unlike those depicted in *The Last Ferry* and *300 Miles to Heaven*, do not identify with their homeland, only with their families.

Skolimowski continues his exploration of the lives of Polish emigrants in London in *Success Is the Best Revenge* (1984), which is the story of a Polish émigré theatre director, Alex Rodak (Michael York, who bears a strong resemblance to Skolimowski himself), trying to stage a play about martial law in London. For his project, Rodak needs a large number of Polish extras and, inevitably, approaches Poles living in London and working there illegally. These people are represented as a materially and culturally impoverished herd, easily excited and manipulated. Rodak gets in contact with them, plays football with them, appeals to their patriotism, but is not really interested in their plight, nor shares with them any values.[2] The only member of this crowd, whom the director endows with an individual identity, Mr. Gienio, is reduced to an animal-like existence. He is practically homeless, camping in the back of a restaurant, deprived of basic amenities and privacy, and plagued by alcoholism. Mr. Gienio claims that he misses his wife and mentions the luxurious presents he recently sent her, but it appears that his wife gave up on him. Hence, it is suggested that this Polish 'herd' leads a ghettoized existence in a multiple sense, being alienated from the British majority which does not understand them and finds them repulsive, their Polish

---

2   For the western viewer Rodak's and, by extension, Skolimowski's disinterest in, even contempt for the working class, as conveyed in *Success* (in the film reciprocated by the workers) might be difficult to reconcile with his unequivocal support of Solidarity which was, predominantly, a workers' movement. This paradox can be explained by the anti-communist character of Solidarity opposition which made it possible for a large section of the Polish intelligentsia to support it, without subscribing to its pro-workers character.

motherland and the educated Poles living in London such as Rodak, who prefer more cosmopolitan company.

In comparison with the illegal Polish migrants, Rodak leads a rather affluent life, living in a spacious and tasteful house and having his sons educated in a public school. However, he is also not free from material problems, related to his work and private life. In order to get funds for his theatrical project he has to enter into a deal with a fellow emigrant, Dino Montecurva, who specializes in pornography and laundering dirty money. On the other hand, Rodak's rather luxurious lifestyle is based on credit, as we learn from a conversation he has with a female bank manager, who criticizes the way he spends the money he previously borrowed, and refuses him a new loan. It can be argued that the official represents an entirely unideological stance in relation to emigration: neither prejudiced towards emigrants, nor in favour of them. For her, people like Rodak are welcome if they add to the wealth and prosperity of Britain; if they fail to do so, they should leave.

The Post-communist Period

Emigration was never as common a phenomenon among Poles as it became after the fall of communism, and especially after Poland joined the European Union in 2004. After abortion and the issues surrounding collaboration with the communist secret services (so called *lustracja*), it has been the most discussed issue in the last five years or so. At the same time, the huge influx of Poles into Britain, resulting from Britain's open borders to the new member states of the EU, has created, among the British media, enormous interest in the newcomers. These movements can be seen in the larger context of the so called 'new migration' in Europe, characterized by greater scale and new directions (countries such as Italy and Spain which were previously were 'donor' countries, now hosting large numbers of migrants), as well the fact that more of these new migrants are women than ever before (see Koser and Lutz 1998).

However, films dealing with emigration have not been as numerous after 1989 as one might expect. More films were actually made about re-emigration (examples are *Kapitał czyli jak zrobić pieniądze w Polsce* [*Capital, or How to Make Money in Poland*] (1989), directed by Feliks Falk, *Dzieci i ryby* [*Children and Fish*] (1997), directed by Jacek Bromski, *Pułapka* [*Trap*] (1997), directed by Adek Drabiński, and *Moje pieczone kurczaki* [*My Roasted Chicken*] (2002), directed by Iwona Siekierzyńska) and about foreigners from the East trying to settle in Poland (such as *Farba* [*Paint*] (1998), directed by Michał Rosa and *Billboard* (1998) by Łukasz Zadrzyński), than about Poles leaving their country. This focus on emigrants in Poland rather than emigrants from Poland, reflects some important phenomena of the 1990s: the mass return of Poles, especially emigrants of the 1980s, to their country, following the fall of communism and the entry of large numbers of citizens from the ex-Soviet Bloc, to Poland. At the same time, it testifies to the previously mentioned difficulty of making films about emigrants from 'outside', so to speak, namely by Polish directors living in Poland.

Polish films about 'emigration proper' include *Papierowe małżeństwo* [*Paper Marriage*] (1992), directed by Krzysztof Lang, *Przeklęta Ameryka* [*Damned America*] (1993), directed by Krzysztof Tchórzewski, *Obcy musi fruwać* [*Stranger Must Fly*] (1993), directed by Wiesław Saniewski, *Trzy kolory: Biały* [*Three Colours: White*] (1994), directed by Krzysztof Kieślowski, *Szczęśliwego Nowego Jorku* [*Happy New York*] (1997), director by Janusz Zaorski, and *Oda do radości* [*Ode to Joy*] (2005), directed by Anna Kazejak-Dawid, Jan Komasa and Maciej Migas. Although this group is rather small, it is worth dividing it further into films made before and after Poland joined the European Union, with *Ode to Joy* being a distinctly post-EU film. I will discuss this film together with Ken Loach's *It's a Free World* which covers the same period.

In comparison with Polish films from the period of Solidarity, movies tackling emigration post-1989 strike one as more critical of the host countries. It could be argued that their main purpose is to destroy the myth of the West as a promised land. This destruction begins when the potential emigrant attempts to reach a foreign country and this proves difficult. It feels like, for the first time after the war, Polish filmmakers realized that to relocate to the West one needed not only a passport but also a visa, and that these were rationed goods. Efforts to acquire a visa or arrange a way to stay abroad when the visa has expired are an important motif of many films. Consequently, illegal deals and crimes such as smuggling forbidden goods, 'paper marriages' and sexual services are rampant. Furthermore, once the protagonists reach the country of their destination they must fight for some measly scraps of Western prosperity, taking jobs the 'natives' do not want such as working in abattoirs, on building sites (often dealing with asbestos) or, if they are women, as sex workers or cleaners. Their degradation and misery is rendered even more visible by our knowledge that some of them, such as Alicja in *Paper Marriage* and Professor in *Happy New York*, are well educated and in Poland they would not accept the jobs they have to content themselves with abroad. In *Happy New York* the characters' miserable positions are accentuated by their penchant for gambling, either on a small scale by regularly buying lottery tickets, or on a large scale, risking everything they have for some uncertain profits. *Mise-en-scène* underscores the characters' problems with assimilation into the host culture while at the same time pointing to their distance from the motherland.[3] In *Happy New York* all the main characters live in a cramped flat in an unpleasant, dilapidated building which looks like a disused factory. The centre of their spiritual life is the Catholic Church; they observe Polish festivals and remain faithful to Polish food rich in protein and strong alcohol. At the same time the director points to their pathetic efforts to fit into the new culture by drawing attention to their corrupted Polish and shiny, kitschy clothes. Nevertheless, these efforts are a new phenomenon

---

3   *Mise-en-scène* refers to the organisation of the frame in the film.

suggesting that, post-1989, the emigrants' attempts at assimilation into their new culture overshadowed their attempts to preserve the old one.

Poles abroad are also often the victims of cheating, either by the natives or by their fellow Poles. For example, Alicja does not receive her full pay for cleaning the office on the pretext that she did her work faster than required. Potejto in *Happy New York* is offered the chance to earn extra money for helping to deliver some furniture and then is drugged, raped and thrown out of the car naked in front of the Polish church, which for this religious man represents utter humiliation. The protagonist of *Three Colours: White* is divorced by his French wife, humiliated by her and deprived of everything he acquired when living in France and what he brought from Poland, including his Polish car.

Not only are the new emigrants rather unsuccessful abroad, but one gets the impression that if they did return to Poland, most of them would also belong, if not to the very margins of society, then at least to the less successful section of the population. This assumption is confirmed by the films about emigrants returning home. They come back because they fail to achieve the success they hoped for; they are neither rich, nor famous and often their personal lives are a shambles. Consequently, they hope that back home they will be more successful, not least because Poland had changed for the better, becoming democratic and capitalist. Yet, paradoxically, this proves to be a major problem for re-emigrants. Poland changed so much while they were away that they hardly recognize it and cannot find a place for themselves. They suffer unemployment or have to take poorer jobs than those they had before, and they cannot communicate with their families and friends who 'moved on' while they remained psychologically in the old Poland. Thus, after returning they also become emigrants of sorts. Moreover, it is more difficult for them to put up with their low social position and sense of alienation in Poland than it was in a foreign country. Needless to add, the emigration after 1989 is no longer political. Broadly speaking it is economic, but not always in the sense of simply improving one's position in comparison with what it was before. Some new emigrants have much higher aspirations than their cinematic predecessors: they want to be rich or famous, have their own businesses, employ others, be creative. Thus their disappointment is greater when they cannot achieve what they aspire to.

As with the 'martial law' films, the post-communist films about emigrants encourage the question: 'Who or what is responsible for these people's exit from Poland and their subsequent misery?' The answer appears to be Poland: the Polish economy or politics. In *Happy New York* this idea is most clearly conveyed by the only intellectual in the group of the emigrants, an ex-academic appropriately called Professor. At one point he says, 'The greatest swindle of communism was the hope of the West – the belief that elsewhere is a better life than in Poland'. In other words, it is not poverty as such that makes Poles leave their homeland, rather a lifestyle below their expectations, combined with the hope that elsewhere they will be more successful. Of course, Professor argues that life in the West and especially in the US is in fact worse than in Poland. Moreover, in the US one is an object of utter exploitation; when somebody's usefulness expires, they are disposed of as a piece of rubbish. It should be added that Professor has serious reasons to begrudge the US as during Solidarity times he was greeted there as a leading dissident and even awarded an honorary professorship at an American university. However, America's good disposition towards him expired when Poland regained democracy. Unable to find employment appropriate to his education, Professor resigns himself to manual work and later, suffering depression and alcoholism, turns to living on the help of his countrymen. One can assume that even if he were not treated as a celebrity by Americans, he would suffer the greatest discomfort due to being reduced to working class status, as in his case the gap between his education and aspirations and his day-to-day existence would be the greatest. The words of Professor are confirmed by the film's narrative. Although *Happy New York* has a happy ending, with the main character becoming rich and his money buying happiness for all his Polish flat mates, its visual style, which is unrealistic, suggests otherwise – there is no happy ending for Polish emigrants. I would argue that *Happy New York* and, albeit to a lesser extent, other films in this group not only represent the lives of Polish emigrants, but project on the West widespread disappointment with the new Poland, which in the words of the Solidarity leaders, principally Lech Wałęsa, was meant to be like a second America or Japan.

While in films like *Happy New York*, *Paper Marriage* or even in films about re-emigration we still experience the finality of one's relocation, *Ode to Joy* accentuates, in a postmodern fashion, the *impermanent* character of one's move to the West. This idea is conveyed by individual stories, especially the first one, whose protagonist, Aga, returns from London to her hometown with substantial savings, thinking that it will be for good, but in the end, when all her money has been wasted, goes there again. It is also reflected in the structure of the film, in which the ending of one episode, where the character goes to England, is followed by the beginning of the next, where another character, who is still in Poland, contemplates the possibility of emigrating. Thus, emigration comes across as a seesaw movement: one goes, one returns, one goes again (see Jaźwińska and Okólski 2001). This film also covers new ground in comparison with earlier films on this subject by showing different types of emigrants and reasons for leaving their country. A search for bread for one's family and oneself and political reasons still play a part in the decisions of the new emigrants, especially in the first episode entitled 'Śląsk' [Silesia]. However, in the two remaining segments, 'Warszawa' [Warsaw] and 'Morze' [The Sea], the main reason to leave is the need for self-fulfilment and a fresh start or even finding an identity, as each departure is precipitated by some kind of personal crisis such as the break-up of a relationship. As Grzegorz Nadgrodkiewicz observes, emigration is thus inscribed in the process of growing up (see Nagrodkiewicz 2007: 166). Going to London and finding some employment there is for these young people a rite of passage. It is worth adding that for them, London functions as myth (see Grochowska 2006), not unlike 'America's' mythological status for their parents and grandparents generations. However, the stuff of this new myth is quite different; London does not promise the characters material wealth, but rather 'wealth of experience': life in the centre of things, which is faster and unpredictable, unlike the monotonous existence in a small seaside resort or in the remnants of communist industrial Poland.

The characters in *Ode to Joy* come from different social strata. On the one hand we have a rather poor Aga (Małgorzata Buczkowska) and rapper Peras (Piotr Głowacki); on the other there is Marta (Roma Gąsiorowska), the rich daughter of a businessman. She travels to London not to work, but to learn English on a course paid for by her father. Hence, it is suggested that class rather than nationality or ethnicity is the most important characteristic to consider in the new migration, although the poor in Poland or, for that matter, in most of the republics of the former Yugoslavia or Romania, are still poorer than their Western counterparts (see Stone 2007).

The authors of *Ode to Joy* tacitly engage in a vision of Polishness in which emigration is viewed as a rejection of the 'Law of the Father', as described by Gombrowicz in his *Trans-Atlantyk*. Aga in 'Silesia' and Wiktor in 'The Sea' leave for London because they reject the values and lifestyle of their fathers who come across as poorly adapted to the new capitalist Poland. This opinion is openly expressed by Aga, who tells her father who is a Solidarity activist fighting against the closure of a coalmine, that she leaves Poland following her survival instinct – staying with him will equal self-destruction.

Although Kazejak-Dawid, Migas and Komasa subscribe to Gombrowicz's view that the young should choose their own ways and privilege the welfare of the individual over that of the nation, their approach was not unanimously shared by the film's reviewers. Some criticized the characters for being selfish and lacking any convictions (see Grochowska 2006; Kłuskiewicz 2006). This criticism can be put in a wider discourse about the character and values of the younger generation of Polish people, those who do not remember or were not even born during the triumphs of Solidarity and martial law. This generation is often described as 'Generation Nothing' (Generacja NIC); the derogatory label connoting such features as lack of ideals and ideas for life, conformism and lack of critical awareness.

Ode to Joy is unique in the way it depicts people who decided to emigrate, but the option of emigration as a way to tackle one's problems is considered by characters of other recent films as well. It is worth mentioning here *Podróż* [*Journey*] (2006) by Dariusz Glazer, whose female protagonist decides to escape from her husband, children and her unfulfilling and poorly paid job and go to London, where her old boyfriend lives. However, she backs off at the last moment, leaves the bus and returns home on foot, through the snow. Of course, this dramatic return underscores the significance of the woman's decision to emigrate, had she done so. For this reason, however, the film does not ring true as it contrasts with widespread knowledge that in real life leaving to work in London nowadays is devoid of the old, 'modernist' finality.

While in Polish films on emigration Poles are inevitably at the centre of the discourse, Ken Loach's *It's a Free World* focuses on emigration as seen through the eyes of the inhabitants of the host country: Britain. Loach's main characters, the two young women Angie (Kierston Wareing) and Rose (Juliet Ellis), owners of an employment agency, are acutely interested in the emigrants – they make their living by finding casual employment for them. They look for jobs not only for Poles, but also for other nationalities such as Iranians. Of this group Poles are in a relatively privileged position because, thanks to Poland being part of the European Union, they can work legally. Others have to arrange false documents and put up with despicable wages and working conditions. Nevertheless, all foreigners in Loach's films end up being exploited: by the agents, ruthless employers who take every opportunity not to pay them, the Mafia and the capitalist system as a whole. Moreover, Loach shows that exploitation breeds ruthlessness and the need for revenge on both sides. An example of this can be seen in the behaviour of the Poles who beat up Angie and later kidnap her son to force her to pay them a large sum of outstanding wages.

Unlike Skolimowski, who in *Moonlighting* and *Success* portrayed Polish workers in London as a faceless mass who due to difficult living conditions practically lost their humanity, Loach attempts to humanize and individualize the migrants. Even the Poles who attack Angie come across not as a brutal herd, but people who have justifiable complaints but are devoid of legal means to articulate them, and are therefore reduced to using brutal force and blackmail. The director depicts most sympathetically a young Polish man named Karol, with whom Angie spends a night in the Silesian town of Katowice and whom she later meets in London. Karol is open-hearted and generous, despite being poor and unlucky. He helps Angie in her dealings with the emigrants and invites her to his caravan, where he offers her Polish alcohol. Handsome and articulate, he awakens sexual attraction in Angie. However, their romance does not blossom because, as the woman puts it, they met at the wrong time. This statement most likely refers to the fact that after numerous romantic disappointments and ending up as a single mother, hardly able to look after her son, Angie associates romance with trouble. The impossibility of their romance might also be read as signifying the impossibility of crossing ethnic barriers but, more likely, it symbolizes the insurmountable gap between the exploiters (even as inept as Angie is initially) and those who are exploited. It is worth mentioning that Lesław Żurek, who plays Karol, was the main character in the third segment of *Ode to Joy* and apparently Loach chose him after seeing him in this film. Even if it was not the case, a viewer familiar with the Polish film might regard Karol's London adventure as an extension of Żurek's character's life as represented in *Ode to Joy*. In both films the main problem for the young Pole is finding his own place in the world, acquiring an identity. It is also worth noting that the only identity the young man is after is an individual one, and he uses a woman as a vehicle to find his place in the world. On the other hand, he does not identify with any real or imagined community, be it Poland, England or even a group of fellow emigrants. Poland for Karol or any other character in the film is an empty signifier; it does not define their values or govern their actions. Wiktor and Karol's 'identity projects' ultimately fail, but this does not mean that they see any alternative.

Loach employs *mise-en-scène* that conveys a sense of the restricted lives of the emigrant. Most of them live in a caravan park and such accommodation is depicted as desirable as an alternative is squatting in cold, disused factories or complete homelessness. The caravan park renders the lives of migrants claustrophobic and tightly controlled. The very space of a caravan is limited; there is hardly enough room to eat or sleep there. Moreover, the caravans stand close to one another, leaving practically no space for privacy. The caravan park is surrounded by a wire which, on the one hand, serves as protection from hostile English neighbours, but on the other marks its territory as a confined place, a prison. This impression is strongest when Angela talks to Iranian children living there through the wire, which brings to mind a concentration camp.

While the lives of the emigrants come across as restricted and claustrophobic, Angie and Rosie are extremely mobile. Angie in particular is always on the move, criss-crossing on her motorcycle the whole of London several times a day. The women are also in charge of vans which take the migrants to their work places; the workers have to wait there passively until the vans are full. Moreover, Angie and Rose 'penetrate' Eastern Europe, as shown in the last scene, where the two women are recruiting people from Ukraine to work in London. This scene testifies to Europe moving eastward; this being an aspect of the larger phenomenon of globalisation. We can guess that as a result of this movement Poland's place in Europe will change – it will become more and more 'Western'. In accordance with his credentials as a chief 'socialist realist' in British cinema, Loach assesses this movement utterly negatively, as leading to the exploitation and misery of migrants and the lowering of moral standards on both sides of the divide: host country and donor country. It is, however, not the loosening of borders which he condemns, but capitalism in the name of which it happens.

Conclusion: Cinema of Scepticism

In conclusion, I would like to reiterate that by and large Polish cinema reveals a negative attitude to the emigration of Poles. Irrespective of whether the films were made in the 1950s or 1990s, they treat an emigrant as an anomaly from the norm and a problem for which somebody is to blame. The characteristics of emigration and responsibility for this phenomenon, however, change as we travel through Polish history. In the first period, which I described as communist, emigration is typically permanent and the emigrants themselves are principally guilty because they prefer an easy life abroad over a modest but honest existence in their own country. In the second period the blame is attributed to the political and economic situation in Poland which virtually forces citizens to escape to seek a decent life abroad. However, even in the films of this period, especially in *The Last Ferry*, it is suggested that the best Poles, the greatest patriots, would never leave their fatherland, but rather work and die for it. Finally, in films about post-communist emigration, emigration is depicted as lacking permanence, like a seesaw movement and Polish capitalism or perhaps global capitalism is guilty of forcing Poles to leave their country, changing them into perpetual exiles, lacking stable homes and stable identities.

Conversely, the films of all types lack happy and fulfilled emigrants, for whom life in a foreign country did not impoverish but enrich them, economically and culturally. If the unwillingness to include such a character in the films prior to 1989 can be attributed to the requirements of censorship in Poland, post 1989 it is less understandable. In my opinion, it might point to the persistence of old ideas of emigration in dominant Polish cultural discourses, for example the idea of fixed identity and a natural homeland. Similarly, it reflects the dominant way of depicting emigration in Eastern and Western or indeed global cinema, good examples being *Dirty Pretty Things* (2002) by Stephen Frears, *Lilja 4-Ever* (2002) by Lucas Moodysson, and *Rezervni deli* [*Spare Parts*] (2003) by Damjan Kozole (see Mazierska 2006). The lack of first-hand knowledge about the lives of emigrants and the attempt to adhere to a certain ideology (such as communist, anti-communist, anti-American) and, consequently, the moralistic tone used in these films, to a large extent explains why the majority of them are of a rather low artistic standard and they age badly. However, it does not always need to be the case. Even the relative artistic and commercial success of *Ode to Joy* points to the possibility of finding a new and polyphonic cinematic voice about migration. My hope is that this voice will find its echo.

References

Aciman, A. (ed.) (1999), *Letters of Transit: Reflections on Exile, Identity, Language and Loss* (New York, NY: New Press).

Barańczak, S. (1992), 'Emigracja: co to znaczy?' ['Emigration: What does it Mean?'] in Fik (ed.).

Bauman, Z. (1996), 'From Pilgrim to Tourist – or a Short History of Identity', in Hall and Du Gay (eds).

Fassman, H. and Rainer, M. (1994), *European Migration in the Late Twentieth Century* (Aldershot: Edward Elgar).

Fik, M. (ed.) (1992), *Między Polską a światem: Kultura emigracyjna po 1939 roku* [*Between Poland and the World: Émigré Culture after 1939*] (Warszawa: Krąg).

Gombrowicz, W. (1953), *Trans-Atlantyk* (Paris).

Grochowska, M. (2006), 'Oda do radości' ['Ode to Joy'], Kino 4, 69–70.

Hall, S. and Du Gay, P. (eds) (1996), *Questions of Cultural Identity* (London: Sage).

Hoffman, E. (1999), 'The New Nomads' in Aciman (ed.).

Jaźwińska, E. and Okólski, M. (eds) (2002), *Ludzie na huśtawce* [People on a Seesaw] (Warsaw: Scholar).

Kita, B. (ed.) (2006), *Przestrzenie tożsamości we współczesnym kinie europejskim* [*The Spaces of Identity in Contemporary European Cinema*] (Kraków: Rabid).

Kłuskiewicz, Ł. (2006), 'Generacja Nicponi' ['Generation of Hooligans'], *Kino* 4, 13–16.

Koser, K. and Lutz, H. (eds) (1998), *The New Migration in Europe* (London: Macmillan).

Mazierska, E. (2006), 'Wszędzie źle, ale w domu najznośniej. Portret emigranta w kinie europejskim po upadku muru berlińskiego' ['Everywhere is Bad, but Home is most Bearable: The portrait of an Emigrant in the Cinema after the Fall of the Berlin Wall'] in Kita (ed.).

Mazierska, E. (2007), *Roman Polanski: The Cinema of a Cultural Traveller* (London: I.B. Tauris).

Miłosz, C. (1992), *Szukanie ojczyzny* [Searching for Fatherland] (Kraków: Znak).

Mrożek, S. (2006), *Baltazar* (Warsaw: Noir sur Blanc).

Naficy, H. (ed.) (1999), *Home, Exile, Homeland* (London: Routledge).

Nagrodkiewicz, G. (2007), 'Śląsk, czyli szkic do portretu pokolenia' ['Silesia, or a Sketch of a Portrait of a certain Generation'], *Kwartalnik Filmowy* 57–8, 160–6.

Stola, D. (2002), 'Milion straconych Polaków' ['A Million Lost Poles'], *Biuletyn IPN* 14.

Stone, R. (2007), 'Notes from Region 2', *Journal of Contemporary European Studies* 15:1, 5–14.

Suder, D. (2003), 'Obraz Polaków na emigracji w twórczości polskich reżyserów w latach 1977–2002' ['Representation of Polish Emigrants in the work of Polish directors in the years 1977–2002'], MA Thesis (Kraków: Jagiellonian University).

PART II
Experiences of Immigration and 'Settlement'

Chapter 6

Shared History? Polish Migrant Experiences and the Politics of Display in Northern Ireland

Maruška Svašek

I first came to Northern Ireland in 1990. I had a strong sense of isolation because there were no Poles at all. It was very hard. When I came back the second time in 2005 my experience was very different. There were many Poles now which was nice. But this also creates a problem. Other Poles may not give a good impression, which affects myself. I want people to have a good view of myself.

This quote comes from a Polish woman in her thirties who is an active member of the Polish Association in Northern Ireland. She is married, has a young child and works as an interpreter in Belfast. The quote illustrates a number of issues that are central to this chapter. First, the historical situation of Polish migration to Northern Ireland is quite specific. Migration from Poland did not begin until the 1990s and has increased substantially since the Polish entrance into the European Union, though levels have dropped in 2008 because of the worsening economic situation in Britain.[1] Even though a considerable number of Polish workers have returned to their home country, the Poles have become the largest minority group in Northern Ireland, overtaking the Chinese. Until recently, the latter were the largest ethnic minority group of around 8,000 people. According to official estimates approximately 40,000 Polish migrant workers resided in Northern Ireland in 2007, while many more have settled in the Republic of Ireland.

Second, many Polish migrants tend to have ambiguous feelings about other Polish migrants. On the one hand, they are happy to speak Polish and make friends with other migrant workers, to occasionally attend Polish gatherings and, especially when they have just arrived, to find support through the Polish Association. Yet on the other, they criticize those who misbehave (often single men who are over for short periods and drink heavily) because their behaviour spoils the reputation of 'Poles' and 'Poland', feeding anti-Polish feelings amongst the local population. As a result, numerous Polish migrants, especially

---

1   Compare, for example, with Polish migration to England that started much earlier (see Burrell 2006).

those who plan to settle in Ireland, consciously aim to behave 'properly' and try to present a positive image of Polishness.

Third, Polish migrants in Northern Ireland find themselves in a place marked by a history of sectarianism and violence that has strongly shaped the experience and perceptions of the local population. Memories of past and present aggression influence the emotional dispositions of local residents as well as their use of space, characterized by spatial strategies that involve, 'complex mapping practices, whereby space is carved into safe and unsafe zones, where both macro and micro-territorial considerations exist, involving respectively the "other side of town" or the "other side of the street"' (Lysaght 2005: 140; Lysaght 2002, 2005; Lysaght and Basten 2002). Many locations are segregated, dividing spaces into areas dominated by Protestants or Catholics (Boal 1969, 1978, 1981, 1982, 1994; Boal and Livingstone 1983; Darby 1986, 1990; Doherty and Poole 1995; Murtagh 1993; Poole and Doherty 1996). Loyalist (Protestant) and Nationalist (Catholic) areas are often marked by flags, painted curb stones, murals and parades (Jarman 1997; 1999). Faced with newcomers, locals who are fixed on keeping residential areas 'to themselves' have frequently reacted to incoming migrants with anti-foreigner sentiments.

Ironically, the improved political situation in Northern Ireland since the 1994 ceasefires seems to have had a negative effect on migrant experiences as 'sectarian conflict has given way to racist offences as new and vulnerable targets were sought' (Hainsworth, undated).[2] While anti-minority sentiments did exist before, they did not receive much political or media attention as politicians and the police concentrated mainly on sectarian violence. In the 1990s, spokespersons from settled ethnic minority groups began calling for an 'all-inclusive peace process'. This happened at the time when large numbers of Poles started arriving in Northern Ireland.

In this chapter, I will focus on Polish migrants who participated in the Shared History project in 2006, a project that intended to stimulate good relations between the minority and majority populations of Northern Ireland. Other groups involved in the project were Cantonese speaking Chinese migrants, Northern Irish Protestants and community workers from five different organizations. The analysis will explore the emotional dimensions of the interaction within the Polish group, and examine how emotional motives informed their representational politics in a context of increasing public and media attention to racial intolerance and anti-migrant feelings.

---

2   Research has shown that members of ethnic minority groups have experienced an increase in racist attitudes and fear that the situation will get worse (Hainsworth, undated; Irwin and Dunn 1997).

Emotions, Migration and Representation

Theoretically, this chapter links up with studies that have explored emotions and the emotional dimensions of human mobility. 'Emotions' should not be perceived as interior psychological states, but rather as dynamic processes that bridge the domain of the individual and the social, and that are central to the experience and management of subjectivity (Lutz and White 1986; Milton and Svašek 2005; Overing and Passes 2000). Through emotional processes, people exist in and relate to the world around them, feel and position themselves vis-à-vis others, and negotiate identities. In my own work I have employed a theoretical framework that combines various schools of thought and examines emotions as discourses, practices and embodied experiences.

The *discursive* dimension of emotions explores how ideas about emotional processes encode knowledge about subjectivity and intersubjectivity (Lutz 1988; Lutz and Abu-Lughod 1990). A discourse of 'fear of strangers' (Csordas 1990; Lock 1993; Lyon 1995), for example, delineates particular others as outsiders who potentially harm or pollute the self. Such discourses, mediated for instance through the media, can shape people's perceptions of particular migrant groups. In various contexts, some migrants, migrant organizations and social workers have aimed to produce effective counter-discourses to undermine negative stereotyping. We shall see that in the Shared History project this was one of the strategies taken by the participating groups.

Emotional *practices*, or partially learned behaviour resulting from the internalization of social rules concerning emotional expression and interaction (Bourdieu 1977), often reinforce dominant discourses of emotions. To stay with the example of 'fear of strangers', this practice may be an almost unconscious part of someone's disposition, and may be performed in many ways; from the selective use of space, avoiding areas one perceives to be dangerous, to the ritual enactment of fear in political rallies, when particular groups are marked as a threat to society. The level of practice often has a performative dimension, where people consciously trigger and manage emotions in themselves and others. People may, of course, also undermine particular discourses through alternative forms of behaviour. It will become clear that in the context of the Shared History project, the participants aimed to overcome potentially fear-triggering experiences of 'difference' through cross-community interaction and communication.

The third level of *embodied experience* focuses on the bodily dimensions of emotional processes and the connection between multi-sensorial perception and interpretation (Leavitt 1996). In the case of 'fear for strangers', physical sensations such as sweating, blushing or an increasing heartbeat are important experiential elements that must be understood in the context of discourses and practices of emotions. Media images of 'dangerous terrorists' and political speeches intended to trigger anxiety about resources in the context of increasing migration can, for example, impact on people's physical reactions to 'strangers' (Ahmed 2004). It will be argued that in the Shared History project bodily co-presence was essential to the creation of trust within the participating groups and between the group members and the project organizers.

Various scholars have recently explored how 'emotions' can be theorized to create a better understanding of human life in a world of movement (Baldassar 2007, 2008; Conradson and McKay 2007; Skrbiš 2008; Svašek and Skrbiš 2007; Svašek 2008; Svašek 2009). The analysis in this chapter will mainly focus on Polish migrant workers and emotional discourses, practices and experiences in the context of the Shared History project. Transnationally mobile people are to some extent conditioned by emotional discourses and practices learnt in their homelands and are often strongly attached to their families and friends 'back home'. In their new surroundings they may be confronted with homesickness and feelings of non-belonging as they encounter unwelcoming attitudes amongst the locals and are faced with the difficulties of finding employment and housing. Coping in their new surroundings, migrants may need to learn to experience and express feelings in new ways or to learn to suppress or manage them differently.[3] In addition, migrants are often pulled into two or more directions, which means that they need to '[unsettle] linear narratives of origin and migration; and [rethink] the relation between embodied subjectivity, place and belonging' (Ahmed 2004: 10). The movement between spheres of belonging, in our case between Poland and Northern Ireland, demands extensive emotional negotiation.

Migrants are not the only ones confronted with change; so are the locals. In a study of the emotional and multi-sensorial dimensions of interethnic living in a suburb of Sydney, Amanda Wise (2009) demonstrated, for example, that elderly inhabitants especially – themselves migrants from Europe – found it hard to cope with the ways in which more recent Chinese migrants had changed the everyday environment. The changes were not only obvious in the sounds, sights, and smells of everyday life, but also in the different emotional dispositions of the Chinese they interacted with, for example in the shops. As it was more difficult for the older population to adjust to the new situation 'their experience of the place [became] imbued with negative affects', and feelings of resentment were directed at the Chinese community. Some of the older inhabitants drew on available representations and discourses that were exclusionary and racist to make sense of their destabilizing experience. Distrust, fear and hatred of 'foreigners' are not however, the only possible outcomes of immigration. Encounters between locals and migrants can lead to a variety of emotional reactions, ranging from avoidance and scepticism to fascination and interest, love and joy, or as demonstrated by this chapter, to hope to improve relations. This chapter will show that representational politics can be an important route to enhancing insider/outsider relations, as strategically distributed texts and images may capture targeted audiences, triggering empathy and pushing them to take on more positive views of each other.

---

3   While some migrants assimilate easily, others may 'attempt to recreate the world they have left behind through active engagement in diasporic communities' (Svašek and Skrbiš 2007: 373).

Anti-racist Policies and Polish Experiences

Before looking in more detail at the project, it is necessary to give some historical background to Northern Irish migrant/minorities policies. By the late 1990s, partly in reaction to demands made by the more settled ethnic minorities, the British Race Relations Act that aspired to counter racism in the whole of Great Britain, was extended to Northern Ireland. The Commission for Racial Equality for Northern Ireland was established in 1997 and the British government began to finance research on racial prejudice in Northern Ireland (see, for example, Connolly and Keenan, 2001). New policies, outlined in a document entitled *A Racial Equality Strategy for Northern Ireland 2005–2010*, identified six major aims, including 'elimination of racial inequality', 'equal protection', 'equality of service provision', 'participation', 'dialogue' and 'capacity building'. The idea of 'dialogue', was central to the Shared History project in which Polish migrant workers participated, reflecting the statement in the document that it was necessary 'to promote dialogue between, and mutual understanding of, different faiths and cultural backgrounds, both long standing within Northern Ireland and recent arrivals to these shores, guided by overarching human rights norms'.

Underlying the notion of dialogue was a discourse of hope, a future oriented emotion that assumed that intercommunity communication would lead to increased trust and better relations. Preventing or tackling racism and the hope that things could change for the better also became a more central element within policing strategies. In November 2006, referring to an interview with Chief Constable of the Police Service of Northern Ireland, Sir Hugh Orde, the *New Statesman* reported that:

> [t]he biggest emerging threat, according to Orde, is racist attacks against immigrants. Northern Ireland now has up to 40,000 Poles (though nobody has any real idea of numbers), along with an array of Slovaks, Lithuanians and others who are prepared to do the cheap labour that locals shirk (Kamppfner 2006).

The article further noted that problems arose when migrants who looked for cheap rental accommodation moved into 'the most dangerous sectarian areas' and became the target of anti-foreigner attacks. Numerous Poles, many of whom had no background knowledge of the complex history and aftermath of the Troubles, had indeed moved into neighbourhoods affected by sectarianism. This could be especially problematic when settling in dominantly Loyalist neighbourhoods, as many local residents perceive the Poles as 'unwanted Catholics'.

At an academic conference about migration in 2006, Barbara Snowarska, a representative of the Polish Association in Northern Ireland, argued that the Poles are generally better off in Catholic neighbourhoods.[4] She described the

---

4   This was a conference I organized in Belfast in November 2006, entitled *Emotional Interaction: Migrants and Local Communities*.

relationship between Polish migrants and Northern Irish Catholics as 'generally friendly and welcoming' because they often 'share the same faith' and 'are perceived as boosting the number of Catholics in the province'. Not wanting to sketch an oversimplified and purely positive picture of Polish–Northern Irish Catholic interaction, Snowarska stressed that there were also 'negative signals, especially in deprived [Catholic] areas where Poles were accused of taking jobs'. She argued, however, that religion had the potential to stimulate good relations, as those who attended Catholic churches had the opportunity to meet Irish people in a context that promoted compassion and peaceful interaction. As we shall see, this issue came up during the discussion amongst the Polish participants of the Shared History project, but was, for strategic reasons, underemphasized in the exhibition.

Discussing connections between Polish migrants and Northern Irish Protestants, Snowarska pointed out it that the situation was 'more complex', as 'the hate of Catholics [by the more extreme Loyalists] is extended to the Polish because they are Catholics'. She emphasized, however, that 'educated Protestants often believe that the Polish have a positive influence on the local economy', and argued that Protestant anti-Polish sentiments were partly caused by socio-economic factors. Most tensions appeared

> in more deprived areas, and in areas such as Donegall Pass where there is sectarianism, and the paramilitaries have a strong influence. If someone enters such a space there may be problems. There can be intimidation or attacks, and children may be calling you names. These instances are often not reported to the police.

The reference to the Donegall Pass area is particularly relevant as one of the groups participating in the Shared History project came from this part of Belfast.

Anti-Polish sentiments are, however, not restricted just to areas of Belfast. On 3 April 2007, the *Belfast Telegraph* reported that there had been a string of attacks in the North West of Northern Ireland.[5] It must also be recognized that the source of conflict does not always lie with the locals. Snowarska stressed that Polish migrant

---

5   Katrina Kordula, founder of the Polish Welfare Association in Derry, commented: 'This is totally deplorable. I believe those who were attacked perceive this to be racist. It is totally disgraceful. If this is young people running about the street and picking these people out as an easy target, then I am asking community leaders and parents to stamp on this now and show those responsible that they are not going to get away with this type of behaviour. We may have to get the message out again that race hate crime will not be tolerated'. The latest attack was described as follows: 'A Polish couple who moved into a flat in the Copperthorpe area of Drumahoe near Derry were forced to flee when thugs threw a firework and bricks through their bedroom window in the early hours of Sunday morning. It is believed that they were living there for less than a week and are too frightened to go back'. <http://belfasttelegraph.co.uk/north-west-edition/daily/article2415442.ece>, accessed 16 April 2007.

workers must sometimes be blamed for causing problems: 'Hostilities are also sometimes caused by Poles, who may see their stay here as a three year holiday. They don't care about the locals, make no attempt to integrate, have parties, drink and make a lot of noise'. The Polish Association of Northern Ireland was concerned about the negative impression such behaviour gave of Polish culture, as a negative press could increase anti-Polish sentiments. We shall see that the Polish migrant workers who participated in the Shared History project aimed to create a more positive image of Polishness through an active politics of emotions.

The Shared History Project: Anger and Hope

As noted earlier, the situation which gave rise to the Shared History project was one in which reports about xenophobia and racism appeared more frequently in the Northern Irish media and where the Race Equality Strategy for Northern Ireland had begun to inform local policy. The emotions expressed in these documents included apprehension and anger, as well as morally-loaded sentiments that were meant as a 'wake-up call' to encourage individuals to take action and change both their own and other people's anti-minority/migrant attitudes. The discourse of concerned outrage was reinforced in public performances of anger in ethnic minority and majority political arenas.

One of the initiators of the project was the South Belfast Round Table on Racism, an umbrella organization that brought together several organizations in South Belfast. On its website, its 'anti-racism statement' announced that:

> [i]f South Belfast is to prosper as a community, then it is essential that all citizens feel they have an equal share in the community and that each citizen is equally valued. Racism should be eliminated wherever and however it occurs, whether in the form of racial discrimination, racial harassment or violence.[6]

Visual symbols on the website showed alliances with organizations at different political levels, ranging from the very local (an emblem of the Donegall Pass Community Forum) to the transnational (a symbol saying 'The European Union against Racism' and a quote by the African American Martin Luther King).

The Donegall Pass Community Forum, established in 1996, also participated. It functioned as the main representative body for Donegall Pass, an inner city 'urban village' dominated by Loyalist paramilitaries. As a sub-committee to the South Belfast Roundtable on Racism, the Forum committed itself to 'challenging racism and racist practices, creating an atmosphere where racism is not tolerated'. Ken Orr, Community Training and Education Coordinator of the Forum noted that as one of the most deprived areas in Northern Ireland, Donegall Pass was

---

6   See   <http://www.donegallpass.org/html/the_south_belfast_roundtable_o.html>, accessed 12 May 2008.

faced with high unemployment, ill health and housing pressures; 78 per cent of the residents were perceived Protestants and many supported the Unionists. The fact that other residents included Chinese people (mainly Cantonese speakers from the Hong Kong area) and migrant workers from Poland, Brazil and the Ukraine meant that the area was an appropriate target for the project. Orr worked with the only 'local' group, formed by members from the Protestant community.[7]

The Chinese group consisted of elderly members of the Hoi Sum Group, who were coordinated by the Chinese Welfare Society, a very active organization that had been established by members of the Chinese minority in 1986. Its former chief executive, Anna Manwah Lo, was Chair of the South Belfast Roundtable of Racism.

The participating Poles were guided by Maya Picard, a French community worker who was employed by South Belfast Highway to Health. This organization was not just focused on migrants but served all residents in the area. Active in deprived areas of South Belfast, it offered health-improving programmes including sports activities, anti-smoking programmes and cheap fruit bags for disadvantaged families. Initially its emphasis had been solely on physical health, but as Picard explained, in 2005 employees in the organization had begun to realize that stress, caused by racism and isolation, was a significant health problem for members of ethnic minority groups who lived in its catchment area.[8] Consequently, the organization began to focus on issues of social and emotional well-being, attempting to stimulate positive interaction between locals and newcomers.

The Polish part of the project was also supported by Karen McCartney, a lecturer from Ulster People's College with experience in exhibition making. She told me in 2008 that the project had been conceived as an opportunity for migrants and locals to share their life stories, and thus, in McCartney's words, to 'learn about each others' communities' and 'build relationships'. Narrative performance was used as a tool to counter negative stereotypical images and replace them by images of shared humanity, creating an atmosphere of trust. A text about the Shared History project, posted on the Internet, explained that:

> [b]y sharing who we are, and how we came to live together in Belfast, we hope that we will build a relationship and trust which will help us work together to make Belfast a better place for all'.[9]

---

7   The all-female Northern Irish indigenous group was relatively small, with three women having the biggest input.

8   Numerous migrants live in the area, and therefore the organization has strong connections with migrant organizations, such as the Chinese Welfare Association, the Islamic Centre, and more recently, with the Polish Association.

9   <http://www.donegallpass.org/html/the_shared_history_project_pag.html>, accessed 3 June 2008.

The narratives were structured along similar lines to assure experiences of 'shared history'. The method increased the possibility of mutual recognition and dialogue, feeding the hope that the project would generate better intercommunity relations. The prescribed structuring metaphor was that of 'the journey', although there was no attempt to force individual narrators into a representational straightjacket. As McCartney explained:

> We helped them to tell their story. 'How did they come here', 'how was their journey', 'how did they settle in', was the main focus for each group. It was left open for each group to interpret these themes. It was important to leave space for positive and negative stories. It was important that they had control over that, that control wasn't taken away from them.

For the largest part of the project, the Polish, Chinese and Northern Irish groups met separately to allow the participants, in a more private sphere, to exchange personal stories. The conversations were taped and transcribed and during the last meeting the individual groups made a final selection of quotes that would then represent them in the exhibition. Group members were also offered a day of photographic training and subsequently collected and made photographs to illustrate their stories. Due to space restrictions, I will not discuss any of the visuals in this chapter but instead will concentrate on oral and textual narrative performance.

At a preview of the exhibition the different groups met and presented their work to each other. The public exhibition was launched in Belfast City Hall and has since been touring different locations in Northern Ireland. I was present during all four meetings of the Polish group, attended the evening when the groups presented their work to each other, and visited the opening of the exhibition at the City Hall. I also interviewed various community workers and four of the Polish group members, whose names have been anonymized. All participants were aware that I was conducting research on the project. As noted earlier, I was particularly interested in the aims of the project initiators, the emotional dynamics within the Polish group during its meetings and the decision making process relating to the content of the Polish part of the exhibition.

The Polish Input: Emotions as Identity Claims

To find Poles who wanted to participate in Shared History, Maya Picard had advertised the project at strategic places frequented by Polish workers, including the Polish Association Northern Ireland, Catholic Churches and English classes for foreigners.[10] I asked some of the participants how they had heard about it and

---

10   The Polish Association Northern Ireland, established in March 2006, is supported by Northern Ireland Council for Ethnic Minorities. Its website states: 'We are delivering support and information to the migrant communities. Our main aim: establishing and

why they had decided to join. Different reasons were mentioned, including 'the opportunity to meet other Poles', 'to practice English', 'to be active and have fun' and 'to communicate something about ourselves and our home country to non-Poles'; the latter was in line with the official intention of the project. A married couple emphasized the importance of projecting a positive image of Poland, which, they said, had been the main reason for their participation. In a similar vein, a 22 year old photography student replied 'It's good for Polish people, and for Irish people to hear something about Polish people ... to improve tolerance'.

During the first meeting on 5 October 2006, seven Poles (five women and two men) showed up, most of them in their twenties. They were relatively recent arrivals and came from a variety of jobs and professional backgrounds.[11] After offering coffee and cakes, Picard and McCartney introduced the project. Picard explained that the aim was to make an exhibition that would consist of both photos and texts, the latter telling 'your stories about how you came here and why you chose to stay', and that the first meeting would focus on 'what is Poland for you? [sic]'. Evidently, this was potentially a highly emotive subject, as migrants often have ambiguous feelings about their homeland and have mixed feelings about their decision to leave. To provide a visual and emotional trigger for the narratives a few maps of Poland were spread out on the table. Picard laughed as she said the obvious: 'this is the map of Poland'. McCartney added half-jokingly: 'this will make you all homesick'.[12] As everyone laughed, the comment had the productive effect of temporarily synchronizing the group members' emotional body language. By increasing the experience of co-presence and commonality, this helped to create an atmosphere in which people were willing to communicate further.

The discussion soon turned to the dire economic conditions in Poland and became more serious. All agreed that the situation back home was 'very bad', and that this had been a major reason for their departure. 'Everybody has left to work abroad, especially specialists', somebody said. Another person noted that the conditions were different in distinct regions, but that people did not choose

---

developing links between local and migrant communities. promoting polish [sic] culture abroad. We organize information meetings for polish community (tax law, employment rights etc), cultural events (Polish Cultural Week). We also provide English classes for adults and every Saturday help polish community solve their problems'.

11   Four had been in Northern Ireland for about a year and a half, and the other three had arrived between three and six weeks ago. In terms of employment, one worked for the Court Service, others were employed as construction worker, interpreter, and caretaker in a hostel. One young woman had done her PhD at Queens University, a young male had had several jobs and was now enrolled for a photography course, and two people were unemployed and looking for work. One had just been sacked from a telephone service company; the other was planning to move to the Republic of Ireland and work in Dublin.

12   The meeting was, however, not marked by nostalgic longing. Most of the participants were young, and had not been away for long. Some said they would probably return to Poland within a year, but none were sure about that. They saw their stay in Northern Ireland as an opportunity to learn English and make money.

to become unemployed: 'People are not lazy; there simply isn't enough work'.[13] Maya and Karen reacted with empathy, removing any suggestion that they, as 'non-Poles', would accuse the Poles of laziness. A female participant said that the economic situation in Poland brought a lot of hardship: 'No work, no money, no perspectives brings a lot of frustration'. The photography student noted that having a university degree did not assure a high salary in Poland, stating that 'nurses and teachers only earn £200 per month. No way you can buy your own place'. The construction worker added: 'The price of living in Poland is very high. Here if you have normal wages and it is cheap to live, you can afford something'. Someone suggested that the economic necessity to look for work abroad should become one of the themes in the exhibition and the others agreed. It was clearly important to the group to counter negative images of Polish migrant workers as 'abusers of the British social system', a conviction that has angered numerous Northern Irish locals.

The shared gloom about the economic situation in Poland and the participants' concern about their perceived collective identity reinforces Parkinson's claim that 'getting emotional is in reality something that people often do actively in order to influence others in support of particular self-presentational goals' (1995: 199–200). In the context of the meeting, the discourse of 'suffering through economic hardship', enacted through performed narrative, verbal intonation and body language, had an aim beyond expressing personal feelings. The narrated feelings were negotiated within the context of the planned exhibition, as the process was at least partly consciously directed.[14] The self presentation as 'victims of poverty' was an active claim, justifying their presence in Northern Ireland. Although it was based on shared embodied memories of their desperation about the situation back home, it also gave a selective account of their motivations to coming to Northern Ireland. Other reasons that were also expressed during the meeting by some participants, such as the desire to see more of the world, were left out. The focus on economic push factors was thus a strategic choice, informed by a collective wish to induce empathy in the viewers.

Under the caption 'Why did we choose to leave home?', a text at the exhibition explained that '[i]t is not easy to get a reasonably well paid job in Poland as there are very few such employment opportunities'. Two of the selected quotes read: 'This is not because we are lazy and choose to live on benefits rather than work. This is hugely frustrating. You start to think: "What am I here for?"'; and

---

13   He said, for example that Poznan was not a bad region but that there was still 13 per cent unemployment. East Poland and Pomerania were much worse with 30 to 35 per cent unemployment.

14   To interpret the interaction as fully conscious would, however be a mistake. As Hatfield et al. (1994) have argued, emotional encounters are often also shaped by unconscious communicative signals.

> Unemployment has reached such a level and competition is so hard even for
> very low paid jobs, that, for example, you need to speak English and German to
> get a cleaning job, and for the same low salary as before!

The message was clearly addressed to the Northern Irish visitors of the exhibition and tried to change negative evaluations of Poles as unwelcome profiteers. As Parkinson (1995: 200) noted, it is important explore the sources of positive identity claims, suggesting that 'our relative social positions within institutions define many of the presentational requirements that are satisfied by emotional performance'. In the case of the Polish migrants, their situation as relatively vulnerable foreigners informed it.

Narrating Positive and Negative Experiences

At the second meeting, due to work commitments only two of those who had attended the first meeting showed up, but five new people came along. The seven participants (one male, six female) had been in Northern Ireland between five months and a year and a half; two of them had arrived with one or more children. The first question ('Why did you leave Poland?') continued the previous week's discussion and, again, the emphasis was on economic necessity. While a young woman remarked that she had always wanted to travel, the other six emphasized the need to improve their financial situation.

When asked why they had chosen to go to Northern Ireland, some stated that they had preferred an English speaking country. They also said that they had little knowledge about Northern Ireland before their arrival. A somewhat embarrassed man noted (although with a humorous undertone) that he had thought that Belfast was in the Republic of Ireland: 'I didn't know Ireland was divided'. Other group members laughed and admitted that they had been equally ignorant; they were surprised when they could not pay in Euros. The sharing of their 'confessions' created a moment of intimacy, of intense shared sociality. In the exhibition, their lack of previous knowledge was commented on in several texts, as it illustrated the difficulties of newcomers, uninitiated into Northern Irish society.

In response to Picard's question about their first experiences in Northern Ireland, some expressed their disappointment with Belfast. Expecting it to be less provincial, more attractive, and having experienced some kind of culture shock, a woman said: 'The first time I thought I was in hell. The buildings and streets are ugly; everything is so dirty, and people have tattoos and piercings'. She also felt that children were rude to their parents and, apologizing herself, said that 'in Poland people are better behaved, more cultural'. One of the male participants agreed.

The above shows that at least some of the participants felt safe enough to express their criticism, using strong, potentially insulting terms like 'dirty' and 'hell'; the organizers had managed to create an atmosphere of trust, crucial to such openness. It must be noted that, in the context of the meeting, the Poles formed a majority, which may have impacted on their willingness to convey their dissatisfaction. As Elizabeth Tonkin (1992: 3) points out, when analysing storytelling, the tellers should not be isolated from the context of interaction with the listeners; the 'characteristics of tellers' have to be connected with 'those of their audiences, and both with the structure of their narrations'.

The Poles did not only complain, however (a very common Polish narrative style according to many Polish migrants I spoke with) – they were also happy to talk about positive experiences. Obviously, their readiness to do so was partly influenced by the knowledge that they would be addressing a Northern Irish audience in the exhibition but they also seemed to express genuine feelings of satisfaction. Texts referring to positive Polish perceptions of the Irish dominated in the exhibition, and appeared under the headings 'Settling In', 'The Helping Hand', and 'More Impressions of Northern Ireland'. To give some examples:

> At first when I came here I was surprised that people here smile and nod and say 'hello' to strangers in the street. In the countryside they do this even more so.

> People here are well mannered – all the bus drivers even are nice. The customers are very polite with them – they always thank the drivers when leaving the bus.

> People on the street are very helpful.

During the meeting the participants also related positive stories about Northern Irish employers. One text in the exhibition referred to a Polish speaker who had been 'very pleasantly surprised by the way my boss behaves towards me', and another mentioned that the boss 'was really helpful when I first arrived'. The participants of the meeting were visibly enthused by these narratives and the positive tone of the stories triggered other optimistic narrative performances. Hatfield et al. (1994) introduced the term 'emotional contagion' to refer to the (partly unconscious) infectivity of people's emotional expressions. These dynamics again emphasize that emotional processes cannot be understood by a focus on the individual, as they are often generated in and formative of social situations.

One story with a 'happy ending' that was included in the exhibition was particularly effective. The discussion theme was 'finding a job' and the first person to speak was the construction worker. He explained that he had found his first job through an agency that looked for workers in Poland. His trip and accommodation had been organized for him, but he had only been given a one week contract. After the job had ended he had been anxious to find more work. He recalled how he had walked from the city centre all the way to Dunmurry (about five miles), asking all the agencies and offices he passed whether they had work for him. The reply was always negative and he had become increasingly desperate. As he was telling his story he was clearly reliving the event, re-experiencing his anxiety. His narrative performance was so powerful that his audience, myself included, were truly captivated and moved by his account, feeling the emotions he expressed as the story unfolded. Building up tension, he recounted how he had finally come across a team of builders working in the street and had asked them, at the end of his tether, for work. 'Not now, maybe in wintertime', they had replied. In desperation, he had demanded access to their boss and had ended up shouting 'I need a job!'. In a dramatic turn, the boss had decided to employ him.

On hearing his account, the audience sighed in relief after the happy ending. Yet the narrative also evoked embodied memories of stress, caused by the need to find or hold on to jobs. After the story, a young woman admitted that during her time at a call centre she had had a hard time trying to understand different English, Irish, Welsh and Scottish accents and had feared she would be fired. This put an additional strain on her and eventually she had been sacked.

Sharing Stories, Emotional Relief and Selective Representation

As noted earlier, sometime after the exhibition I interviewed Anna about her involvement in the Shared History project. She referred to the emotional impact the sessions had made on her and the personal relief she had felt from exchanging migrant experiences with other Poles. She explained:

> It was most difficult to talk about the situation in Poland. People don't want to admit that they have economic problems. Some left because they got divorced, and wanted to start a new life. Or they have to pay alimentation, or support sick parents. They feel like a 'feeding man'. They may be torn inside. I also feel that a bit. I miss out on student life. But my parents do not have so much money to support me. Telling how you looked for a job, or about the journey you made to get here, I felt embarrassed. But then again it's my achievement that I am here. [One man], for example, told how he screamed that he needed a job. He was desperate.

When I replied that the way he had told the story was funny, and that we had all laughed about it, she commented: 'Yes that was maybe therapeutic. But ok, nothing … it gave relief. Everybody laughed and nobody pointed at you. There was trust and understanding in the group, empathy'. At another point in the interview, she said:

> It was a good way to express yourself. If people have a problem, they can say so. They could talk about being homesick, worries about money, and discrimination. It was good to hear stories and tell them, and to meet friends. It was the first time I met Maria, I live a minute from her house and we have become friends.

Another woman 'came out' with a moving story about how she had been mistreated and bullied when she had worked at a Northern Irish mushroom farm. Although it was visibly painful for her to remember her past suffering, and she said she would not go into detail as it was too hard to talk about it, she seemed to welcome the empathetic reactions she received from the group.

Researchers of traumatic experiences have found that telling stories about past suffering can be a helpful tool in the healing process (see, for example, Leys 2000). This seemed to fit the aim of the South Belfast Highway to Health organization, that is 'to support individuals and groups in developing confidence and community skills by providing health and wellbeing training and programmes'. McCartney emphasized, however, that the Shared History project 'did not claim to have any therapeutic objective', even though this may have been a welcome outcome to some of the participants. The main aim had been to work towards an exhibition that would increase trust and promote tolerance.

In the last meeting, when texts and images were selected for the display, it was decided that the mushroom farm story should not be directly mentioned in the exhibition as it was atypical in the group. McCartney commented: 'I think that many in the group felt it was too negative an experience to present to an outside audience'.[15] Some of the Polish participants I spoke with confirmed their reluctance to present an overly negative image of Polish experience to the Northern Irish public as their aim was to trigger a more positive interest in Poland and the Polish people. Not wanting to misrepresent the diversity of experiences, however, the group decided to add an explanatory text under the caption 'Getting a job', which said: 'People have had different experiences of employment in Northern Ireland. Whilst many in the group have been treated fairly and lawfully by their employer, this has not been the case for others'.

McCartney pointed out that the participants were given the freedom to select the texts that would appear in the exhibition, and that this form of empowerment was an important part of the project.

> Whenever we negotiated with them what would go into the display, they wanted more positive images of the Polish. So we put more in. They were sensitive about it ... Whenever we were selecting texts, they felt too many sob stories would not be good. There was a debate in the group. Some liked to tell the more negative stories in the exhibition, others wanted certain negative things to be said but were more cautious. They wanted to emphasize the positive stories. We talked to them about it during and outside the meetings and exchanged emails. The general feedback was that they wanted a more positive story. They brought more stuff in to emphasize the positive side of the story. The exhibition took the feedback into account.[16]

---

15   She further explained: 'There was a debate about this. The selection for the exhibition had to be negotiated. They were in control ... We had made the commitment to them at the beginning that they would be in final control of what was put into the exhibition'.

16   McCartney noted that decision grew out of consent. 'To be truthful, it was very organic. Individuals had different aims. A lot of it was social, they met other Polish people

Since the immediate background to the project was the struggle against racism and anti-foreigner sentiments, I asked McCartney why these issues had not been central to the display and whether they were downplayed on purpose. She replied that the project coordinators would have accepted the inclusion of experiences of xenophobia in the exhibition if the group's members had wanted to highlight these within the framework of the pre-chosen theme of 'the journey'.

The relative silence about experienced problems becomes all the more apparent when contrasting the content of the exhibition with exchanges about Polish migrant life on the Internet. In his 'Irish Diary', the Polish blogger 'MacKozer' claimed, for example, that '[s]ome of my friends have no good memories from the Protestant areas of Belfast. They were told very seriously that Catholics, especially Poles, are not welcome there. They had no problems in Catholic districts'.[17] References to Protestant–Catholic tensions were in fact totally absent from the exhibition, as were the suggestions that Poles were often better received in Catholic areas. Interaction with Northern Irish Catholics was only indirectly mentioned. Under the caption 'The Helping Hand', a text said that in 2005 the priest of the Good Shepherd Church in Belfast had asked the Poles in attendance whether he could help them with anything. When they had replied that they needed to improve their English, he had organized weekly lessons in his Parish. At the first meeting 25 non-Poles attended, outnumbering the 15 Poles.

When Pawel told the story about the helpful priest, it was clear from his intonation and body language that he was grateful and had enjoyed the meetings, and that the friendly attitude of the Priest had decreased his feelings of non-belonging. In the exhibition the section on the helpful Priest alluded to the identification of Catholic Poles with Northern Irish Catholics, but without politicizing their shared religious identity. The strategy was clearly not to antagonize, but instead to be positive and to open up a dialogue with all citizens of Northern Ireland.

Evidently, the Polish group members were individuals with different backgrounds, outlooks, and opinions, and the exhibition was the result of both dialogue within the group and compromise by individual participants. While all Poles in the project eventually accepted the politics of optimistic reporting and self-presentation, some had done so reluctantly. As Anna explained,

> I like the truth. Others kept it more polite and 'cheesy' (she laughs). The farmhouse slave story, I would keep it in. It is inconvenient but important. We don't have to censor or be polite and act as if there is never any discrimination. You have to cope with it.

---

and exchanged stories. Only then most realized that there was going to be an exhibition. It was an organic process because the project grew slowly and in the end there was a consensus. It was, however, hard to reach. There were a lot of people involved, and they had different backgrounds and experiences'.

17   See <http://www.drakkart.com/eire2/>.

Conclusion

This chapter has shown that emotional processes are crucial to narrative performance and textual representation. It has demonstrated that the social, political and historical contexts in which stories are told must be taken into account when analysing communicative interaction. Furthermore, the ways in which individual narrators manage their emotions and project notions of individual and collective self are influenced by their familiarity with particular discourses and practices of emotion, and are shaped by embodied memories of earlier emotional encounters. When analysing human emotions in the context of human mobility, it is also crucial to look at the predicaments and emotional habitus of both migrants and members of local communities.

As was clear in the Northern Irish case, the troubled past of Protestant–Catholic tensions affected how specific groups of incomers were perceived and treated, and perceptions of Poles as Catholics shaped Protestant–Polish emotional interaction. The historical context of Polish entry into the European Union, which legally allowed Poles to work in Britain, also influenced Northern Irish attitudes. The sudden increase of foreign workers shocked many locals, who feared losing their jobs or felt unable to compete with the low paid, hardworking Poles. Another historical factor that was taken into account was the implementation of anti-racist policies as a result of demands by settled minorities for an all inclusive peace process.

The Shared History project was initiated as a consequence of anti-racist and reconciliation politics, and was shaped by both positive and negative emotional experiences. Feelings of dissatisfaction with and anger about racism and xenophobia were the driving factor. The project coordinators intended to create a framework in which a more positive dialogue between indigenous and incoming groups could develop. Through expressions and enactments of anger and hope during the group sessions and the opening ceremony, they called for the improvement of insider/ outsider relationships.

The Polish sessions allowed the Polish participants to share good and bad experiences and created a social context in which their identity as migrants was emphasized and negotiated. Exchanging stories of economic and social hardship created a trustful environment and had a positive impact on at least some of the individuals involved. This shows that narrative performance does not just produce meaning but also allows for emotional interaction between tellers and their audiences.

The Polish group understood the project not only as a way of socializing with other Poles and migrants but also as a strategic tool, to reach out to Northern Irish society. With regard to the latter, they decided to prioritize the more informative stories of 'life in Poland' and accounts of positive interaction with the Northern Irish locals, translating them into texts for the exhibition. Their politics of representation was not only informed by the official project's discourse of hope through dialogue but also by their own urge to create a positive image of

Polishness, thus stimulating peaceful emotional interaction with the locals. Their hope was that this would increase their own sense of belonging.

References

Ahmed, S. (2004), *The Cultural Politics of Emotion* (Edinburgh: Edinburgh University Press).

Baldassar, L. (2007), 'Transnational Families and the Provision of Moral and Emotional Support: The Relationship between Truth and Distance', *Identities* 14:4, 385–409.

Baldassar, L. (2008), 'Missing Kin and Longing to be Together: Emotions and the Construction of Co-presence in Transnational Relationships', *Journal of Intercultural Studies* 29:3, 247–66.

Boal, F. (1969), 'Territoriality on the Shankill-Falls Divide, Belfast', *Irish Geography* 6, 30–50.

Boal, F. (1978), 'Territoriality on the Shankill-Falls Divide, Belfast: The Perspective from 1976', in Lanegrin and Palm (eds).

Boal, F. (1981), 'Residential Segregation and Mixing in a Situation of Ethnic and National Conflict: Belfast', in Compton (ed.).

Boal, F. (1982), 'Segregating and Mixing: Space and Residence in Belfast', in Boal and Neville (eds).

Boal, F. (1994), 'Encapsulation: Urban Dimensions of National Conflict', in Dunn (ed.).

Boal, F. and Livingstone, D. (1983), 'The International Frontier in Microcosm: the Shankill-Falls Divide, Belfast', in Kliot and Waterman (eds).

Boal, F. and Neville, D. (eds) (1982), *Integration and Division: Geographical Perspectives on the Northern Ireland Problem* (London: Academic Press).

Bourdieu, P. (1977), *Outline of a Theory of Practice* (Cambridge: Cambridge University Press).

Burrell, K. (2006), *Moving Lives: Narratives of Nation and Migration among Europeans in Post-War Britain* (Aldershot: Ashgate).

Compton, P. (ed.) (1981), *The Contemporary Population of Northern Ireland and Population-related Issues* (Belfast: Queen's University Belfast Institute of Irish Studies).

Connolly, P. and Keenan, M. (2001), *The Hidden Truth: Racist Harassment in Northern Ireland* (Belfast: Northern Ireland Statistics and Research Acency).

Conradson, D. and McKay, D. (2007), 'Translocal Subjectivities: Mobility, Connection, Emotion', *Mobilities* 2:2, 167–74.

Csordas, T. (1990), 'Embodiment as a Paradigm for Anthropology', *Ethos* 18:1, 5–47.

Darby, J. (1986), *Intimidation and the Control of Conflict in Northern Ireland* (Dublin: Gill and Macmillan).

Darby, J. (1990), 'Intimidation and Interaction in a Small Belfast Community: The Water and the Fish', in Darby et al. (eds).

Darby, J., Dodge, N. and Hepburn, A.C. (eds) (1990), *Political Violence: Ireland in a Comparative Perspective* (Belfast: Appletree Press).

Doherty, P. and Poole, M. (1995), *Ethnic Residential Segregation in Belfast* (Coleraine: University of Ulster, Centre for the Study of Conflict).

Dunn, S. (ed.) (1994), *Managing Divided Cities* (Keele: Keele University Press).

Hainsworth, P. 'Cause for Concern: Racism in Northern Ireland', <http://www.thevacuum.org.uk/issues/issues0120/issues05/is05artcaucon.html>, accessed 12 May 2008.

Hatfield, E., Cacioppo, J.T. and Rapson, R.L. (1994), *Emotional Contagion: Studies in Emotion and Social Interaction* (Cambridge: Cambridge University Press).

Irwin, G. and Dunn, S. (1997), *Ethnic Minorities in Northern Ireland* (Coleraine: University of Ulster, Centre for the Study of Conflict).

Jarman, N. (1997), *Material Conflicts: Parades and Visual Displays in Northern Ireland* (Oxford: Berg).

Jarman, N. (1999), *Displaying Faith: Orange, Green and Trade Union Banners in Northern Ireland* (Belfast: Institute of Irish Studies, Queens University Belfast).

Kamppfner, J. (2006), 'Divided in Peace', *New Statesman* 20 November.

Kliot, N. and Waterman, S. (eds) (1983), *Pluralism and Political Geography: People, Territory and State* (London: Croom Helm).

Lanegrin, D. and Palm, R. (eds) (1978), *An Invitation to Geography* (New York, NY: McGraw-Hill).

Leavitt, J. (1996), 'Meaning and Feeling in the Anthropology of Emotions', *American Ethnologist* 23:3, 514–39.

Leys, R. (2000), *Trauma: A Genealogy* (Chicago: University of Chicago Press).

Lock, M. (1993), 'Cultivating the Body: Anthropology and Epistemologies of Bodily Practice and Knowledge', *Annual Review of Anthropology* 22, 133–55.

Lutz, C. (1988), *Unnatural Emotions: Everyday Sentiments on a Micronesian Atoll and Their Challenge to Western Theory* (Chicago: University of Chicago Press).

Lutz, C. and Abu-Lughod, L. (eds) (1990), *Language and the Politics of Emotion* (Cambridge: Cambridge University Press).

Lutz, C. and White, G. (1986), 'The Anthropology of Emotions', *Annual Review of Anthropology* 15, 405–36.

Lyon, M. (1995), 'Missing Emotion: The Limitations of Cultural Constructionism in the Study of Emotion', *Cultural Anthropology* 10:2, 244–63.

Lysaght, K. (2002), 'Dangerous Friends and Deadly Foes: Performances of Masculinity in the Divided City', *Irish Geography* 35, 51–62.

Lysaght, K. (2005), '"Catholics, Protestants and Office Workers from the Town": The Negotiation of Fear in Northern Ireland', in Milton and Svašek (eds).

Lysaght, K. and Basten, A. (2002), 'Violence, Fear and the Everyday: Negotiating Spatial Practice in the City of Belfast', in Stanko (ed.).

Milton, K. and Svašek, M (eds) (2005), *Mixed Emotions: Anthropological Studies of Feeling* (Oxford: Berg).

Murtagh, B. (ed.) (1993), *Planning and Ethnic Space in Belfast* (Belfast: University of Ulster Centre for Policy Research).

Overing, J and Passes, A. (eds) (2000), *The Anthropology of Love and Anger: The Aesthetics of Conviviality in Native Amazonia* (London: Routledge).

Parkinson, B. (1995), *Ideas and Realities of Emotion* (Routledge: London).

Poole, M. and Doherty, P. (1996), *Ethnic Residential Segregation in Northern Ireland* (Coleraine: University of Ulster, Centre for the Study of Conflict).

Skrbiš, Z. (2008), 'Transnational Families: Theorising Migration, Emotions and Belonging', *Journal of Intercultural Studies* 29:3, 231–46.

Stanko, E. (ed.) (2002), *The Meanings of Violence* (London: Routledge).

Svašek, M. (ed.) (2008), 'Transnational Families: Emotions and Belonging', *Journal of Intercultural Studies* 29:3.

Svašek, M. (forthcoming), 'On the Move: Emotions and Human Mobility', *Journal of Ethnic and Migration Studies*.

Svašek, M. and Skrbiš, Z. (2007), 'Passions and Powers: Emotions and Globalisation', *Identities* 14:4, 367–83.

Tonkin, E. (1992), *Constructing Our Pasts: The Social Construction of Oral History* (Cambridge: Cambridge University Press).

Wise, A. (forthcoming), 'Sensuous Multiculturalism: Emotional Landscapes of Interethnic Living in Australian Suburbia', *Journal of Ethnic and Migration Studies*.

Chapter 7

Recent Polish Migrants in London: Accessing and Participating in Social Networks across Borders

Louise Ryan, Rosemary Sales and Mary Tilki

Over the last 20 years there has been growing interest in the role of social networks in facilitating migration as well as in the transnational networks that are fostered and maintained post-migration (Gurak and Caces 1992; Faist and Ozveren 2004). Networks are increasingly seen as crucial to understanding patterns of migration, settlement, employment and links with 'home' (Boyd 1989; Castles and Miller 2003). As Gurak and Caces (1992: 151) argue: 'Networks link populations in sending and receiving societies in a dynamic manner. They serve as mechanisms for interpreting data and feeding information and other resources in both directions'. Thus the process of network building depends on and in turn reinforces relationships across space, linking migrants and non-migrants (Boyd 1989). These relationships and contacts may influence decisions to migrate, provide money to finance moves and, after migration, provide accommodation, jobs, information and emotional support (Boyd 1989: 651). Networks may also be a key element in facilitating community formation and permanent settlement (Portes 1995).

This chapter focuses on recent Polish migrants to London, drawing on a one-year study which examined their migratory experiences and networking strategies.[1] Since EU enlargement in May 2004, official statistics suggest that Eastern European migrants have arrived in almost every region of Britain (UK Border and Immigration Agency et al. 2007). Thus, this wave of migration has been more geographically dispersed than all previous waves of migrants which tended to be concentrated in particular regions or cities (Pollard et al. 2008). Nonetheless, despite the dispersion of recent migrants, the highest number of applications for National Insurance Numbers (NiNos) has been in London, with the Worker Registration Scheme (WRS) also showing London as a key destination between 2004 and 2007 (UK Border and Immigration Agency et al. 2007). Statistics from NiNos and WRS also indicate that migrants in London are very diverse, including

---

1   Recent Polish Migrants in London: Networks, Transience and Settlement, funded by the Economic and Social Research Council (RES-000-22-1552). The grant holders were Louise Ryan, Rosemary Sales and Mary Tilki. Bernadetta Siara was the Research Fellow on the study.

a wide range of different types of occupations and professions. Using purposive sampling our study aimed to include this diversity of backgrounds and experiences within London.

There has been a long history of Polish migration to the capital and areas such as Hammersmith and Ealing, in West London, have been associated with Polish communities since the end of the Second World War. The previous generation of migrants established Polish churches, clubs and community organizations, but, as we discuss later in this chapter, the relationships between these formal networks and the newly arrived Polish migrants are complex and shifting. It is also apparent that recent migrants are not simply congregating within areas traditionally associated with the Polish community. Official statistics suggest that newly arrived Poles are spread across all London boroughs, making up significant proportions of the overall population in areas such as Westminster (5.5 per cent) and Camden (2.8 per cent) (Pollard et al. 2008).[2]

Our study was primarily qualitative, using interviews and focus groups with recent migrants as well as interviews with key informants with knowledge of the Polish community and recent migration patterns. A total of 46 recent migrants took part in three focus groups and individual interviews. The 30 individual interviewees were split equally between the sexes but the focus groups were largely female. The majority of respondents were aged between 21 and 39, with approximately 20 per cent aged between 40 and 59. This roughly reflects the age ratio of Polish arrivals in Britain (Kohn 2007). Just over half had children. The majority of these lived with them in London but almost a quarter had children living in Poland. More than a third of participants were working in professional occupations in London with the remaining two thirds either in manual jobs or not in employment, mainly due to caring responsibilities. A higher proportion had had professional jobs in Poland, suggesting some deskilling.

The chapter explores the different ways in which participants access, use, form and maintain networks.[3] We begin by discussing, in more detail, different types of networks and their role in migration and settlement. We then examine firstly, the role of pre-migration networks in encouraging and facilitating the migration process through, for example, assistance with employment and accommodation; secondly, the dynamism and make-up of networks in the post-migration period, for example the extent to which networks may gradually extend through new friendships and weak ties; thirdly, migrants' involvement with transnational networks and their changing relationships and roles over time. Finally, we consider some of the limitations and constraints of migrants' social networks.

---

2   In areas traditionally associated with Polish communities, new migrants made up slightly smaller proportions of the overall population – Hammersmith and Fulham (2.0 per cent) and Ealing (1.5 per cent). Other London boroughs with significant numbers of new Polish migrants included Kensington and Chelsea (1.4 per cent) and Southwark (1.3 per cent) (see Pollard et al. 2008).
3   For a fuller discussion of social networks and social capital see Ryan et al. 2008.

Conceptualizing Social Networks

The analysis of social networks is a cross-disciplinary field involving, for example, sociology, geography, economics, cultural and political studies (Mailfret 2007) and they have been studied at a variety of different levels and analysed according to their size, depth, strength and longevity (Willmott 1987). Rather than consisting of one clearly defined theoretical and methodological approach, network analysis has been described as 'a loose federation of approaches' (Emirbayer and Goodwin cited in Vertovec 2001: 7) ranging from descriptive to highly technical analyses which rely on complex computer packages to detect and measure network formats (see for example, Degenne and Forse 1999; Scott 2000). The latter may not necessarily be useful when studying how networks perform in practice and the richness of social relationships that underpin them. Morgan (1990) has suggested that a structural analysis of networks needs to be supplemented by studying social support and personal relationships to enable a more meaningful understanding of how varied forms of support are given and received, an area to which migration researchers have made important contributions.

Migration studies have, however, been criticized (see for example Wierzbicki 2004) for using the concept of 'network' in loose ways which may deprive it of real meaning. Writing in the early 1990s, Gurak and Caces argued that there had been little cross citation between work done by sociologists on network analysis and migration scholars researching migrant networks. They strongly urged migration researchers to engage with sociological analyses of networks and to use concepts such as 'strength of ties' (Granovetter 1973) and the 'spatially dispersed' nature of networks (Wellman 1988) in the study of migrant networks (Gurak and Caces 1992, 160). It is also important to consider the dynamism of social networks and the tensions and fractures that may occur in networks of friends and acquaintances over the lifecourse (Cochan et al. 1990). Nonetheless, a decade later, Vertovec (2001) highlighted continuing weaknesses in the ways migration scholars use the concept of networks. He argued that while one can study networks without resorting to mathematical equations, researchers of migration would be well advised to take note of some of the specific concepts and terms in social networks analysis. Analysing the durability, intensity, multiplexity, frequency and density is especially useful in providing a deeper understanding how migrants' networks function and change over time (Vertovec 2001).

It is useful to distinguish between the different types and levels of social support that networks may provide (Morgan 1990). Schaefer et al. (cited in Oakley 1992) differentiated between emotional, informational and instrumental (or practical) support. We would also add companionship and socializing (Ryan et al. 2008). These different types of support may be provided by different people in varied ways and at different times. For example, emotional support in combating homesickness and loneliness involves a good deal of trust and empathy. This support may come from close friends and relatives or a partner including those living outside one's immediate environment (Granovetter 1973) as regular communication is maintained through, for example, telephone conversations (Wellman 1988). In this way, transnational links with people 'back home' may continue to play a supportive role for migrants. Information, such as how and where to register with a doctor or which is the best school in the area, may be sought from different sources such as work colleagues or neighbours who are more familiar with the local environment (Coleman 1990: 310). Thus, informational support may be provided by transient acquaintances, or 'weak ties', who have the necessary knowledge and know-how but are outside one's intimate social circle (Granovetter 1973). Practical support such as accommodation or financial assistance may be provided by a combination of kinship and friendship networks. Companionship and socializing may involve varying combinations of casual, transient and long-established relationships (Ryan et al. 2008).

As Wierzbicki (2004) has argued, migration researchers often take for granted that migrants arrive and simply slot into networks that provide them with jobs, housing and emotional support, or as Gurak and Caces (1992: 152) suggest, researchers 'tend to treat networks as sets of kin (and sometimes friends) who are always present in migrations'. Because of the loose ways in which networks are conceptualized insufficient attention has been paid to how migrants access existing networks or establish new ties in the 'host' society. For example, the same, small group of trusted friends and relations may provide all these different forms of practical and emotional support. Such a tight network, which Portes (1999) terms 'multiplex', may represent strong, dense and enduring relationships but may equally indicate a lack of weak ties and an over-reliance on a small, 'closed' network (Coleman 1990). The existence of a circle of friends and relatives does not in itself mean that appropriate support is always available or forthcoming (Gottlieb 1981). For example, friends may not have the material resources to provide the kind of support that migrants require. In addition, it is important to consider the dynamic nature of networks since the networks that migrants encounter when they first arrive are unlikely to remain static, especially if migrants experience social and geographical mobility within the 'host' society (Ryan 2007; Ryan et al. 2008).

The Role of Pre-migration Networks

The stories told by our participants of practical assistance received from friends already in London reflect the descriptions in other research (Jordan and Duvell 2003). The experience of Kasia and Marek was typical of many for whom migration was facilitated by networks already established in Britain.[4]

> When I came for the first time, I had two friends here, who had come a month earlier and ... they reserved a room for me. (Kasia, aged 26)

---

4   We would like to thank all the people who took part in this study. The names of all participants have been changed.

I wouldn't have come here without knowing what to expect. I had friends here who organized my accommodation and work … So everything was arranged. (Marek aged 30)

While Polish friends were an important source of information and practical assistance for newly arrived migrants, over time participants often developed new relationships and found alternative sources of information and support. Kasia had remained within her close-knit group of Polish friends but was aware of the limitations this placed on her: 'That's why I can't learn English and it is upsetting me … I have the feeling that I am not learning anything and it's disappointing. I only spend time with Poles'. Her experiences can be interpreted in terms of high levels of 'bonding' but low levels of 'bridging'. Bonding involves the process of establishing ties with people similar to oneself in some important way, for example people of the same nationality, language group or ethnic background, while bridging involves ties with people who are different from oneself (Putnam 2007). Marek, on the other hand, migrated into a ready-made circle of Polish friends in London but became frustrated and deliberately sought to establish networks with a wider range of people: 'The people I was surrounded by didn't have a clue about anything'. In order to improve his language skills and get a better understanding of London, he moved into a flat with a group of Australians: 'I realized that if I kept on living with Poles, I would never learn the language'. Mikolaj (aged 25) also described how he had 'lived only with Poles, I only rented accommodation with Poles. Certainly it made me feel safer'. But after living in London for more than a year, he now feels more confident, better able to cope and less reliant on his exclusively Polish flat mates and he said: 'Now there's no problem, I can live with anyone'.

Many other respondents migrated through family networks and for most this was an initial stepping stone. Bozena came with her husband and young child. Neither she nor her husband spoke any English and their migration process was eased considerably by her sister who provided accommodation and helped Bozena's husband to find temporary work in the construction industry. After six months he found a permanent job in London and the family moved to a flat of their own, becoming less reliant on relatives. Through her daughter's school, Bozena has made new friends with other mothers. She said 'they have children like me, so we have something in common'. Thus in addition to her close-knit family network, Bozena began to establish new local friendships. She now attends English classes at a local college in South London and is keen to improve her language proficiency. Her story suggests the dynamism of social networks over time as well as the variety and complexity of network formation. She maintained strong kinship ties with her sister, but the level of dependency appeared to diminish over time as she and her husband became more confident about living in London. Her new ties were important in creating a sense of familiarity and attachment to the neighbourhood, as well as providing a way into local, mainly school-based, networks.

While Bozena was able to establish new friendships, others remained reliant on dense family networks. As Kelly and Lusis (2006) suggest, this may reflect migrants' lack of other social resources. Bernard, who is 48, migrated to London for what he called 'family-related' reasons. Following the break-up of his marriage in Poland, he decided to join his two sons who were working in London. He now lives with his younger son and works in the building firm owned by his elder son. Thus, Bernard has a strong family network in London which may be described as multiplex. He receives a range of different support from the same, small group of people, including accommodation and employment but also emotional support. In addition, as he does not speak much English, he is reliant on his sons for information. Although he has lived in London for over two years, he has limited contact with people outside of his close-knit family network and has not managed to establish any new friendships or get to know his neighbours. Most of his leisure time is spent with his son's family. His situation suggests 'network closure' (Coleman 1990). Although he feels 'alienated' from British society, Bernard is planning to stay in London for some time, 'maybe even permanently'.

The existence of a family network does not necessarily mean that support is forthcoming. Friends and relatives may encourage or facilitate migration but provide limited support once the new migrant arrives. Aneta (aged 21) decided to come to London because she had two sisters already living in the city. Both sisters were married and their own family responsibilities meant they provided little in the way of practical or emotional support to Aneta. 'I visit my sisters [but] they don't help. They said "if you want to come, but we won't be helping you"'. Through a casual acquaintance, also Polish, Aneta found out about job vacancies at a hotel in south London and quickly established a circle of friends with whom she now socializes. Her experience not only reveals that familial support cannot be taken for granted, but also suggests the importance of transient acquaintances, or 'weak ties'. These were important to many of our respondents in finding employment and accommodation and other practical information. They may also provide more general information about the wider society and thus help migrants to reach out beyond their immediate network of family and close friends (Williams 2006).

The transient contacts described above may be regarded as horizontal linkages, since they involve other migrants who occupy similar social locations (see Ryan et al. 2008). It may be particularly difficult for newly arrived migrants to establish weak ties vertically and this ability to extend one's networks may be related to other factors such as age, language and family circumstances. We return to this point below.

Arriving Without Networks

While many of the people we interviewed migrated through family and friendship networks benefiting from practical and informational support upon arrival, this was not the case for everyone. Some had arranged jobs through agencies before arriving in London. Agnieszka and Ewa, both professionals, secured their posts and accommodation before leaving Poland:

> I came to Great Britain feeling 100 per cent secured because I had found a job in Poland. The interview took place in Poland, I knew I was going to have accommodation guaranteed for three months. Maybe that's why I chose this job, because it was easy to come here. (Agnieszka, a graduate aged 31)

The absence of a network of friends and relatives waiting to welcome them was not problematic for these young professionals and both quickly made friends through their work. For others, however, the lack of networks in London was more problematic. Several respondents spoke about arriving in London, usually at Victoria coach station, without any pre-arranged accommodation or employment and without contacts or networks. Tomek, aged 33, reflected back on when he had first arrived in London a few years previously. He had travelled by bus with a friend:

> I came without any idea of what to expect, not knowing anyone here. We spent a few hours at the station, then we met some Poles. They helped us to organize accommodation, which was the most important thing. (Tomek)

It was not just younger people who arrived in this way. Malgorzata at 57 one of the oldest of our interviewees, arrived with her adult daughter in 2002. As this was prior to Polish accession to the EU, they were not allowed to work legally and came on tourist visas:

> It was four years ago. And the coach left for Poland and we stayed with our travel bags on the pavement. We didn't have accommodation, we had money but no accommodation and we stood with these bags ... It was really stupid because the evening was coming and we didn't have a place to stay ... my daughter didn't speak English either, only 'goodbye' and 'sorry'. (Malgorzata)

In a shop window the women saw advertisements in Polish for cleaners. They phoned one of the telephone numbers and spoke to a man who agreed to collect them from the station and drive them to his house. Despite the obvious risks involved, Malgorzata and her daughter were exhausted and decided to take a chance with this stranger. Perhaps they felt safer because they were two women together. The man made them tea while they cleaned his house. He also helped them to find accommodation for the night. Shortly afterwards both women found jobs as cleaners in a hotel. Having lived in London for several years, Malgorzata had expanded her circle of friends and said she has plenty of people with whom she can socialize. She had also been joined by another daughter. However, language remained her greatest problem and prevented her from making contacts with English-speaking people. She remained within ethnically-specific but spatially dispersed networks and avoided contact with non-Poles. Her situation was far from unique.

Hanna (aged 48) also had no pre-existing networks upon arrival and spoke no English. Like Tomek and Malgorzata, she migrated before 2004, working initially as an undocumented migrant. Hanna's early experiences in London reveal the vulnerability of her position, her susceptibility to exploitation and her dependence on exclusively Polish networks. They also highlight the usefulness of transient acquaintances. She said: 'Poles helped me to stand on my own two feet'. Through these Polish contacts she got a series of 'illegal' jobs one of which was in a factory: 'I worked there for four months … £2.50 an hour, 12 hours a day or 12 hours a night with a half hour break, the conditions were terrible, a nightmare'.

Eventually things did improve for Hanna. EU accession gave her the opportunity to regularize her migration status and to take up legal employment thus considerably improving her pay and working conditions. Her new status also enabled her to facilitate the migration of her two daughters who have recently joined her in London. Hanna's story illustrates high levels of bonding within her networks. She received considerable emotional support and practical assistance from friends and acquaintances but these were usually other migrants who occupied a similar social position. Her location within a dense but disadvantaged community of migrants may be regarded as providing important support but did not improve her access to better economic opportunities through engaging in bridging beyond her specific social network.

The vulnerability of those migrants who arrive without either clear plans or reliable networks was clearly illustrated in the story of Jacek, a 25-year-old chef. Initially Jacek had not intended to migrate but he was persuaded by a neighbour, recently returned from Britain. 'I would not have gone but he convinced me that there is so much work abroad, and it is easy to get work'. This returnee gave Jacek some addresses of other Poles to contact in Britain. Thus, when Jacek arrived in Britain in 2002, accompanied by another friend, Adam, he had no firm job offers or accommodation arrangements but instead was reliant on contacts he had never met – 'friends of a friend'. Jacek and Adam travelled to a seaside town where the contacts were supposed to find them work in a hotel. However, there was no job and no accommodation so the two men ended up sleeping on the beach:

> And we slept the second night on the beach, but it was warm, so it was OK and then came the third day, it was the same situation I didn't know what to do. (Jacek)

Jacek then contacted another friend who was working on a farm in the Midlands and he encouraged Jacek and Adam to join him. For three months they worked long shifts packing vegetables and slept in caravans on site. During this time tensions grew between Jacek and Adam and the latter returned to Poland. Once again Jacek used his network of acquaintances and old friends to facilitate his search for a better job and improved lifestyle. He managed to find the telephone number of someone he had known in primary school, but not seen for years, who lived in London. The man promised to help Jacek find accommodation in London.

> He picked me up from Victoria station, we went to Battersea to the flat, we talked for two or three hours then he left. He had brought me a small radio and alarm clock. He also gave me an A–Z map of the city and that was it. I was on my own in a strange city. (Jacek)

Since that time, Jacek has hardly seen this old schoolmate although they both continue to live in south London. Like Hanna, Jacek has shown remarkable resilience given all the setbacks he encountered and has managed to find himself work in London. But Jacek's story also reveals that networks can be unreliable and fleeting. Networks may be a source of emotional support but friendships, such as between Jacek and Adam, can come under strain especially in stressful situations. Weak ties and casual acquaintanceships may be very useful, such as the contact from primary school, but they may also be temporary, not providing any ongoing support. Thus, rather than taking migrants' networks for granted, it is important to examine not only the diversity of roles and resources and their usefulness and reliability but also the dynamics of relationships over time.

Extending Networks

Gurak and Caces (1992: 165) suggest that 'While most networks may originate as tightly knit kin networks, the underlying needs for diverse resources (aid with legal systems, better employment, improved housing, schooling options etc.) should predispose migrants to open up their networks and involve specialized elements in them'. The migration strategies of the professionals in this study were often markedly different from those of other migrants, and involved developing contacts with other groups rather than maintaining exclusive ethnic networks. They tended to develop both professional and personal relations with a wider group of people, including both Poles and non-Poles. Some had pre-existing contacts with British professional networks. Czeslaw, a 44-year-old doctor, came to Britain to pursue further training. He spoke fluent English and had contact with several British professionals within his specialist area of medicine who advised him to come to London. Czeslaw is aware that he had a relatively easy migration experience:

> I have to say that I had a soft landing here. I had friends, I had people who helped me from the very beginning ... there were no problems. ... When I didn't know something, I had somebody to ask. (Czeslaw)

His experiences provide an example of 'bridging' social networks as he was able to access people within his profession who could assist him. He has made several friends since coming to London: 'various nationalities, mostly British, of various origins ... I don't have many social contacts with Poles ... maybe with two people in similar professions'. His social networks are shaped by employment and the contacts he forms at work rather than specifically ethnic or migrant circles.

Ewa (aged 30) had no networks upon arrival in London but she quickly made friends with her co-workers. She spoke fluent English and enjoyed establishing friendships with people from a variety of backgrounds. Although Ewa describes herself as a religious person and regularly attends mass at a Polish church, she is not actively involved in Polish organizations in London. She says that she does not need to rely on Polish groups because she has the skills to find her own way in British society. That is not to imply that she is disconnected from other Polish people. She has facilitated the migration of several close friends from Poland to London. Her circle of friends in London now includes newly formed relationships with non-Poles as well as enduring friends from Poland.

Amelia arrived in London in the early stages of her first pregnancy, having migrated primarily to join her husband. She recalled: 'When I was pregnant it was a terrible time ... I didn't have any friends, my family was not here'. At that time Amelia's transnational networks with family in Poland proved particularly important. Her father had retired and was able to visit for extended periods to help look after the baby, while Amelia started her degree at a London university. Because she spoke fluent English and had access to a wide range of people through university, Amelia was able to establish quite diverse networks. As the mother of a small baby, she also had opportunities to create new friendships through local mother and baby groups. She has built up a network of practical support, especially around reciprocal childcare:

> My neighbour from Holland has the telephone number of the nursery. If something comes up she will go and collect Jan if they cannot get hold of me. My friend Anna, the Polish one, would help with collecting Michal from school, sometimes I help her ... Mary [an English woman] is another one I sometimes use, but not very often because she has four young children of her own. I think in the case of Mary it is me who helps her a lot. (Amelia)

As Ryan (2007) suggests, having children seems to enable migrant women to access particular types of localized networks for example, through play groups or schools. This allowed Amelia's networks to shift from almost exclusively transnational (her parents) to predominantly localized (friends and neighbours). While Amelia and Bozena both made new locally-based friends through their children, this was not the case for everyone. Marzena and her husband have found it difficult to establish friendships in their neighbourhood although they have lived in London for several years, both speak English and regard themselves as sociable people:

> Well, I don't want to make English people sound unfriendly. They are just a bit more distant. I mean, I have been living now in the same apartment for three

years and I have got neighbours in the same building but apart from occasionally saying 'hello', exchanging pleasantries, you know, there is no such a thing as inviting each other into our homes. Wherever I have lived in London people just stick to themselves. (Marzena)

She contrasts this with her experience in Italy prior to migrating to Britain where 'we were constantly guests of our neighbours, and they were in our place, organizing lunches and dinners together and barbecues'. Marzena's difficulties in establishing local contacts may be partly because she has no children and therefore does not participate in networks around school and childcare. By contrast, she has made friends with people of varied nationalities through the large office where she works as an administrator.

Several other participants socialized with people at work and the type of employment and of co-workers was crucial in shaping these social networks. People who worked predominantly with other Poles may have limited opportunities to establish new friendships with non-Poles. Tomek, for example, has lived in London for over five years but says that all his friends are Polish. The workforce of the building firm where he works is almost entirely Polish. In addition, he spends a good deal of his spare time on his hobby, a biker club, which also involves an almost exclusively Polish group:

I have a lot of friends ... there is a pub by the North Circular which many Poles come to because it's a bikers' pub, people usually come there on motorbikes. I also have a motorbike, I meet my friends who have motorbikes and we have a good time there. (Tomek)

Thus while this kind of leisure activity provided an opportunity to broaden his social circle, it appears to have reinforced his entirely Polish social networks. Tomek's wife and sister also live in London thus he also has a strong kinship network. It would be inaccurate to describe his social networks as 'closed' since he has been able to establish new friendships through work and the biker club, but Tomek's social location, job, hobby and kinship networks appear to provide little opportunity to meet people other than Poles and he seems to feel no need to seek out non-Polish friends.

Transnational Networks

Both Coleman (1990) and Putnam (2000; 2007) regard mobility as a key barrier to accessing and maintaining social networks. As Putnam notes, it takes time for a mobile person 'to put down roots' (2000: 204). Coleman argues that 'individual mobility' is potentially destructive of social capital (1990: 320). By contrast, it is the dynamism and dispersal of networks that is particularly relevant to the study of migrants' social ties. Far from being reified or static, networks are often fluid, changing as the needs, circumstances and expectations of the participants alter and develop over time (Morgan 1990). Rather than being rooted in specific local formations, such as neighbourhoods, migrant networks may be dispersed over a wide geographical area, including transnational ties (Portes 1995).

Our respondents used text messages, cheap phone calls and e-mail to maintain contact with home. Aneta's comment was fairly typical: 'I call Poland constantly because calls are cheap'. Like several of our respondents, Aneta said that her closest emotional support came from her best friend in Poland. 'I try to call her at least once a week. I need to talk and she is the first person I call'. Many respondents phoned close relatives in Poland at least once a week, but daily phone calls were not unusual. Darek's wife, who still lives in Poland, is his main source of emotional support although his daughters who live in London provide a great deal of practical support. He phones his wife every evening using a cheap phone card, often talking for several hours. Contact with parents, especially mothers, in Poland was also very important. Marzena said: 'I phone my mother every day, even if it's just for a few minutes'. For Marek, although he has made many friends in London, his mother in Poland is still his primary source of advice and support: 'Certainly the person who can advise me is my mum, who I trust, and I can ask her about everything'. In terms of network analysis, mothers or best friends in Poland may acts as 'lynchpins' (Williams, 2006) connecting different people within a larger network. Through passing on news, gossip, information, a lynchpin can help to keep people up to date with what is going on across the network.

In spite of the importance of these transnational sources of emotional support or advice, one cannot underestimate the significance of proximity in relation to practical, hands-on support and assistance (Wellman 1979; Oakley 1992; Ryan 2007). Childcare, for example, cannot be done at a distance, and as well as relying on local networks, many respondents described how relatives, usually parents, came to London on extended trips to help look after children. Since Iza's (aged 25) baby was born in London she has relied on support from Poland for help with childcare: 'Firstly, my mother-in-law came when the baby was a month old and she stayed for six months and then I asked my mum if she could come … and Mum stayed'. Iza and her husband, Staszek, present an interesting example of the ways in which transnational attachments may shift over time. In addition to Iza's mother, other relatives have also migrated to London during the last three to four years. Staszek set up his own building firm and encouraged his brother and father to come and work with him. Iza's sister and several cousins also moved in London. Thus, the extended family, including three generations, has been reconstituted through migration. This process of family reunion has impacted on transnational ties. Iza and Staszek rarely visit Poland and have no immediate plans to return.

Transnational networks not only facilitate migration but may also encourage and enable return. Conradson and Latham (2005) in a study of migrants from New Zealand living in London, show that the maintenance of transnational networks can reinforce the temporary nature of migration. They go on to argue that researchers need to take a longer term perspective and study the composition and dynamism of networks over time: 'we need a much stronger sense of the durability and forms of interaction that comprise the networks through which global mobility takes place' (2005: 301). Transnational networks and ties to the home base 'change once larger migrant communities are established abroad' (Wallace 2002: 617). As has been argued elsewhere (Ryan 2007; Ryan et al. 2008), the reliance on transnational networks may diminish when local sources of support have been established. For Amelia, her sources of local support around childcare are gradually replacing her reliance on transnational kinship networks. Thus, the relationship between local and transnational networks is complex and shifting.

'Poles Don't Help Each Other'

Despite the high levels of practical, information and emotional support that many respondents received from Polish friends and relatives, the idea that Poles do not help each other was a recurring theme in many interviews. Several respondents said that Poles may deliberately compete and undermine each other. Marysia said that many Poles were reluctant to pass on information about their employment 'because they are afraid that you will take up their place'. Competition between Poles for employment was a theme running through many of our interviews. Bozena, for example, stated that while she and her family were away on holiday, her husband was cheated out of his job in London by another Polish man. Several respondents mentioned the issue of jealousy among Poles. Marzena said: 'Complaining and jealousy are our worst features. If you are happy, [they ask] why are you happy? You shouldn't be happy'. Very similar words were used by Marek: 'Poles are vicious, they can't be happy at someone else's happiness, they don't understand that there is strength in the group'.

In spite of these criticisms, respondents usually emphasized that their own circles of Polish friends and relatives were very supportive and trustworthy, providing practical help and emotional support. This suggests a binary opposition between particular Polish networks and a more general population of Polish migrants who were constructed as unhelpful and even dangerous. This point came out very clearly in Kasia's narrative, as she was careful to differentiate her friends from the general population of new Polish migrants in London: 'If I go out somewhere, it's with Poles and we don't go to typically Polish places. I have never tried these places for Poles, but I have heard a lot of bad things, so it doesn't appeal to me … I have a lot of friends and I don't need to get to know new ones'.

Coleman (1990: 304) discusses at length the importance of trust in social relationships, arguing that 'a group whose members manifest trustworthiness … will be able to accomplish much more than a comparable group lacking that trust'. Migrants, however, have complex relationships with the wider migrant 'community'. Most interact and engage with very specific groups of friends, family and acquaintances and while these may be made up of varying numbers of co-ethnics they are often distinguished from the wider and more generalized ethnic 'community' (Kelly and Lusis 2006). In fact, as researchers of other migrant groups have noted, the wider community may be perceived in negative terms as a source of competition, pressure or even danger (Williams 2006). Our findings that recent Polish migrants tend to regard the wider Polish 'community' with wariness and suspicion are supported by another study of this group (Eade et al. 2006).

These observations highlight potential tensions within migrant communities. Migrants who are reliant on community networks may be particularly exposed to competition, rivalry and jealousy. Indeed, research suggests that migrants who maintain strong ties only with groups of co-ethnics may be socially disadvantaged (Wierzbicki 2004) and immersion in ethnic specific networks may also be associated with a lack of resources and can foster dependency and ghettoization (Griffiths et al. 2005). As Kelly and Lusis (2006, 842) argue, 'although migration studies often celebrate the use of networks in the integration of new immigrants, this utilization should perhaps more accurately be interpreted as an indication of how comparatively bereft of social contacts, and the value they provide, immigrants really are'. This point was made by Czeslaw, who, although a medical professional and able to operate independently of Polish networks, made some interesting observations on how these networks may operate: 'there are many alienated people ... they stay in a ghetto, don't have any contacts with non-Poles ... one speaks English a bit, so he deals with everything, and the rest completely depends on him' (Czeslaw). He added that this dependency on other Poles could also result in frustration and disappointment. Relying on other Poles for employment, accommodation, communication and information can lead to unrealistic expectations as well as competition and rivalry. Our study suggests that the Poles who were most dependent on these types of networks were also the most critical of their fellow Poles.

We also found evidence of wariness in relation to the formal Polish networks which had generally been established by earlier generations of Polish migrants. The new migrants tended to use these networks for instrumental reasons rather than being actively involved or forming deeper connections. They thus remained 'weak ties' which provided access to certain forms of support. Many participants attended Polish churches for example, seeking information, practical and social support as well as for religious reasons. One participant in a focus group described how she sought help from this source:

> When I went ... I needed a form from the priest that we are Catholics to enroll my daughter at school. I started talking to him and he told me ... that he would have a job for me. If I wanted, he could help me look for a job. (Basia)

Several also sent their children to Polish Saturday Schools and some attended a mother and toddler group within an established community centre. Few, however, had any social or family ties to the older generation of migrants. As one Parish priest put it:

> We can talk about unity under the roof of the Church, where people gather and
> pray together and the church is probably a very important element of integration
> for these various groups. But outside one can't talk about unity. (Key informant)

We also interviewed people who had little connection with any Polish organizations
or groups. Some respondents saw the older generation of migrants, and the
organizations they had founded, as closed to them and not relevant to their needs
or situation. Most of our participants remained detached from, and wary of, such
organizations. As one participant put it:

> The old Polonia, who don't go to Poland, who don't have contacts with people
> who have problem … they have no idea, they are not sympathetic to Poles. They
> are afraid of these Poles that they may rob them, they will cheat them … they don't
> trust them at all. They want to show that they are somebody in this country. …
> (Hanna)

Older migrants, for their part, had ambivalent attitudes to the new migrants. Their
motives for migration and their attachment to Poland had been very different.
Furthermore, while welcoming new members of the community as providing a
new lease of life to the old Churches and other institutions, they may also resent
people who they saw as using the services without having provided the labour
needed to set them up and run them. As one older established migrant put it:

> They worked really hard to establish all those organizations, societies, schools,
> parishes, parish buildings, clubs, whatever. We didn't get any support from the
> British government, it was all our own sweat and blood. Now these young people
> come over and think they are entitled to it. Of course they are. It's what it's here
> for, but on the principle: give and take. You can't just take, take, take and expect
> my generation to go on giving. (Female key informant)

There is evidence of the development of some new organizations which reflect the
needs of the new migrants, while some older organizations are attempting to adapt
to the needs and opportunities posed by the new wave of migration.

Conclusion

Our research suggests the importance of a social networks perspective, combined
with analysis of social support (Morgan 1990), in understanding the experiences
and strategies of migrants as they negotiate their way in a new society. Access to
and participation in social networks in the 'host' country cannot simply be assumed
or taken for granted and we argue that there is a need for detailed examination of
how migrants actually access, establish and maintain networks. In particular it is
necessary to consider the factors that may facilitate or hinder access to networks,

the different types and levels of support that may be available from a range of networks and the diverse, dynamic and dispersed nature of the networks both temporally and spatially.

We have explored here the varied ways in which recent Polish migrants may access and participate in different types of networks at different times and in different locations. It is important to avoid generalizations about migrants networking strategies and opportunities. Our study included migrants from a range of occupations and educational backgrounds as well as different ages and family situations. Their various strategies reflected the difference in the opportunities and obstacles they faced. Language emerged as a crucial factor affecting their ability to extend and develop networks. While those with poor English language skills may receive a great deal of practical and emotional support from tight-knit groups of relatives and friends, such networks may lock them into specific sectors of employment that are already oversubscribed by migrants, thus exacerbating competition and jealousy.

While we have not attempted a specifically gendered analysis of network formation and participation here, some differences between men and women were clearly apparent. For those with young children, mothers were more likely than fathers to talk about networks in terms of their children, reflecting similar findings by Salaff and Greve (2004) and Ryan (2007). Many mothers described how they had accessed new networks through playgroups and schools and the ways in which childcare impacted on their use of social networks. These often necessitated quite complex reciprocal childcare arrangements with other mothers in the local area or by bringing relatives from Poland to help look after children. By contrast, men tended to form new networks through work (as did those women who were in employment) and through leisure activities.

Ties to the 'home base' change with the passage of time (Wallace 2002: 617) and it is apparent that migrants accessed social support through a combination of new and well-established networks involving contacts in both the country of origin and within the new environment. The majority of participants in our study had been in London for less than five years and their networks are still developing and changing. New technology facilitates the continuity of transnational networks and many of our participants maintained close and regular links with Poland. Nonetheless, more localized networks were also used as sources of practical support. It remains to be seen how the balance between transnational and local networks will change over time.

References

Boyd, M. (1989), 'Family and Personal Networks in International Migration', *International Migration Review* 23:3, 638–70.
Castles, S. and Miller, M. (2003), *The Age of Migration: International Population Movements in the Modern World* (Basingstoke: Palgrave).

Cochran, M., Larney, M., Riley, D., Gunnarsson, L. and Henderson Jr., C. (1990), *Extending Families: The Social Networks of Parents and their Children* (Cambridge: Cambridge University Press).

Coleman, J. (1990), *Foundations of Social Theory* (Cambridge, MA: Harvard University Press).

Degenne, A. and Forse, M. (1999), *Introducing Social Networks* (London: Sage).

Duck, S. and Cohen Silver, R. (eds) (1990), *Personal Relationships and Social Support* (London: Sage).

Eade, J., Drinkwater, S. and Garapich, M.P. (2007), *Class and Ethnicity: Polish Migrant Workers in London – Full Research Report*. ESRC End of Award Report, RES-000-22-1294 (Swindon: Economic and Social Research Council).

Faist, T. and Ozveren, E. (eds) (2004), *Transnational Social Spaces: Agents, Networks and Institutions* (Aldershot: Ashgate).

Granovetter, M. (1973), 'The Strength of Weak Ties', *American Journal of Sociology* 78:6, 1360–80.

Griffiths, D., Sigona, N. and Zetter, R. (2005), *Refugee Community Organizations and Dispersal: Networks, Resources and Social Capital* (Bristol: The Policy Press).

Gurak, D. and Caces, F. (1992), 'Migration Networks and the Shaping of Migration Systems', in Kritz et al. (eds).

Jordan, B. and Duvell, F. (2003), *Migration: The Boundaries of Equality and Justice* (Cambridge: Polity).

Kelly, P. and Lusis, T. (2006), 'Migration and the Transnational Habitus: Evidence from Canada and the Phillipines', *Environment and Planning* A 38:5, 831–48.

Kohn, M. (2007), 'A Very Modern Migration: The Polish Presence in Britain', *Catalyst Magazine* <www.catalystmagazine.org>.

Kritz, M.M., Lim, L.L. and Zlotnik, H. (eds) (1992), *International Migration Systems* (Oxford: Clarendon Press).

Mailfret, K. (2007), 'New Farmers and Networks: How Beginning Farmers Build Social Connections in France', *TESG* 98:1, 21–31.

Morgan, D. (1990), 'Combining the Strengths of Social Networks, Social Support and Personal Relationships', in Duck and Cohen Silver (eds).

Oakley, A. (1992), *Social Support and Motherhood* (Oxford: Blackwell).

Pollard, N., Latorre, M. and Sriskandarajah, D. (2008), *Floodgates or Turnstiles? Post-EU Enlargement Migration Flows to (and from) the UK* (London: Institute for Public Policy Research).

Portes, A. (ed.) (1995), *The Economic Sociology of Immigration* (New York, NY: Russell Sage Foundation).

Portes, A., Guarnizo, L.E. and Landolt, P. (1999), 'The Study of Transnationalism: Pitfalls and the Promise of an Emergent Research Field', *Ethnic and Racial Studies* 22:2, 217–37.

Putnam, R. (2000), *Bowling Alone: The Collapse and Revival of American Community* (New York, NY: Simon & Schuster).

Putnam, R. (2007), '"E Pluribus Unum": Diversity and Community in the Twenty-First Century. The 2006 Johan Skytte Prize Lecture', *Scandinavian Political Studies* 30:2, 137–74.

Ryan, L. (2007), 'Migrant Women, Social Networks and Motherhood: The Experiences of Irish Nurses in Britain', *Sociology* 41:2, 295–312.

Ryan, L., Sales, R., Tilki, M. and Siara, B. (2007), *Recent Polish Migrants in London: Social Networks, Transience and Settlement* (London: Social Policy Research Centre, Middlesex University).

Ryan, L., Sales, R., Tilki, M. and Siara, B. (2008), 'Social Networks, Social Support and Social Capital: The Experiences of Recent Polish Migrants in London', *Sociology* 42:4, 672-90.

Salaff, J. and Greve, A. (2004), 'Can Women's Social Networks Migrate?', *Women's Studies International Forum* 27:2, 149–62.

Scott, J. (ed.) (2002), *Social Networks* (New York, NY: Routledge).

UK Border Agency, Department for Work and Pensions, HM Revenue and Customs and Communities and Local Government (2007), Accession Monitoring Report May 2004–December 2007. <http://www.ukba.homeoffice.gov.uk/sitecontent/documents/aboutus/reports/accession_monitoring_report/report14/may04dec07.pdf?view=Binary>, accessed 11 May 2008.

Vertovec, S. (2001), *Transnational Social Formations: Towards Conceptual Cross-fertilisation* (Oxford: WPTC-01-16).

Wallace, C. (2002), 'Opening and Closing Borders: Migration and Mobility in East-Central Europe', *Journal of Ethnic and Migration Studies* 28:4, 603–25.

Wellman, B. (1979), 'The Community Question: The Intimate Networks of East Yorkers', in Scott (ed.).

Wellman, B. (1988), 'Structural Analysis: From Method and Metaphor to Theory and Substance', in Scott (ed.).

Wierzbicki, S. (2004), *Beyond the Immigrant Enclave: Network Change and Assimilation* (New York, NY: LFB Scholarly Publishing).

Williams, L. (2006), 'Social Networks of Refugees in the UK', *Journal of Ethnic and Migration Studies* 32:5, 865–79.

Willmott, P. (1987), *Friendship Networks and Social Support* (London: Policy Studies Institute).

Zontini, E. (2004), 'Immigrant Women in Barcelona: Coping with the Consequences of Transnational Lives', *Journal of Ethnic and Migration Studies* 30:6, 1113–44.

Chapter 8

UK Poles and the Negotiation of Gender and Ethnic Identity in Cyberspace

Bernadetta Siara

This chapter analyses the ways in which Poles who migrated to the United Kingdom after the enlargement of the European Union in 2004 use the Internet as part of their migration experience. The Internet is widely used by these migrants in a variety of forms; many Poles use an array of Internet portals for obtaining practical information related to their lives in the UK. However, Poles also participate in a diverse range of Internet forums which provide them with an opportunity to discuss various matters connected to their experiences in the UK.

This chapter will focus primarily on discussions relating to gender and ethnic identity held by Poles on one specific Internet forum. The decision to research this issue was triggered by my own frequent visits to different forums used by post-accession Poles in the UK. Whilst reading the discussions on the forums, I observed that gender and ethnicity were often an integral part of the debates and I decided to analyse them in more depth. Acknowledging that both gender and ethnicity are socially constructed categories, I adopted social constructionism as a conceptual framework for the analysis and I looked at what type of discourses on gender and ethnicity have been constructed by Poles using one specific Internet forum. The analysis of these discussions shows that this Internet forum may be used not only for creating various discourses on gender and ethnic identity, but also for negotiating gender and ethnic relations between UK Poles.

As some authors claim, gender practices may be negotiated when people migrate and encounter different socio-cultural influences (McIlwaine et al. 2006). The Poles who have migrated to the UK potentially encounter a different approach to gender issues in the UK in comparison to the rather conservative position in Poland. In fact, as this analysis will show, for some Poles gender and ethnicity-related issues seem to be crucial within their wider experiences of migration to the UK, as they grapple with a reconfiguration of their identities within their new multicultural environment. As Polish women in the UK were typically criticized by Polish men participating in the forum, this analysis applies a feminist perspective and focuses on discourses related to gender and ethnicity expressed by *both* Polish women and Polish men participating in the forum.[1]

1　It is important to note that this chapter will consider discourses of heterosexuality only – homosexuality among Polish migrants is a hugely significant issue, with anecdotal

This chapter will address several issues. Firstly, it will consider the current state of gender relations in Poland, so that the significance of gender in the forum discussions can be clearly understood. This is then followed by a description of general Internet usage among Polish migrants, and an explanation of the methodology and approaches used to research the Internet forum, its users and the analysed discussions. Finally, three key themes presented in the forums will be analysed; gender roles (the physical appearance and behaviour of Polish women and men in the UK), the sexuality of Polish women and Polish men in the UK, and inter-ethnic relationships and Poles in the UK.

Gender Relations in Poland

It is important to start with the context of this analysis – gender relations in Poland. Patriarchy is still considered to be the main cultural force concerning gender relations in Poland and as a result, women are expected to fulfil certain gender-specific roles and follow a specific behavioural code (Duch-Krzystoszek 1997; Szarzynska-Lichton 2004; Gontarczyk 1995; Platek 2004). In contemporary Poland, conservatively defined female gender roles are also strongly supported by the Catholic Church (Szarzynska-Lichton 2004; Pankowska 2005; Duch-Krzystoszek 1997). Accordingly, and as described by Fres (2002), women are supposed to focus on the expectations of others rather than themselves, so as to fulfil their roles of wives and mothers rather than pursue their own goals and dreams in life. Fres further argues that specific standards for the behaviour and appearance of women are also dictated by Poland's patriarchal culture. Women are therefore expected to be passive rather than have their own opinions, especially when these opinions are contradictory to those of men. In terms of physical appearance, women are pushed into a system of activities which, according to Korzinska (2003), is a very effective way to control them. As Melosik (2002) maintains, such an approach reinforces the interests of patriarchy as women focus on body-related activities (i.e. dieting, exercising) rather than on other aspects of life.

   This patriarchy, along with the powerful rhetoric of the Catholic Church, also heavily influences attitudes to sex in Polish culture (Hauser et al. 1993). As Graff (2001) claims, in patriarchal cultures rules concerning sexual activities are set by men. Therefore, as a result, male 'sexual promiscuity' is not seen as problematic in the same way that female sexual activity is (Timm and Sanborn 2007). Men in patriarchal cultures are allowed to have sexual desires, but women are not (Abbott et al. 2005). Such a phenomenon is often described as 'double standard morality',

---

evidence suggesting that many gay Poles have left Poland precisely in order to move to a more liberal environment with regard to homosexuality. The discussants on this particular forum, however, do not talk about these matters, although perhaps their exclusive focus on heterosexual relationships does underline the heteronormative nature of contemporary Polish culture.

entitling men to sexual freedoms which are at the same time denied to women, and allowing men to have many sexual partners, but women only a few (Abbott et al. 2005; Hauser et al. 1993). As Lees (1997) has argued, when women do express sexual desires they risk being negatively labelled – according to Melosik (2002), in patriarchal societies men tend to characterize women who engage in sexual activities as 'easy'. At the same time they also identify women who are not sexually active, considering them to be 'suitable' for long-term relationships i.e. 'good candidates for wives and mothers' (Melosik 2002: 55). In patriarchal societies women's sexuality is often talked about, perceived as being integral to their reputation, and such a tactic is used to control their sex-related behaviour (Lees 1997). The idea of women becoming sexually active may lead to anxiety amongst men, as they become afraid of losing power over women (Melosik, 2002). According to Timm and Sanborn, 'male dominance in its patriarchal form has been based upon the sexual control of women' (Timm and Sanborn 2007: 216). Foucault (1978) maintains that dominant discourses influence ways of thinking about sexuality and sexual relations; in Polish culture it is patriarchy that continues to shape popular perceptions regarding sexuality.

The focus of this analysis, of course, is on gender relations in the context of Polish migration to the UK in the post-2004 period, where the migrants come into contact with people from other ethnic groups and cultures, and experience different cultural attitudes to gender relations in comparison to Polish ones. Over 80 per cent of people who have come to the UK from Poland are between 18 and 34 years old, and many of them were reported as single (Home Office et al. 2007). These statistics are especially important for the part of the analysis relating to inter-ethnic relationships. With such a young age structure among the migrants, it is highly likely that many of these people would start relationships in the UK. It is also likely that some of these relationships could be inter-ethnic – something which would be considered a normal occurrence in a multicultural environment. As Rodriguez Garcia (2006) claims, the growing number of inter-ethnic relationships and marriages generally is a consequence of international migration. However, the attitude of UK Poles to ethnic relations in the UK may play a crucial role in this area. Following their recent research amongst Poles in London, Eade et al. (2007) claimed that some Poles feel hostile about multiculturalism in London and express racist opinions, but at the same time for many other Poles the experience of multicultural London appears to be positive and enriching. These issues will be discussed in more detail in the latter part of this chapter.

Internet Usage by Poles in the UK

Poles in the UK use the Internet in a variety of ways. Many Poles use websites extensively in their daily lives; the most common ones include general UK Polish Community websites, but some of them focus on communities based in specific cities in the UK.[2] Poles use these websites in multiple ways, particularly instrumentally for getting practical information relating to employment (such as job opportunities), accommodation (relating both to renting, but also buying properties in the UK), healthcare (which include queries related to GP and specialist services, but also contacts and information about Polish doctors in the UK), education (i.e. information on primary and secondary schools), and various family and children-related matters. Poles also use websites for getting advice about different issues connected with life in the UK, such as dealing with the Police, information on paying taxes, National Insurance numbers, self-employment, the Worker Registration Scheme and bank accounts, but also information about Polish institutions in the UK including the Embassy and Consulate.

Other forms of Internet use include e-mail correspondence facilities and also various communication tools such as Skype and the Polish version – Gadu Gadu [Talk Talk], which allow Poles in the UK to communicate not only with people based in the UK, but also outside, in Poland, which is especially crucial for sustaining links with their family members and friends based there.[3] Many of these Internet portals also host various forums and chat rooms, which Poles not only use instrumentally, but also socially for keeping in touch with the Polish community in the UK. This may be seen as especially important not only for creating a feeling of belonging to the Polish community by being able to meet other fellow Poles and make friends, but also for discussing a variety of issues related to their everyday lives in the UK.

Researching Internet Forums

Through participating in the Internet forums held on the Internet portals, then, Poles have an opportunity to discuss various issues connected with their experiences and identities in the UK, including gender and ethnicity. This chapter presents a discursive analysis of the discussions relating to these issues. The analysis focuses on the debates based on one specific forum hosted on the Internet portal of one newspaper in Poland, and considers several specific discussions relating to different gender and ethnicity aspects of identity.[4] All the analysed discussions took place in 2006, so two years after Poland's accession to the EU. This means that many users may have taken part in the forum discussions while they were in the process

---

2   For example, <www.mojawyspa.co.uk> [My Island], <www.gbritain.net>, <www.britaintown.com>, <www.polonia-uk.com> nationally, and <www.mojbristol.co.uk> or <www.liverpool.one.pl> regionally.

3   Through the use of cameras, microphones and earphones Skype not only allows a user to speak with the other person, but also to see them. Gadu Gadu only allows a user to write to the other person.

4   For ethical reasons such as the possibility of tracking the Internet forum users both the name of the newspaper and the name of the forum will be kept anonymous.

of establishing themselves in the UK and familiarizing themselves with the new multicultural environment. I did not take a part in the discussions myself; they were initiated and moderated by forum users themselves. This forum's users were mostly anonymous; they frequently used nicknames and very seldom used their real names. Sometimes their IP addresses appeared next to their nicknames, which may operate against their anonymity.[5] As already noted, both women and men participated in the dialogues, but, significantly, the discussions analysed from this forum were usually initiated by men, who appeared to have a greater need to talk about such identity-related issues. The dialogues started either from questions or expressions of concern and criticism, for example: 'If I was ever getting married, then only to a Polish woman'; 'Is it true that Polish women in England usually start relationships with non-Poles?'.

From a methodological point of view these specific discussions took the form of focus groups 'delayed in time'; opinions might have been posted within minutes, hours, days, weeks or even months (Ignatio 2005). Out of the all the discussions only those relating to gender and ethnic issues were selected – fourteen in total. Each of the discussions involved between 30 and 120 posts. As all the discussions were carried out in Polish, the analysis was carried out in Polish. Only after the main analytic concepts were established, were they then translated into English. The discussions were analysed using a critical discourse analysis approach, which is generally focused on the processes of social and cultural change, so it is very relevant in this case.

Such analysis of discourses on gender roles, sexuality and ethnicity typically explores patterns in and across written statements and identifies 'the social consequences of different discursive representations of reality' (Phillips and Jorgensen 2002: 21). This analysis also focuses on the 'order of discourse' – it looks at different discourses that cover the same ground, identifying where different discourses with different meanings compete in the same discussion space, and investigating where a particular discourse is dominant. However, as Fairclough (1992) claims, critical discourse analysis is not sufficient by itself for the analysis of wider social practice, so this study also employs a feminist perspective by looking at relations between women and men, treating femininity and masculinity as socio-cultural categories (Gontarczyk 1995), and also focusing on 'how gender ideologies are re(produced) and contested' (Litosseliti 2006: 57). This analysis concentrates primarily on perceptions, within the constructed discourses, of expectations concerning women, and also women's physical appearance and their sexualities (Litosseliti 2006; Ramazanoglu and Holland 2002). In addition, as the discussions focused on ethnic relations, the analysis also looks at perceptions of ethnic 'otherness' by the forum users. As is to be expected, the distinction between what is a 'gender' or 'ethnicity' thread is sometimes blurred, as ethnicity as an analytic theme was often embedded in gender ideologies. Nevertheless, the

---

5   However, for any quotes mentioned in this publication any nicknames or real names have been anonymized for ethical reasons.

different ways in which the themes of gender, sexuality and ethnicity emerged within the data have been compared and contrasted, with ensuing interpretations made based on textual evidence (Tonkiss 2005). As the analysis concerns a relatively small number of discussions, it is unlikely that the findings would be widely representative; however the study presents important potential for theoretical generalizations about the negotiation of gender relations by Polish women and men in the UK (Tonkiss 2005). The following themes will now be analyzed: the physical appearance and gender-related behaviour of Polish women and men in the UK; the (hetero)sexuality of Polish women and men in the UK; and inter-ethnic relationships between Poles and people of other ethnic origins.

Gender Roles: Physical Appearance and Gender-related Behaviour

In terms of gender, the debates often concentrated on Polish women in the UK. Some users, mostly self-reported males, praised the physical appearance of Polish women and claimed they are 'the most beautiful in the world', 'attractive', 'well-dressed', 'more feminine' and 'thinner' in comparison to women of other ethnic origins. For example, one user wrote that: 'Polish women are the most beautiful women in the world, if you see a good looking woman, it is surely a Polish one'. This may be interpreted as a part of Polish 'ethnosexual mythology', which envisions members of a given ethnic group, in this case Polish, as exceptionally attractive and beautiful (Nagel 2003), and may also be connected to the specific cultural pressures concerning women's physical appearance in Polish culture. Polish public opinion (especially on the part of males) judges the way women look harshly and women are generally expected to meet specific standards in their appearance, for example by 'looking after themselves' and dressing in a feminine way (Melosik 1996, Fres 2002). As Nagel (2003) maintains, in any society there may be a dominant discourse of sexuality that defines socially approved women's and men's bodies. Importantly, however, there was also strong disagreement on the forum with this discourse, with some users calling such an approach a 'myth of good looking Polish women', and claiming that beautiful women exist in every ethnic group. These users also argued that the concept of beauty depends on an individual's taste rather than culturally set preferences.

Often the physical appearance and behaviour of Polish men in the UK were discussed in response to debates relating to those of women. Firstly, some users maintained that in contrast to this image of Polish women, some Polish males have a poor level of personal hygiene and bad taste in clothes. These men, however, instead put the apparent lack of interest of Polish women in them down to their lack of money, something observed by one forum user: 'The problem is – greasy hair or short cut, smelly t-shirts remembering old times, jeans and white Reebok shoes … and he is trying to convince himself and everybody else that it's because of money … '. This could be interpreted as a lack of self-awareness amongst some Polish men, who perceive that having substantial financial resources is the most important way to attract women, and certainly some men were criticized by both male and female forum users for not looking after themselves, but at the same time expecting the same from women. It seems that physical appearance is not considered to be important by some Polish men with regard to themselves, which can arguably be put down to the patriarchal culture, where no strict rules as such concerning physical appearance are set for men.

Secondly, some users, self-reported as males, had a very negative image of other Polish men in the UK, claiming that they are 'blunt primitives' in terms of how they perceive gender relations, and that they have conservative attitudes towards women, especially when compared to men of other ethnic origins, usually English men in this case. These users claimed that some Polish men have a so called 'Taliban mentality', and assume that a woman should be 'virtuous', not too self-confident, and that she should fulfil her household and sexual duties:

> The fact is that some of them have heavy make-up, which provincial men of a Taliban mentality don't necessarily like, as a woman needs to be virtuous.

> And with a Taliban mentality amongst many Poles it's not really funny – what makes them different from the Taliban is that their Talibanness is hidden behind a 'European' screen, and after a few vodkas it comes out – woman is for cooking, a man can betray, a woman can't, a man likes sex, a woman has to, a woman with make-up is a slut, and it's even worse if she is self-confident.

Many female users held similar views about some Polish men and were also critical of them, especially the ones who have a conservative worldview strongly grounded in Catholicism, and expect women to undertake all the household and childcare duties and not to concentrate on having a career, or being socially active:

> … every second Polish man … if he listens to Radio Maria and has subscribed to Our Daily or something like that. According to them such woman should stay at home, clean, look after the family, cook, and in the meantime give birth to children and not to focus on silly things like a career or social life.[6]

As this section shows, the 'myth' of Polish women's physical appearance and expectations about their gender-related conduct, as well as the issue of Polish men not looking after themselves but expecting women to, were hotly debated within these discussions. Some male users supported traditional perceptions of women's gender roles, whilst such outlooks were strongly challenged by female users and other male users.

---

6   Radio Maria is a radio station in Poland devoted to a conservative audience, and Our Daily is a similar magazine, also devoted to a conservative audience.

The Sexuality of Polish Women and Men in the UK

Debates about gender also concentrated on the sexuality of Poles in the UK. Perhaps not surprisingly, the focus of the discussions was most frequently on the sexual lives of women rather than those of men.

Some self-reported male users commented that many Polish women in the UK are sexually active, and this was clearly perceived negatively by them. One user especially gave relationship advice to other Polish men, suggesting that if they were looking for a serious relationship with a Polish woman they should go back to Poland and meet a woman there instead, as women in Poland would not be so liberal in terms of their sexuality:

> 90 per cent would do it with just about anybody, going for money, with some exceptions, which confirms the rule. A Polish woman, yes, but surely not one that has been here for x months or years, as there is high probability that she is already 'used up', if anything then take one from Poland or meet during a journey.

As Timm and Sanborn maintain, gender ideologies rest on so called 'accepted standards of sexual behaviour' (2007: 173). Lees (1997) also points out that women are often portrayed as those who are sexually used rather than those who actively initiate sexual encounters, particularly in patriarchal cultures. Certainly many of the male forum users expressed the need to control the sexual activities of Polish women in the UK, and having been brought up in a culture often described as patriarchal, they may see themselves as responsible for overseeing the sexuality of Polish women away from Poland.

At the same time, however, other (self-reported) male and female forum users created a counter-discourse on sexual double standards, arguing that Polish men who have sex with various women, often not their partners, are not criticized for it and are often perceived as being 'sexually attractive'. According to one user:

> There is an understanding that men get stronger by 'scoring' women, but a woman doing similar loses in their eyes, and that's how men put blame on women … and what about if a woman also wants to have a life and be happy?

These forum members, therefore, actively challenged the patriarchal assumptions of some of the treads. They claimed that women, just like men, have their sexual needs and have a right to fulfil them for their own pleasure. Some users argued that decisions about the sexual activities of women should be made only by women themselves:

> If they want to, they can sleep with whom they want – it's their business. It is strange, a chick sleeps around – it's a slut, a mate sleeps around – he is popular,

a good chat and everything perfect. They want to sleep around, let them do it …
– it's their business.

As these examples demonstrate, this forum became an important site for the contestation of the sexuality of Polish women in the UK, providing a safe, anonymous space for traditional/patriarchal and more liberal views to be aired and negotiated.

Inter-ethnic Relationships and Poles in the UK

The forum discussions also focused on inter-ethnic relationships between a Polish person and someone of another ethnic origin, and again the same themes of physical appearance, gender-related behaviour and sexuality were often a crucial part. The main point which was made on the forum about these relationships was the observation that most inter-ethnic couples involve a Polish woman and a man of another ethnic origin, but it is rare to find a relationship which is the other way round, with a Polish man and a woman of another ethnic origin involved. This claim led to an intermingling of debates about ethnicity, gender and sexuality.

Some self-reported male users claimed that Polish women get into inter-ethnic relationships for financial reasons, particularly women on low earnings in the UK:

> Even a child knows why a woman who graduated from an economic school, or even not, is looking for a foreigner. She doesn't want to work for five pounds, but she wants to drive her bottom in a Land Rover, own houses. I wonder how it is in relation to women who are successful in the UK, surely there are less of them in such relationships. [7]

Others claimed it was an old myth that marrying a foreigner guaranteed a better standard of living for a woman. However, the financial aspect of relationships appears to be an important consideration for some Polish men, especially considering the claim by some men that Polish women do not establish relationships with them exactly for this reason. The analysis shows that some Polish men in the UK see financial resources as an important part of their migration experience, and of their post-migration relationships.

Many male users expressed their negative and often racist attitude to inter-ethnic relationships between Polish women and men of other ethnic origin (different nationalities, religions or 'races'). Some of them claimed that such relationships have got only one aim – a sexual one, where Polish women are sexually 'used' by men of other ethnic origins:

---

7   An economic school is a secondary school which focuses on economics.

> They [men of other ethnic origins] are interested in any girls, and if Polish
> women are easy and go for money, they don't have many problems in attracting
> them. But they don't respect them and only treat them as toys in bed.

Muslim men in particular were singled out – something already suggested with the 'Taliban' remarks – with some male forum users claiming that Muslim men in the UK go out with Polish women purely for sexual reasons. These users claimed that their knowledge of these issues came from discussions with Muslim men who seemed to perceive of Polish women as 'easy', actively and willingly engaging in sexual activities. As Nagel (2003) argues, each society constructs sexuality in its own way, using a dominant sexuality paradigm that defines a socially approved choice of partners and acceptable sexual desires. In this case, the 'rules' seem to suggest that Polish women should only be intimate with Polish men, while at the same time being 'virtuous' and 'submissive'. Moreover, this analysis also shows that essentialist perceptions of ethnic otherness are very powerful in these opinions – the process of identity ascription develops in relation to men of other ethnic origins. Any behaviour observed on an individual level is immediately generalized and ascribed to all the men originating from a specific ethnic group (Pierik 2004).

This discourse claiming that Polish women are 'sexually used' in inter-ethnic relationships rather than being decision makers arguably objectifies them. As discussed earlier, the depiction of women as being sexually passive rather than active is common not only in patriarchal societies, but also in nationalist contexts, and much has been written about this phenomenon. Nagel (2003: 160), for example, argues that 'the national state is essentially a masculine institution attempting to regulate women's sexuality'. Yuval-Davis and Anthias (1989) also claim that male nationalists often commodify women and do not consider them as having rights of their own. In order to reinforce ethnic boundaries, it is argued that nationalists not only enforce in-group sexual purity, but also construct negative stereotypes about the sexuality of ethnic Others (Nagel 2003). In such a situation, 'women's sexual rule breaking' can also be used 'as an opportunity to reinforce and re-establish sexual and nationalist hegemony' (Nagel 2003: 142). This clearly resonates with the Polish case study.

However, these discussions are also about expressing negative attitudes towards ethnic 'otherness' and therefore inter-ethnic relationships, and not just about gender. Due to the migration of these Poles to the UK, contact with people of other ethnic origins has increased, both economically and sexually, and therefore 'ethnic differentness' and tensions related to it have become magnified (Nagel 2003). To use Nagel's (2003: 17) arguments again, 'interethnic sexual contact remains an inevitable feature of migration'. However, at the same time, 'in some cases ethnic identities are strengthened in immigrant communities' and ethnic boundaries may become barriers to intimate contact (Nagel 2003: 16). The evidence from the forum does suggest that some Polish male users are trying to strengthen Polish identities and ethnic boundaries in this new context. Nagel (2003) also distinguished four different types of ethnosexual contact: settling (manifesting itself in establishing long-term liaisons), sojourning (brief or extended contacts), adventuring (casual encounters) and invading (assaults). She argued that ethnosexual adventuring and invading are more prevalent than settling and sojourning, and that these contacts tend to lead to more 'recreational sex'. Whatever type of ethnosexual contact takes place between Polish women and men of other ethnicities in the UK, there are some Polish men who try to prevent Polish women engaging in it, appearing as uncomfortable with inter-ethnic long-term relationships as they are with more casual encounters.

As with the debates on gender, however, robust arguments were made against such views on the forum, and some forum users described this negative attitude to inter-ethnic relationships as 'narrow-minded' and argued that such negative comments towards inter-ethnic relationships were expressed by frustrated and jealous Polish men; they claimed that 'normal' men do not care who Polish women have sex with and why:

> Whenever in the forum there is a connection between 'man of other skin colour – Polish woman', frustrated men with complexes come out with comments about 'them doing it with Arabs' … think about it boys … it is quite sad … some kind of jealousy comes out of you, and it comes from what? I think a poor sexual life and 'exciting' situation in the lower parts below the belt. Because what normal person would care about these statistics of who has sex with whom and for what reason? What does it matter to you?

Some aspects of this discourse take the debate back to the perception of women's sexuality in Polish culture, as discussed earlier, but the risk of being labelled negatively (called a slut) is increased by entering a relationship with a man of a different ethnic background. To quote Nagel (2003: 20) again, 'in such a case, an individual's decision with whom to have sex ceases to be a personal choice, but becomes an ethnically loaded public act which others in the community claim the right to define, judge, and punish'.

This counter-discourse, however, was strong, with some male participants also arguing that Polish men expressing such sexist and racist attitudes to Polish women entering inter-ethnic relationships should be more self-critical, as women not only have a right to sexual desires of their own, but also to establishing relationships with people of their choice:

> What? She doesn't have a right to fulfil her needs? What's the problem? … oh … because she chose a man of other skin colour … it hurts … we are the best, Polish men. Only because of the great choice of females in our country we got confused … so if a Polish woman … finds an Arab man … and she is not impressed with our drinking records, or our discussion about the fortunes we say we make here, if they prefer a coloured man, they are sluts, and that's it … it's not that we are bumpkins … we blame them again …

Others argued that Polish women are not the property of Polish men, and that their actions are their private matters: 'Do Polish women BELONG to us? Let them do what they want and with whom they want'. Some explanations were given for these views – for example, it was claimed that some of the male forum members may be frustrated as they feel they are losing control over women's lives and sexuality, and think that they are 'losing' Polish women as potential partners:

> Girls! Don't worry about what these half-brains are writing about. Polish men who write so are desperate, they are nobody in the UK. ... And their most basic problem is a lack of woman, they are bitter, they are jealous about women who are in any relationships. Because all they have is masturbation at night. That's the truth, and admit it you losers, Polish women don't want you ... That's why it hurts you.

These debates illustrate the sexual anxieties that may prevail amongst some Polish men in the UK, and it is these anxieties that perhaps lead these men to criticize the 'sexual looseness' of Polish women in the UK, and to try to re-enforce 'the patriarchal order' they are used to (Nagel 2003).

Interestingly, some male participants did express their potential interest in establishing relationships with women of other ethnic origins, and claimed that nobody would probably mind this, as they are men and the focus of social control is only on Polish women. Again, criticisms were made of the 'primitive', 'pathetic' outlook that many Polish men had on life and women. As before, Polish men were advised by their male compatriots to look at themselves more critically and change their views on these issues – change their approach to become more equality focused and less controlling – which would stop women turning to men of other ethnic origins:

> I am not surprised Polish women prefer [men of other ethnic origins], it's not about money, but because men from Poland are used to the family pattern where a woman needs to fulfil all the requirements: working mother, loving wife, and good cook, and in order to get married she needs to have a perfect body shape, and reputation, and she needs to represent her man really well, you are pathetic, that's why THEY DON'T WANT YOU!

> Mates, have some respect for women. It seems to you that only the fact that you come from Poland makes some kind of übermensch [superman] of you. It's a mistake. Change your worldview ... and Polish women will stop running away to [men of other ethnic origins]. I am telling you this as a man.

Many women made similar arguments, this time also stereotyping men of other ethnic origins and claiming that they seem to have a more equal approach to their female partners in relationships. Englishmen were often given as an example; they were perceived as 'nice', 'looking after themselves', 'respectful of women' whom they treat as partners, and, in contrast to Polish men, they also share household duties. Some female members reiterated the claim that Polish women enter relationships with Englishmen because Polish men have a 'primitive outlook' on women and do not respect them:

> Surely I prefer an Englishman to a Polish man – Englishmen look after themselves, they have no complexes, they have a sense of humour, they are intelligent, they treat women differently, they don't see women only as potential cooks and cleaners.

> Polish female – English male, I definitely recommend :-))) … he will wash up the dishes, he will help to cook, he cleans better than me and additionally he is so nice.

The 'ethnosexual cosmology' (Nagel 2003) is a very interesting aspect of these debates, as some male users stated that relationships between Polish women and English men are more acceptable than with men of other ethnic origins, arguably presenting a sexist and racist outlook on inter-ethnic relationships. In fact, the expression of very racist *and* sexist opinions led in one case to the establishment of a new forum by one of the users, where men sharing racist and sexist attitudes could express such opinions without being challenged as closely.

These views were still contested by other forum users, however. Some users claimed that using such negative terms to describe people of other ethnic origins emanates from the fear that such people feel towards 'otherness' and belies a narrow minded personality, arguing that the only way to overcome this fear is to get to know a person from another culture, but the problem is that not everybody is ready or willing to do so. These users criticized racial and religious stereotypes and called for more tolerance and understanding of 'ethnic differences'. Some users even talked about how their views had changed, going from quite extreme prejudice to more openness, through their personal experiences with people of other ethnic origins:

> Until recently I have thought, as do most people, that all Muslims are bad, murder poor Christians, and it would be better to remove all of them … but I changed my mind, when I got to know a wonderful man, who turned out to be a Muslim … this man is one of the funniest, the most hardworking and the nicest people I know …

Similarly, several women in relationships with men of other ethnic origins spoke about how satisfying their relationships are:

> I have the most wonderful man under the sun, he is from an Islamic country, he doesn't beat me, he doesn't make me stay at home, we do everything together,

I didn't get to like him for his skin colour, but for his personality and how wonderfully he treats me.

I can say that I am in a relationship with a 'British Indian'. We have been together for five years, and we have been married for two years. We are very happy.

Many women claimed there are not enough 'decent' Polish men in the UK, dividing the 'available' Polish men into the following categories: 'tracksuits', 'frail students', 'manual workers' and 'skaters smoking marihuana'. They argued that the choice of men is limited in comparison to men of other ethnic origins in the UK and that is the reason why they become interested in them. Moreover, some women maintained that people look for partners on their 'social and cultural level', and in that case personality plays a greater role than ethnicity in the choice of a partner. Rodriguez Garcia (2006) observed a similar phenomenon in his research on inter-ethnic relationships, where social class factors played a bigger role in establishing inter-ethnic relationships than the ethnicity of potential partners. There was a strong discussion on this issue, with other users claiming that Polish women who establish inter-ethnic relationships are attracted by the other person's otherness, but at the same time they do not take the other person's culture seriously enough. According to some participants it is important to understand the differences in a potential partner's culture, as the position of women may vary in other cultures and in some there is little gender equality. Some of these women commented that they were happy to have friends of other cultures, but they would not start relationships with men coming from other cultural backgrounds for gender-related reasons.

As these arguments all demonstrate, the issue of Polish women establishing inter-ethnic relationships appears to be firmly embedded in the negotiation of gender relations between Polish women and men in the UK, and an important factor in locating Polish migrants in wider and more ethnically diverse social networks more generally in the UK.

Evaluating the Forum Discussions

As this analysis has shown, in presenting their opinions some male forum participants referred to patriarchal perceptions of the roles of women and recalled this 'cultural myth' of what women should be like. This could be interpreted as their need to reaffirm certain cultural perceptions and, in this case, patriarchal understandings of gender. However, some other male users criticized the cultural expectations about women's roles in Poland, perhaps wanting to escape from these specific cultural expectations of how women should look and behave. At the same time, women argued against the patriarchal approach and called for a change in the perception of gender roles of women and more equality for them. As Domanski (1995) argues, a 'traditional' approach to gender is prevalent in Poland, but it is often women who reject it. Blair (1998) argues that cyberspace offers an opportunity for women to enter a discourse from a position more 'levelled' with men and that it empowers them, and this has been apparent in the on-line activities of many of the female participants. They may feel freer to voice their opinions than they would be in a 'real-life' situation. It is also important that it is not only women who challenge these views, however. The roles that other men have been fulfilling in supporting some of the opinions expressed by female users present a significant dynamic for change, particularly with their attempt to compare the more traditional and patriarchal attitudes of Polish migrants to the notorious extreme conservatism of the Taliban, possibly to shame the Polish men into rethinking their stance on gender.

Evidently, practices connected with women's sexuality are also fiercely discussed amongst Polish migrants in the UK. Many male forum users do not seem to have appreciated the 'relaxation of sex-related rules' amongst Polish women in the UK. However, women appear to be 'freeing' themselves from rules concerning sexuality that are specific to the Polish culture. This has been recognized as more common amongst other ethnic groups (Ahmed 2006), when women 'free themselves' through migration from specific cultural norms and men find it difficult to accept, but in general migration can be especially empowering for women. Many female and some male forum users argued against the 'controlling' attitude of some migrants and called for a more equal approach to the sexual lives of women, where they would decide for themselves about their sexual activities. This may be a result of observing the more liberal approach to sexual politics in the UK.

As McIlwaine et al. (2006) argue, gender practices are often renegotiated when people migrate and when they encounter different socio-cultural influences. As the analyzed discussions show, Polish females and males in the UK – or at least those on this forum – do actively negotiate gender relations. Their migration to the UK has given them an opportunity to start the process of reworking their values and norms in relation to gender issues. Whilst many men refer to a more traditional outlook on gender relations prevalent in Polish culture, many women and some men are calling for change and for more empowerment for women. Mahler and Pessar (2006) have noted that migrant women often experience gains in personal autonomy, independence and greater gender equality, whereas men lose ground, and I think that a similar process can be observed amongst Polish women and men in the UK. However, this issue requires more investigation, with more research needed with other respondents in different contexts, but also into other matters surrounding sexuality such as homosexuality.

It is also apparent that the subject of inter-ethnic relationships between Polish women and men of other ethnic origins is embedded in this negotiation of gender relations. Some male forum users expressed overtly racist attitudes to inter-ethnic relationships. This may be due to the fact that Poland is not as ethnically diverse as the UK; post-2004 EU enlargement migration to the UK has offered many forum users an experience of living in a multicultural society and an opportunity for contact with people of other ethnic origins, and it is quite likely that this has been the first experience of ethnic diversity for many of these forum users. As Arif and Moliner (2007) claim, migration experiences may strengthen ethnic identifications and the negative perception of ethnic otherness. However, according to Nagel, although enforcement of ethnosexual rules focuses on maintaining ethnic solidarity, at the same time it may also 'mobilize opposition' and lead to 'building of bridges across ethnic divides' (Nagel 2003: 21). The analysis shows that this is exactly what may be happening. Many female and some male users thought there was a need amongst Poles in the UK to rethink their attitudes to ethnic issues and people of other ethnic origins; they called for more openness and a greater effort towards getting to know and understand people of other ethnicities.

It can be argued that these forum debates have led to the creation of various discourses on gender and ethnicity among Polish migrants. The debates usually started from a question or a 'heated' opinion, and this was then followed by a discussion where specific discourses were constructed. The discussions often ended with opinions arguing against stereotypical perceptions and promoting equality. When opinions became too offensive, for example when they used swear words, they were removed from the debates by other users. Sometimes this led to changing a nickname in order to be able to maintain a continuous part in the debate. There were limits to the views which could be expressed and therefore the debate's parameters were constantly reassessed and negotiated, making the discourse construction a 'messy', contested and ongoing process.

These discourses constructed within the forum discussions can be defined in the following way:

- Discourse of patriarchy promoting a traditional outlook on gender issues and therefore gender inequality. Within this discourse the following discourses were created:
  - Discourse of control over women's lives, choice of the potential partner and sexuality
  - Discourse of expected women's submissiveness and fulfilling the needs of others
  - Discourse of expectations about women's physical appearance
- Discourse of gender equality and rights arguing for establishing the same rules for women as for men and criticizing patriarchal approach. Within this discourse the following discourses were created:
  - Discourse of women's rights
  - Discourse of women's needs and the right to fulfil them
  - Discourse of choice – so women can choose their own way of living
  - Discourse of women's private 'sexual freedom'
  - Discourse of women's empowerment
- Discourse of ethnic intolerance and stereotypes. Within this discourse the following discourses were created:
  - Discourse of ethnic stereotypes ascribing characteristics of a certain 'group member' to the whole ethnic group

- Discourse of racism promoting racist attitudes to people of other ethnic origins
- Discourse of ethnic tolerance. Within this discourse the following discourses were created:
  - Discourse arguing against cultural stereotypes by criticizing any generalizations (for example, seeing everybody as an individual rather than a member of a specific ethnic group)
  - Discourse of openness to 'ethnic otherness'

These are the main discourses identified in the analysis, however individual users may have chosen to create their own, often quite hybrid, discourses that could include elements of discourses described above. In terms of the 'order of discourse', in relation to gender, the discourse of patriarchy strongly set in Polish culture seems to be a dominant one. However, the discourse of gender equality and rights does come into play. In terms of the 'order of discourse' in relation to ethnicity, the discourse of intolerance appears to be dominant and it may be connected to the lack of experience with multiculturalism, but also quite a strong prevalence of nationalism amongst Poles. However, the discourse of tolerance also emerges, which may be connected with experiences of living in the UK's multicultural society. The analysis exposed a multitude of voices reflecting multiple positions and perspectives on gender and ethnicity issues. As the focus of the analysis was primarily on gender issues, it can be stated, referring to Timm and Sanborn (2007), that modern gender relations are built, not by replacing earlier approaches, but by layering on new interpretations. Such a process may often result 'in contestation but never in total victory for one gendered ideal over another' (Timm and Sanborn 2007: 210).

This discursive analysis shows that the meanings of gender, sexuality but also ethnicity are socially constructed and these meanings may be heavily contested once living in a multicultural environment. Based on this analysis I argue that the gender norms embedded in ethnicity-related issues amongst Poles in the UK are changing. Some forum users are challenging gender and 'ethnosexual hegemonies' and are becoming gender and 'ethnosexual resisters, innovators, and revolutionaries' (Nagel 2003: 261).

Conclusions

To conclude, it can be argued that these debates are important for those who have migrated, where their identities and values come into contact with the new reality of a multicultural society, and these discussions appear to be a crucial part of the negotiation of their own identities. For many Poles it is an opportunity to enact their values, which may be more traditional or more liberal in terms of gender or ethnic relations. As Slater and Miller (2000) claim, the Internet can be understood in terms of the liberation of new and fluid identities, but also the reparation of old allegiances such as religion and nation. The analysis of the discussions on the Internet forum shows that many female users and some male users call for a change in gender and ethnic relations, whilst other male users would like to maintain the more traditional approach.

These discussions help individuals to 'position' themselves vis-à-vis both the forum group by reconfirming their Polish values and attitudes, and the new society they are in by finding their way in multiculturalism, where various attitudes and approaches meet and co-exist. As Abbott et al. (2005) claim, in cyberspace gender inequalities are transferred from real life into the virtual space. Although this migration might have provided Polish women with an opportunity to liberate themselves from subordinate gender roles, in a way these traditional gender roles are still perpetuated in the UK by many male forum users (DeLaet 1999; Mahler and Pessar 2003). However, it appears that many Polish women feel more autonomous and independent, whilst Polish men feel threatened (Mahler and Pessar 2006). Gender practices are therefore negotiated by Poles who have migrated to the UK, with Polish women becoming more empowered (McIlwaine et al. 2006). Polish female emigration has already been referred to by Coyle (2007), following her work with women's organizations in Poland, as an escape from the conservative gender environment in Poland. As Ramazanoglu and Holland (2002) also argue, women's situations can be transformed through the production of new discourses and this appears to be happening amongst some forum users.

These kinds of debates are possible because of Internet technology which allows many Poles coming from various parts of Poland and living in various parts of the UK to meet at the same place – a virtual space – which probably would not be possible in 'real' life. Moreover, cyberspace offers them anonymity, so they feel free to express their ideas, sometimes very controversial, but also their fantasies and frustrations. This Internet forum in particular also provides an opportunity for Poles to debate these gender and ethnic-related issues in their own language – again, opening up virtual space for an accessible discussion of these matters.

This analysis has concentrated only on the discussions which the Poles created in relation to ethnic and gender identity, but these chosen debates have enabled the portrayal of issues arising among Polish migrants in the UK relating to gender and ethnic identity which are happening in a virtual space, hidden away from everyday social life, but which are at the same time also a part of it. It can be argued that the analyzed Internet forum is a part of the social reality of Poles in the UK, as the discussions carried out there are embedded in other non-virtual social spaces, and that these Internet forums may be a platform for creating new approaches to gender and ethnic identity.

References

Abbott, P., Wallace, C. and Tyler, M. (2005), *An Introduction to Sociology: Feminist Perspectives* (London: Routledge).

Ahmed, N. (2006), 'Transference or Transformation? Traditional and Transmuted Gender Roles'. Paper presented at European Association of Social Anthropologists Conference, University of Bristol, 18–21 September 2006.

Blair, C. (1998), 'Netsex: Empowerment Through Discourse', in Ebo (ed.).

Coyle, A. (2007), 'Resistance, Regulation and Rights: The Changing Status of Polish Women's Migration and Work in the "New" Europe', *European Journal of Women's Studies* 14:1, 37–50.

Domanski, H. (1995), 'Rownouprawnienie. Stereotyp tradycyjnego podzialu rol' ['Equality: The Stereotype of the Traditional Division of the Roles'], in Titkow and Domanski (eds).

Duch-Krzystoszek, D. (1997), *Malzenstwo, seks, prokreacja. Analiza socjologiczna* [*Marriage, Sex, Procreation: A Sociological Analysis*] (Warsaw: IFIS PAN).

Eade, J., Drinkwater, S. and Garapich, M.P. (2007), *Class and Ethnicity: Polish Migrant Workers in London – Full Research Report*. ESRC End of Award Report, RES-000-22-1294 (Swindon: Economic and Social Research Council).

Ebo, B. (ed.) (1998), *Cyberghetto or Cybertopia?: Race, Class, and Gender on the Internet* (London: Praeger).

Fairclough, N. (1992), *Discourse and Social Change* (Oxford: Polity Press).

Fairclough, N. (1995), *Critical Discourse Analysis: The Critical Study of Language* (London: Longman).

Foucault, M. (1978), *The History of Sexuality* (Harmondsworth: Penguin).

Fres, M. (2002), 'Falszywe cialo. Psychoterapia w problemach dziewczat wkraczajacych w patriarchat' ['Psychotherapy and the Problems of Girls Entering Patriarchy'], in Radkiewicz (ed.).

Funk, N. and Mueller, M. (eds) (1993), *Gender Politics and Post-Communism: Reflections from Eastern Europe and the Former Soviet Union* (London: Routledge).

Gontarczyk, E. (1995), *Kobiecosc i meskosc jako kategorie spoleczno-kulturowe w studiach feministycznych* [*Femininity and Masculinity as Socio-cultural Categories in Feminist Studies*] (Poznan: Eruditus).

Graff, A. (2001), *Swiat bez kobiet; plec w polskim zyciu publicznym* [*The World Without Women: Gender in Polish Public Life*] (Warsaw: W.A.B.).

Hauser, E., Heyns, B. and Mansbridge, J. (1993), 'Feminism in the Interstices of Politics and Culture: Poland in Transition', in Funk and Mueller (eds).

Home Office, Department for Work and Pensions, HM Revenue & Customs and Communities and Local Government (2007), *Accession Monitoring Report May 2004–December 2006*. <http://www.ukba. homeoffice.gov.uk/sitecontent/documents/aboutus/reports/accession_ monitoring_report/report10/may04dec06.pdf?view=Binary>, accessed 11 March 2007.

Ignacio, E. (2005), *Building Diaspora; Filipino Cultural Community Formation on the Internet* (London: Rutgers University Press).

Korzinska, A. (2003), 'Uroda, małżeństwo, macierzyństwo jako komponenty tożsamości plci' ['Beauty, Marriage, Maternity as Components of Gender Identity'], in Radkiewicz (ed.).

Kuczynska, A. and Dzikowska, E. (eds) (2004), *Zrozumiec plec. Studia interdyscyplinarne II* [*Understanding Gender. Interdisciplinary Studies II*] (Wroclaw: Warsaw University Press).

Lees, S. (1997), *Ruling Passions: Sexual Violence, Reputation and the Law* (Buckingham: Open University Press).

Litosseliti, L. (2006), *Gender and Language: Theory and Practice* (London: Hodder Arnold).

Mahler S. and Pessar, P. (2003), 'Transnational Migrations: Bringing Gender In', *International Migration Review* 37:3, 812–46.

Mahler, S. and Pessar, P. (2006), 'Gender Matters: Ethnographers Bring Gender from the Periphery toward the Core of Migration Studies', *International Migration Review* 40:1, 27–63.

McIlwaine, C., Datta, K., Evans, Y., Herbert, J., May, J. and Wills, J. (2006), '"Arriving on High Heels": Gender and Ethnic Identities among Low-Paid Migrant Workers in London'. Paper presented at COMPAS Annual Conference 2006, University of Oxford, 5–6 July 2006 <http://www.geog.qmul.ac.uk/globalcities/reports/docs/workingpaper4.pdf>, accessed 15 September 2006.

Melosik, Z. (1996), *Tozsamosc, cialo, wladza* [*Identity, Body, Power*] (Poznan-Torun: Edytor).

Melosik, Z. (2002), *Kryzys meskosci w kulturze wspolczesnej* [*The Crisis of Masculinity in Contemporary Culture*] (Poznan: Wolumin).

Miller, D. and Slater, D. (2000), *The Internet: An Ethnographic Approach* (Oxford: Berg).

Mohammad-Arif, A. and Moliner, C. (2007), 'Introduction. Migration and Constructions of the Other: Inter-Communal Relationships amongst South Asian Diasporas', *South Asia Multidisciplinary Academic Journal* <http://samaj.revues.org/document136.html>, accessed 8 January 2008.

Nagel, J. (2003), *Race, Ethnicity, and Sexuality: Intimate Intersections, Forbidden Frontiers* (Oxford: Oxford University Press).

Phillips, L. and Jorgensen, M. (2002), *Discourse Analysis as Theory and Method* (London: Sage).

Pierik, R. (2004), 'Conceptualising Cultural Groups and Cultural Difference: The Social Mechanism Approach', *Ethnicities* 4:4, 523–44.

Platek, M. (2004), 'Hostages of Destiny: Gender Issues in Today's Poland', *Feminist Review* 76:1, 5–25.

Radkiewicz, M. (ed.) (2002), *Gender-Kultura-Spoleczenstwo* [*Gender-Culture-Society*] (Kraków: Rabid).

Radkiewicz, M. (ed.) (2003), *Gender w kulturze popularnej* [*Gender in Popular Culture*] (Kraków: Rabid).

Ramazanoglu, C. and Holland, J. (2002), *Feminist Methodology: Challenges and Choices* (London: Sage).

Rodriguez Garcia, D. (2006), 'Mixed Marriages and Transnational Families in the Intercultural Context: A Case Study of African-Spanish Couples in Catalonia', *Journal of Ethnic and Migration Studies* 32:3, 403–33.

Seale, C. (ed.) (2005), *Researching Society and Culture* (London: Sage).

Szarzynska-Lichton, M. (2004), 'Stereotypy plci i ich realizowanie w rolach zyciowych w kontekscie historycznym i kulturowym, szkic' ['Gender Stereotypes and Life roles in a Historical and Cultural Context'], in Kuczynska and Dzikowska (eds).

Timm, A. and Sanborn, J. (2007), *Gender, Sex and the Shaping of Modern Europe: A History from the French Revolution to the Present Day* (Oxford: Berg).

Titkow, A. and Domanski, H. (eds) (1995), *Co to znaczy byc kobieta w Polsce* [*What Does it Mean to be a Woman in Poland*] (Warsaw: PAN IFiS).

Tonkiss, F. (2005), 'Analysing Text and Speech: Content and Discourse Analysis', in Seale (ed.).

Yuval-Davis, N. and Anthias, F. (1989), *Woman-Nation-State* (Basingstoke: Macmillan).

Chapter 9
'This is Special Humour': Visual Narratives of Polish Masculinities on London's Building Sites

Ayona Datta

Figure 9.1   Ryszard's picture, taken to illustrate workplace cultures

It was a joke, a kind of joke. Ah – ah well I was speaking, you know, just let – let's at least say something about, you know, builders – building, in building sites, so – Well, yeah he [English colleague] did it [held poster] so I took a picture of him. ... Yeah, sexy old British singer, yeah, I don't know who he [sic] is but, I – I thought it was, er, *Daily Sport*, you know this paper, *Daily – Daily Sport* – it's got nothing to do with sport you know ... So that – that's something which is quite common in building sites these things. (Ryszard, interviewed in English)

Ryszard's photograph and narrative represents the building site as a masculine space where particular versions of normative and heterosexual masculinities are practiced by builders. Such perceptions of builders and building sites are common in the UK where a large majority of white working-class men are employed and who, within this confined space, can engage in varieties of gender performances that would under other circumstances be considered sexist and derogatory to women. These performances include pin-ups of nude women, sexist jokes, sexual boasting, sports-talk, as well as teasing and cat-calls to women who come near or pass by building sites. Yet, Ryszard's narrative hides another perception of this 'white masculine' space – a perception that is becoming increasingly apparent after 2004 with the visibility of a large minority of Polish migrants like Ryszard within building sites. As a photograph taken at my request to illustrate his 'life in London', it is his critique of the aggressive and normative masculinities practised by his English colleagues on-site – practices which Ryszard often feels uncomfortable with.

Ryszard's visual narrative of the building site highlights many issues. Firstly that the building site is not just a place of manual labour, but is also a place of social interaction between different men. Secondly, in the aftermath of EU expansion, new Polish migrants who interact with the 'home' population and with each other on building sites are articulating new gender identities based on differences in gender performances. Traditionally seen as the workplace of the 'white working-class' (including Irish, Turkish Cypriot and Australian migrants), the insertion of Polish migrants in these places has further fractured its 'whiteness' with perceptions of ethno-national 'otherness'. Thus building sites, as places where the production process since 2004 has been to a large extent driven by migrant labour from Eastern Europe, have through the social relationships between these diverse actors, also become sites of social constructions of Polish masculinities.

In this chapter, I engage with these issues to suggest how social interactions on building sites shape the construction of Polish masculinities. I do this through visual narratives – a combination of participant photographs and semi-structured interviews, which illustrate how Polish builders reshape new spaces and identities to construct 'others' on building sites. I will focus particularly on social interactions on small building sites to examine how gendered performances of humour, teasing and socializing among different workers contribute to the wider construction of Polish masculinities and their differentiations with other 'white' builders in London.

Polish Masculinities?

Recent scholarship on masculinities in the West has suggested that masculinity is one of the many social and political constructions that shape gender relationships within particular contexts. There is no singular form of masculinity – rather there are multiple masculinities, each of which is geographically and temporally specific. As Berg and Longhurst (2003) suggest, masculinities are 'highly contingent, unstable, contested spaces within gender relations' which make them crucial to the production and transformation of identities. Masculine identities are shaped in different material contexts under different conditions of gender relationships, spatial practices and bodily performances. The location and materiality of the body (incorporating its representational, discursive and performative aspects) is crucial to how masculinity is experienced, read and constructed (Nast and Pile 1998). This is particularly significant in building work where employment is a performance undertaken by embodied, gendered and sexed individuals – work which is mainly done by able-bodied and physically strong men. Furthermore, and of crucial importance for this chapter, masculinities are understood to be produced from their mutually constitutive relationships with other identities of class, race, nationality and ethnicity that operate in different places.

Masculinities have been well researched in the West within the geographies of work – largely focusing on white working-class unemployment in the aftermath of Fordist manufacturing. In the UK, this has been marked by a 'crisis of masculinity' (McDowell 2003) in which the taken for granted associations between manliness and manual work were affected by men's anxieties about loss of employment. Yet, despite the increasing visibility of East- and East-Central European men in building sites in the West, research on Polish or East-European masculinities in these contexts have been largely overlooked within this literature. Much of the work on gender identities in Eastern Europe has been around the politics of gender and class after transition into 'post-socialist' states (Einhorn 2006; Gal and Kligman 2000; Heinen 1997; Kligman 1996; Smith et al. 2008; Watson 2000). This literature has articulated the politics of gendered empowerment among women in Poland but does not pay specific attention to the construction of masculinities (except for Watson 1993). Only a handful of studies have very recently focused on Polish migrants in the UK (Eade et al. 2006; Jordan 2002; Spencer et al. 2007), examining the construction of class identities and social networks among Poles. While this range of literature on geographies of work and on post-socialism provide important scholarship on the transformation of gender identities, none of them have paid specific attention to the ways that Polish men's bodily practices and performances during manual work shape ideas of gender differences and masculinities.

Masculine identities and gender relationships, as they take shape among Polish male migrants in the UK today, are connected to their wider socio-political, historical and geographic contexts – the socialist state, the Polish republic and the UK labour market. The socialist state in Poland had offered very few versions of masculinity, emphasizing the importance of the Polish family with men as breadwinners and head of households, while simultaneously usurping men's patriarchal authority over this family (Watson 1993). Socialism however, produced 'workers' of the state – labels that were written on both male and female bodies, but which also created a 'factory world' (Kenny 1999: 406) that was primarily masculine and largely available to men. Men as physically strong workers and loyal party members were provided self-identification with economically productive roles.

Biological differences between male and female bodies were seen as justifications of their differing gender roles within the workplace (Fidelis 2004), with sex-specific legislations that sought to 'protect' women from heavy manual work in 'masculine' industries of construction, factories and shipbuilding. Yet within this factory world, there existed a variety of support structures. Under socialism, trade unions and workplaces were responsible for social provisions at work – toilets, changing rooms, childcare, pubs and restaurants. This allowed workers to get changed after work and to socialize in pubs and restaurants. Particularly for men, pubs and restaurants became not simply a place of leisure but also a place where they could exchange news and provide support during difficult times. These places have continued to remain significant as support structures during unemployment in post-socialist Poland. Thus, although gender roles were largely defined on the basis of men's and women's differing relationships to labour with the male working body becoming central to masculinity, places of manual work during socialism and after have always been more than just 'workplaces' – they were also places of support and of social interaction.

Transition from state socialism in 1989 was seen as creating opportunities to enact traditional masculine roles by men that would provide them with more participation and control over both public and private spheres – a role that had been largely erased by the socialist state. In the aftermath of state socialism, Watson notes that 'it is the rise of masculinism that is the primary characteristic of gender relations in Eastern Europe today' (Watson 2000: 71). This is evident in the simultaneous political empowerment of men and exclusion of women, justified through essentialized gender differences. The new civil society has produced 'sharp ruptures with the past – not only in practices, but also in representations' (Gal and Kligman 2000: 83) of masculinity through subjectivity, sense of self and the body – the aggressive, market-driven and competitive male body providing new representations of masculinity in post-socialist Poland. While there used to be fundamental tensions between the socialist state and men's empowerment, in the newly formed Polish republic the main point of reference has become the Polish nation with men as its main drivers. Manual work however, has had an increased impact on the lives of men – with the downsizing of state-owned heavy industries, particularly manufacturing and construction, leading to a rise in unemployment among men in these sectors (Kligman 1996).[1] Furthermore, unemployment has largely affected the lower and upper end of the age spectrum, being persistently high among young people and among older workers above 50 years (Smith et al. 2008). Under such conditions, households have found a variety of coping strategies with labour migration to the West seen as a regular option. Indeed, as Iglicka

---

1   While male unemployment has been increasing in traditional blue collar sectors, Kligman (1996) notes that female unemployment continues to be higher and more persistent. Women are less likely to become employed and less likely to be retained during downsizing.

(2001, 6) notes, since the 1990s, emigration from Poland has 'slowly become the domain of blue-collar workers unable to adapt to market requirements'.

The transition from state socialism to capitalism to EU citizenship has meant transformations in power relationships and new forms of identity politics around nationhood and gender. This is particularly evident among those men who move to the UK, where they are confronted with new socio-cultural structures embedded within public and private realms of home, workplace and the city. After the new Polish migrants arrive in London, their ideas of masculinity, nationhood, work and sense of self are continually reshaped in their new social, political, economic and spatial contexts. As I noted elsewhere (Datta 2009), earlier perceptions of difference get translated and transformed under these contexts as new attitudes towards others are formed in new places, under different structures of power. Under such conditions, masculinities among Polish male migrants in the UK are constructed in opposition to 'others' who they interact with in different places – often through discourses of gendered nationality and gendered ethnicity (Datta 2008).

Researching Polish Migrant Men in London

This research is part of a wider project exploring East- and East-Central European construction workers' experiences of home, work and migration in London in the aftermath of the EU expansion in 2004. The project used a qualitative methodology of visual narratives – a combination of semi-structured interviewing and participant photographs. There were two stages in this – an initial information gathering interview with participants after which they were provided with a disposable camera to take pictures of their 'life in London'. In the second interview, their photographs were used to solicit the contexts and meanings of their experiences.

From 2006–2007, 20 Polish men were interviewed in English and Polish. For the Polish language interviews, I made use of an on-site Polish translator who translated and transcribed these interviews into English. The interviews were conducted after work or at weekends, sometimes in participants' houses, in the Polish community centre, coffee shops or pubs. These participants were young – between 24–47 years but with only two above 40 years. They had all arrived in the UK as economic migrants between 1996 and 2006. Those who came to the UK before 2004 had arrived as students or tourists and worked illegally until the EU expansion. Although most of them are single in the UK, virtually all of them lived with their parents or partners (and children) before they arrived in London, whom they visit regularly. For some older participants, relationships with their partners broke down soon after they moved to UK, and in a few cases new relationships have formed in the UK. Only two of them had worked in building sites before but most of them had been engaged in some kind of blue-collar work in factories in Poland. Most participants therefore had begun their employment in London on building sites as labourers and progressed to more skilled trades over time. The labour shortages that existed in the construction sector helped to provide them with steady employment which was also seen as better than other sectors such as agriculture, fishing, cleaning or hotels and catering. Almost all of the participants worked in the home refurbishment sector, where they were part of a group of four to ten builders, usually renovating houses in London's affluent and up-and-coming neighbourhoods. Their employers were usually small-time contractors – often English but also of other minority white populations such as Turkish Cypriots, Iranians or Australians. Most of them had been hired through word-of-mouth so it was not surprising that participants usually knew each other on building sites.

At a time when the 'Polish builder' has become a much debated subject in the UK, participants actively used their photographs to provide narratives of difference on building sites – primarily in relation to English workers. This meant that a large number of these pictures were taken of building sites and of themselves working there. Their photographs drew upon ideas of nationality and gender differences, which are evident in the ways that bodies and spaces were narrated in the interviews. This was also often extended to me as an Asian woman researcher – participants were gentle and chivalrous, opening doors, apologizing for occasional swearing and insisting on paying for my drinks. At the same time, some would express surprise at my ownership over the research, asking my Polish translator whether I really was her 'boss'. Thus age, gender, ethnicity, race and language played to a large extent into our research relationships and clearly reflected participants' self-positioning within these contexts – an aspect that is also borne out in their visual narratives.

Yet, although race was a common theme around living experiences in London, work experiences were primarily constructed around gender and ethno-nationality. Participants' discussions of 'English' builders referred largely to the white 'home' population which included second generation Irish and Turkish Cypriot workers. 'Polishness' on the other hand referred to an ethno-national territory, whose subjects shared a particular moment in history – arriving in the UK after or just before 2004. The visual narratives of participants therefore should be seen as reflecting such wider constructions of nationality, ethnicity and gender that are set in particular historical and political contexts.

Polish Builders in London

The construction industry in London employs approximately 230,000 people (including manual, professional and administrative occupations), which constitutes five per cent of its labour force (HPSC 2005). Manual workers (including carpenters and joiners, bricklayers, painters and decorators) represent 73 per cent of this total.[2] The current construction workforce is male (91 per

---

2   http://www.constructionskills.net/pdf/research/2004_market_assessment.pdf.

cent) and white (87 per cent) (HPSC 2005).[3] A recent research report (IFF 2005) suggests that approximately 30 per cent of construction workers in London are from outside the UK, while minorities such as Irish, Scottish and Welsh make up a high proportion of the white workers. During 2004–2005, the largest official numbers of non-UK entrants in the construction sector have been Polish (13,115) (Home Office 2007). These numbers exclude those who work as self-employed – a common phenomenon in the construction sector, and with various challenges to the accuracy of these official numbers (see Currie 2006 for elaboration), it is expected that Polish workers comprise a large minority of white manual workers in the construction sector.

From 2005 until very recently, increasing house prices and reducing affordability in London had transformed the housing refurbishment sector into an important part of the construction industry, amounting to £4.88 billion in 2005 – a share of 46 per cent of the construction sector output and three per cent of the total UK economy (HPSC 2005). Since 2004, East- and East-Central European workers have become increasingly visible within construction – those who were employed illegally before 2004 have now taken on more skilled and entrepreneurial work, and those coming fresh into the sector have largely entered as low-paid labourers. This has been possible due to the highly casualized and temporary nature of construction work – employment is usually word-of-mouth and payment is cash-in-hand. The fast turnover of home refurbishment projects however, requires a steady supply of cheap labour which the new Polish migrants have been able to provide. Their employment has largely been through their Polish social networks, which means that making and maintaining social networks in order to be employed on building sites becomes crucial for those without English language skills. Equally for those who have acquired English skills, making and maintaining new kinds of social networks through their English colleagues becomes critical to find new and better sources of employment.

Studies on construction workers (Applebaum 1981; Paap 2006; Freeman 1983) have highlighted the ways that social interactions during building work produces particular bodily performances – horse-play, physical jousting, bellicosity, as well as practices of sports talk, sexual boasting, pin-ups of nude women and cat-calls. Freeman (1993: 725) contends that this 'hardhat' image of construction workers becomes a 'magical object, conferring masculinity on its wearer' and allows male bonding. Scholarship on manual work such as in the case of dock workers (Gregory 2006) has often identified these practices and performances as making demanding labour more bearable. This range of literature clearly suggests that workplaces of manual labour are more than just places of work – they form key sites of social interaction among manual workers. This becomes even more relevant in the case of home-refurbishment projects in the UK, where most employers do not

---

3   A national study in 2000 of non-UK born construction workers found that 30 per cent were Irish, 13 per cent were from the Indian sub-continent, ten per cent were from the EU, six per cent were from non-EU Europe and 12 per cent were 'other whites'.

provide social amenities such as toilets and washrooms, but expect workers to use the toilets within the homes that they refurbish – practices that often make builders more comfortable in each other's bodily presence. Further, the particular geographies of the building sites as enclosed spaces cut-off from the rest of the city encourage particular forms of socialization among male workers that would be considered inappropriate under other circumstances.

As Cornwall and Lindisfarne (1994: 37–8) argue, 'Not only "being a male", but "being male" can be interpreted differently in different circumstances'. The building site therefore is a particular place of male bonding and masculine performances that have until very recently been conceptualized as a place of white working-class masculinity. In fact, although 'whiteness' on construction sites has always been read as 'Englishness', white workers in the British building industry have always included a significant minority of Irish migrants since the nineteenth century (Clarke 1992). Yet, often their common language and assumed cultural similarities are taken to represent an assimilated white 'English' population – indeed this is a cultural construct which much of the Polish participants often align themselves with. Thus, while the politics of Englishness and whiteness are already complex on building sites, the visibility of a large number of Polish men within its spaces after 2004 adds a further complexity to the masculine performances of builders. Polish masculinities under such contexts take shape not just around the exclusion of women from these spaces, but also around discursive constructions of Englishness and Polishness, old and young, masculinity and femininity within building sites. While 'whiteness' is seen as sufficient cultural capital by Polish migrants to find employment (Eade et al. 2006), the discursive construction of a sophisticated and gentle Polish worker in opposition to English workers also distinguishes themselves from the 'home' population and provide counter-narratives of their perceived marginalities on building sites (Datta and Brickell 2009).

Polish masculinities, as they take shape in London's workplaces, are reflective of the wider historical construction of gender under socialism and its translation within more market-driven capitalist economies in Poland and UK. The building site for the Polish men forms both a nodal point of concrete social relations and a conceptual or discursive space of gendered ethno-national identification in which more nuanced and in-depth insights into gendered differences are constructed and shaped. Social interactions reflect their location within the wider geographies of the city – as low-paid migrant men often without sufficient language skills. These are places where they are able to accumulate sufficient social and cultural capital to get access to employment and basic services in London. These places also form sites of social support for new Polish migrants and provide varieties of knowledge to access and maintain links with Poland. Thus although social interactions on building sites have been conceived as processes of 'stress-relief' and 'male bonding' in earlier literature, the visual narratives of the Polish participants suggest that they incorporate a much wider range of processes that shape the social construction of masculinities among Polish migrant men in London. Such constructions refer to the varieties and forms of differences encountered in the workplace and the ways that these provide the contexts and coordinates for more nuanced understandings of gendered bodies and their spaces.

Visual Narratives of Polish Builders in London

Working on home refurbishment projects is different from that of other construction and building projects. Firstly, this work can be completed in a shorter period of time and involves a smaller number of workers, which increases the amount of interaction between them to complete the project. The manual nature of this work means that workers take frequent breaks during the day, which allows them to interact in ways that are not always related to work. Secondly, the small-scale nature of this work means that most workers are hired through social networks and word-of-mouth recommendations. Under such circumstances, most participants knew each other, indeed some of them had been neighbours or friends back in Poland. They had found employment through each other, some were sharing accommodation in London and most of them also socialized outside the workplace. Their familiarity with each other played a key role in shaping social interactions on building sites in ways that often created divisions between Polish and non-Polish workers. This was related partly to participants' lack of 'cultural capital' in the form of English language skills which produced distinct patterns of socializing and interaction – between Polish and English and between Polish and Polish. Such interactions were also based upon different perceptions of bodies and gender performances – while most Polish participants would engage in sexual jokes and humour, they would simultaneously express discomfort with jokes from their English counterparts. The production of 'others' was then mobilized through perceived ethno-national differences produced from particular interactions of socializing, humour and teasing, which were then mapped onto their bodies and spaces.

Changing Clothes

For most of the participants, differences between them and other builders began with how their bodies were seen and read. Building work was physically strenuous and the requirements of bodily versatility to do different kinds of work were felt very strongly among the participants. Yet, building work was also more than that – it was messy – especially in the home refurbishment sector, where participants would be painting, tiling or plastering all day, which would mark their bodies and clothes. The 'typical' builder's body – wearing thick clothes, marked with paint and grease and carrying tools on public transport is a common image of builders in London – was also a practice which most participants did not find desirable. Often participants, especially those who were more recent migrants to London, would change into working clothes in the morning and change back into everyday clothes before they left the building site in the evening. As Jan commented:

Figure 9.2   Jan's picture of a colleague on-site

> Well, I usually get changed at work, because if we have some sort of flat or refurbishment, then you can easily get changed, and sometimes after work, instead of going straight home, as I said, I would go to downtown, to have a look at the shops, eat something, so not really in dirty clothes ... In Poland still, there is this kind of habit to always change at work, there was no such thing as someone dirty going on a bus because he is going to work, you will not find that in Poland. Here, I noticed that there is a lot of people commuting [not changed], but I still have this habit from working in Poland ... so I usually commute [dressed] normally. (Jan, translated from Polish)

Other participants suggested that changing on-site was 'a very Polish thing'– indeed they reinforced that the Polish working body cannot be identified outside the workplace. These accounts reflect certain cultural differences between the working body in Poland and England – where the former is not visible within urban space. Working in the home refurbishment sector, Jan noted, provided them with the opportunities and places where they could change between work and everyday clothes – the toilets in these homes allowing them the privacy to continue this practice. As we shall see next, such places within their building sites became important not just in the way that they allowed these cultural practices to be sustained, but also produced new forms of interaction between Polish men.

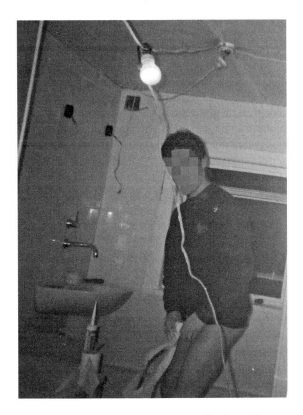

Figure 9.3   Michal's picture of his colleague in the toilet

Teasing and Socializing

Studies on shop floor culture describe interactions between workers as 'aggressive, sexist and derogatory, humorous yet insulting, playful but degrading' (Collinson and Hearn 1996: 68). These range from teasing and physical jousting to opening the door while changing and hiding tools and clothes. As Freeman (1993: 731) suggests, the peculiar social geography of urban building sites promotes shared masculine activities that provide 'a way to glue together a work force in an endless process of recombination'. In such interactions the toilet remained a regular site of such activities (Applebaum 1981).

Participants often indulged in similar crude teasing but only with other Polish workers. A particular feature of this teasing was the way that this was situated in the toilets of the homes they refurbished – places where they also changed into work clothes. This 'playfulness' is illustrated in Michal's photograph of his friend changing in the toilet when he had suddenly opened the door. Michal explained that there was always a convivial atmosphere among them in the building sites where this kind of teasing was taken light-heartedly and assured that his friend had not been offended. Although they were also housemates, Michal refrained from such behaviour at home. Furthermore, Michal clarified that this kind of teasing only occurred between Polish workers – he could not imagine interacting with English workers in this way. The sense of enclosure provided by the building site, which promotes such exchanges between Polish men, served in bringing them simultaneously closer together and further away from non-Polish workers.

These separations were due partly to a lack of English language skills among new Polish migrants, but also due to the fact that these men formed an intricate social support structure that allowed them not just to keep in touch with news and events in Poland, but also to create new social networks. These networks were important since they could lead to employment or accommodation or even friendships. Conversations were usually in Polish in order to keep their discussions private from their non-Polish supervisors. These conversations were an important source of support for many of those who had arrived in London recently, but they were also different across age-groups:

> Because there are mostly older people there, I am the youngest one, there are usually people over thirty, for example they still talk about what is going on in Poland, how their kids are doing, because they have kids in general, you know [pause] well how they help him, if they send them money, how they send it, the best ways to send it, the least commissions, the quickest ways, these sort of subjects. (Jan, translated from Polish)

Jan notes that these subjects, while common among older Polish builders were not ones that he usually engaged with. As for the other younger single participants, coming to the UK provided them for the first time with opportunities to leave home and be more independent. Jan and his friends therefore were more engaged with a different aspect of life in London – discussing differences between women's bodies:

> And about [discussing] women rather it is about the ones that pass by, 'oh, this one is very pretty' for example. Why she is pretty, what we like for example about the Indian ones, Japanese and black ones, in what ways they are different to Polish ones, because obviously, you pick on what is different from Polish women. (Jan, translated from Polish)

The particular work cultures that enable these varieties of discussions combine with the physical geographies of these building sites that bring together Polish men in one place, producing specific kinds of social interaction and masculine performances. Significantly, they also reflect the construction of masculinities through men's specific locations within gender relations in their families. The older men who have partners and perhaps children relate to their gendered roles as breadwinners and patriarchal figures within the household, while the younger men who are single and have for the first time left their parental home in Poland reflect more 'laddish masculinities' (McDowell 2002). While the former reflects gender roles that are intent on sustaining transnational links between Poland and England to situate themselves within a Polish family, the latter uses precisely the absence of their responsibility towards a Polish family to engage with a variety of youthful masculine behaviours.

Although Jan and many like him without English skills were limited in their interactions with other non-Polish builders, there were those who had sufficient language skills to cultivate acquaintances with English builders. This formed a way to tap into a different kind of social capital which the English workers were seen to belong to. Going out for drinks after work was a common way to accumulate this capital, but it was during these moments that differences between them became apparent to the participants:

> I'll give you a difference between drinking with a Polish man or Polish girl and drinking with English people. It's like, when you live with Polish, at some point you would go, on a little bit heavier things to talk about. … you know, more about your problems, maybe, maybe your feelings, maybe, you know, some things and people can help you. That's why we drink. We like drinking and socializing and have fun. It's forbidden in Britain. It is forbidden because I have, innocently have done it few times, being Polish still and you know, I said something that wasn't funny. The silence came on, few minutes of silence, and then someone cracked a joke, turning what I said into a joke and everything was good again. And I find it quite, quite a difficult sociological issue within Londoners. (Karol, interviewed in English)

Karol describes the moment when differences between English and Polish ways of socializing are experienced. While teasing and conversations can be interpreted as part of the wider language skills that keep workers of different nationalities separated, Karol's experiences of socializing suggests how differences are constructed between male builders through drinking. For Karol, drinking with Polish men allows him to discuss the more personal aspects of his life – aspects that might not always be 'funny'. This became particularly significant when he was going through a divorce and wanted to discuss this with friends. What he describes as a 'sociological' issue among Londoners is an observation based upon a geographical ethno-nationality where 'Londoners' refer largely to English workmates. This sociological problem arises from his expectations of a different kind of interaction – where socializing and drinking are connected and allow the sharing of intimate and personal experiences between friends. In London however, drinking with English workmates has reinforced for him the separation between drinking and friendships, the former with English colleagues from the building site and the latter with Polish friends.

Figure 9.4   Karol's picture of drinking beer

'This is Special Humour'

Such constructions of differences were deeply embedded in their interactions within and beyond building sites. As a workplace that employed only physically able men, these differences were marked on their bodies through their nationality, language and ethnicity. Whiteness and being male remained a commonality among the participants and other builders on the site. These commonalities however, did not mean that women were excluded from their interactions. On the contrary, sexual boasting and sexual jokes were part of the inherent work cultures – a phenomenon that has been reported in other studies of construction workers (Applebaum 1981; Freeman 1983; Paap 2006). The all-male workforce and restrictions on entry and exit made them isolated from urban spaces, which often served to safeguard the 'unacceptable' behaviours of builders. As Ryszard commented, 'you cannot get accused of chauvinism or something, saying sexist jokes, or something like that. [Laughing] So, you can be not very nice, you can swear, always swear'.

It is worth noting that 'being nice' seems to require that women are to be protected from overtly masculine performances – an attitude which reflected particularly traditional ideas of gendered differences among the participants. Women were seen as feminine and sensitive and men were seen as masculine and physically strong. This was reflected on by many participants as one of the reasons why women were not present on building sites. As Karol stated, 'there couldn't be a feminine builder, that's just impossibility to me'. The physical body of the heterosexual male builder was what women had to be protected from – it was impossible for participants to perceive of women working in the building site alongside male builders who were often bare-chested and 'with hair that long in his legs' (Karol). Those women who did work on building sites were perceived as lesbian – they were 'scary' since they swore like men and were labelled as 'butch'. The participants' ideas of masculinity were therefore centred on the aggressive male body of the builder, a body that was partially clothed and heterosexual, and hence threatening for women. Women who did enter this space were those who were able to confront this male body and were therefore homosexual. These traditional ideas of gender differences were used to justify the 'rightful' exclusion of women from building sites.

Although participants held traditional ideas of masculinity and femininity, unlike their English colleagues, much of these ideas did not translate into overt masculine performances. While they would discuss women's bodies among themselves as in the case of Jan earlier, translating this into overt and aggressive performances was seen as unacceptable among participants. Sexual aggressiveness among their English colleagues nevertheless was a common feature on building sites – catcalling, teasing and staring at women near the building site. Although seen as humour among their English colleagues, this was nevertheless a version of masculinity that most participants expressed discomfort with:

> Do you know how many times I've been embarrassed when I'm driving in a van with two English builders and they open the window and go, 'hey, love'. And I'm like Jesus Christ! It just makes you feel like – 'I don't want to be involved in this'. … But you can't say that you know, 'cause he'd say 'you're a poof' … You know, it makes them probably feel more manly if they sort of seem to be interested in a girl on the street with a nice ass. And they make sure they know it. (Karol, interviewed in English)

Karol articulates the different nuances of masculine performances – while for the participants the building site can only include the woman as a lesbian builder, overt sexual performances by men which are directed at women are considered unacceptable. Significantly, these aggressive masculinities also demand heterosexual compliance from other less aggressive men such as Karol. It is during these moments that 'whiteness' among builders gets fractured along gendered ethno-national lines. Karol went on to discuss the differences in their interactions with other women by describing the English builder 'as simple as a bloody wooden chair' and the Polish builder as men with more 'finesse' (Datta and Brickell 2009). In this discourse of the 'English builder', Polish men were simultaneously depicted in their 'otherness' to Englishness as more subtle and sophisticated gendered subjects in their interactions with both men and women on building sites.

Despite such nuances of acceptable and unacceptable masculinities among English and Polish men, participants also reported on a form of humour that

**Figure 9.5   Picture taken by Dawid of his Polish friend with whom he
shares jokes**

was shared solely amongst Polish men. This humour was often a caricature of sexual violence, but its context was specific to participants' own socio-political histories.

> Dawid: Oh, [jokes] about the life. It's sometimes about the life, sometimes we have a – okay, this is only rude jokes that – and um, it's too difficult to catch the sense of humour what we have. You know, for, okay, like. No it's rude, that maybe I ... Okay, okay. Sense of humour like, how you can rape really big fat woman.

> Ayona: Do you have an answer to that?

Dawid: Of course, always we have. I must just translate this one. Take her on his [sic] forehead next to the wall, splash her arse, and then after three waves you can come in.

Clearly hesitant to share this with me, Dawid admitted the rudeness, but clarified that it is a Polish 'joke' – one made under very difficult and often extreme circumstances of growing up in a socialist regime where these were everyday coping mechanisms. Moreover, it was only made with a group of people who would immediately understand its context and relate to it politically and historically:

I must translate because … all of the jokes what we have are from our country as well. From the period when we had the different political system. … *This is special humour* [my emphasis]. First you must understand the situation, second you must compare the situation with everything what these people did, you know, to survive, to have any money. … Maybe someone can say 'this was rude, this was wrong'. Maybe. But you have not been there. (Dawid, interviewed in English)

Watson (2000: 204) notes that in socialist Poland, 'although the rulers were male, it was not "men" who ruled'. Thus, although Dawid acknowledges the sexist violence in their jokes, he contextualizes these jokes within the hardships of a socialist regime. These jokes are narrated in Polish among those of the same generation and in so doing, reinforce particular forms of masculinity that are constituted by the intersection of generational experiences and gender roles within a socialist moment. While these 'jokes' are about sexual violence, they are also seen as a coping tactics during the violence of survival facing these men in 1980s Poland. Such survival refers to the 'emasculation' of men in the hands of the socialist state and the erosion of their patriarchal authority in public and private spheres. It is worth noting that Dawid's construction of Polishness refers to the particular ethno-national territory of Poland, and particular subjects of this political territory, who at a certain moment in history chose to migrate to the UK. This description of 'Polishness' does not include the wider Polish diaspora within London – those who came after the Second World War or indeed any of the second generation Poles. This is evident in the way that Dawid cautions those who are likely to judge the nature of these jokes, by referring to them as 'those who have not been there'.

Significantly, the experiences of women are absent in the recounting and interpretation of such 'humour', which reveal the central features of Polish masculinities on building sites – a discursive space where gender identities are constructed with reference to socio-historical and cultural contexts of Polish men that distinguish them from 'other' men across ethno-national categories. Such masculinities are mapped onto Polish male bodies and spaces in ambiguous ways – where engaging in crude sexual 'humour' is not necessarily perceived as sexist; where the heterosexual working male body is central to masculinity but its visibility outside the workplace is considered undesirable; and where 'Polish' gender performances although largely compliant with their English counterparts, are constructed in opposition to Englishness.

Conclusions

I began with the photograph taken by Ryszard, which for many exemplifies workplace cultures on building sites in the UK. The visual narratives of Ryszard and other participants on the other hand complicate this seamless construction of what has until very recently been perceived as a 'homogenous white masculinity' of builders. Their location as white men within the 'home' population allows them to actively construct, reshape and complicate hegemonic white masculine performances on building sites. The insertion of a large number of Polish men in London's home refurbishment sector bring to the fore hitherto 'invisible' differences between white manual workers – through alternative discourses of ethno-nationality, gender roles and gender performances. They highlight the changing configurations of masculinity that are taking shape through other social categories and that have become relevant after 2004. These masculinities are mapped onto bodies and spaces of Polish builders in ways that are always relational and constructed in opposition to the 'otherness' of English builders. Although discursive oppositions might have been constructed during the successive waves of 'white' migrants (Irish, Turkish Cypriots and Australians) in the building industry since the nineteenth century, the constructions of Polish masculinities are clearly significant as they highlight how EU expansion after 2004 has shaped perceptions of difference within workplaces of manual labour. While notions of difference in the West has largely been constructed by over-racializing the experiences of non-white 'others' (Mac an Ghaill 2000) the visual narratives of Polish builders suggest how 'otherness' is constructed through their gendered experiences of a socialist past, and migrant experiences within capitalist labour markets in the EU.

The building site as the workplace of manual labour has acquired a central role in these constructions – as exclusive places of male bodily performances which allow socialization between workers, they are now also sites of difference between those who speak English and those who speak Polish. Although they might have traditionally provided spaces of stress-relief from manual work, they are also now spaces of support and networking among migrant Polish men. While social interactions form integral elements of work cultures on building sites, they also provide ways in which both social and cultural capital can be accumulated by Polish migrants, and highlight the processes through which differences between bodies and masculinities are then fractured along gendered ethno-national lines. These differences are apparent through bodily attire, ways of drinking and socializing, sexist humour and the construction of opposing versions of 'Polish and 'English' masculinities. The particular social and cultural geographies of building sites make such differences more apparent between Polish and English workers in the ways that they are performed by gendered bodies within such confined spaces.

Through particular ways of socializing, teasing and humour then, Polish workers perform different versions of masculinity that are, above all, always constructed in relation to the 'otherness' of English builders. The versions of Polish masculinities on the building site highlight the sophistication of Polish men in comparison to the aggressiveness of English men, and draws careful distinctions between the rude jokes of Polish builders and the rude behaviour of English builders. Thus Polish masculinities, as they take shape on building sites, are primarily about the nuances of gender performances in ways that they differ from English men and are then mapped onto bodies of particular gendered ethno-national subjects. These versions are further fractured across generations – between younger and older Polish men, those who grew up in socialist Poland, and those who did not, those who have gender roles as breadwinners and those who are engaged in more 'laddish' masculinities.

Watson notes that 'in Eastern Europe, deep-seated notions of gender difference often go hand in hand with a lack of any real sense of gender inequality' (Watson 2000: 71). The visual narratives of the Polish participants suggest complex constructions of gender identities and masculinities that make references to a socialist past where the struggles of men to 'survive' are seen as justifications of crude humour around sexual violence. These struggles construct ideas of a heterosexual masculinity that does not necessarily regard women as objects of sexual violence, but rather men as the 'victims' of a socialist state. Polish masculinities as constructed by participants are embedded in their emasculation under socialism and in their new roles as politically empowered workers within capitalist economies – an identification that excludes the wider Polish diaspora living in the UK. Polish masculinities constructed under such conditions evoke particular socio-political and historic moments that connect its subjects through a common experience, which is more about men's experiences and less about gender relations with women.

Above all, this chapter illustrates that building work is far more than 'just work' – this work implants the Polish migrants within a whole socio-cultural structure that is new to them and it provide spaces where their subjective locations vis-à-vis ethnicity, race, whiteness and gender within wider British and Polish societies are negotiated and transformed. Building sites are not just places of work; they are simultaneously places of social interaction which provide support systems and social networks to Polish migrants. While the role of manual work in the construction of masculinities has been well-researched, the role of social interactions in such contexts has been largely overlooked. Yet, as the visual narratives suggest, social interactions during manual work are critical to the construction of migrant experiences and of 'other' masculinities in the UK after 2004.

Acknowledgements

I wish to thank the Suntory Toyota International Centres for Economics and Related Disciplines (STICERD) in the London School of Economics for the New Researcher Grant, which funded this research. I also wish to express my heartfelt gratitude to the participants who kindly devoted their time to answering questions and taking pictures. Thanks also to Katherine Brickell and Magdalena Maculewicz for their valuable contributions towards the fieldwork.

References

Applebaum, H. (1981), *Royal Blue: The Culture of Construction Workers* (New York, NY: Holt, Rinehart and Winston).

Berg, L. and Longhurst, R. (2003), 'Placing Masculinities and Geography', *Gender, Place, and Culture* 10:4, 351–60.

Collinson, D. and Hearn, J. (1996), '"Men' at 'work'": Multiple Masculinities/ Multiple Workplaces', in Mac an Ghaill (ed.).

Cornwall, A. and Lindisfarne, N. (1994), *Dislocating Masculinity: Comparative Ethnographies* (London: Routledge).

Currie, S. (2006), 'Free Movers? The Post-accession Experience of Accession-8 Migrant Workers in the United Kingdom', *European Law Review* 31:2, 207–29.

Datta, A. (2008), 'Building Differences: Material Geographies of Home(s) among Polish Builders in London', *Transactions of the Institute of British Geographers* 33:4, 518–31.

Datta, A. (2009), 'Places of Everyday Cosmopolitanisms: East-European Construction Workers in London', *Environment and Planning A*.

Datta, A. and Brickell, K. (2009), '"We have a Little Bit More Finesse as a Nation": Constructing the Polish Worker in London's Building Sites', *Antipode: A Radical Journal of Geography*.

Eade, J., Drinkwater, S. and Garapich, M.P. (2007), *Class and Ethnicity: Polish Migrant Workers in London – Full Research Report*. ESRC End of Award Report, RES-000-22-1294 (Swindon: Economic and Social Research Council).

Einhorn, B. (2006), 'Gender(ed) Politics in Central and Eastern Europe', *Journal of Global Ethics* 2:2, 139–62.

Fidelis, M. (2004), 'Equality through Protection: The Politics of Women's Employment in Postwar Poland, 1945–1956', *Slavic Review* 63:2, 301–24.

Freeman, J. (1983), 'Hardhats: Construction Workers, Manliness, and the 1970 Pro-war Demonstration', *Journal of Social History* 26:4, 725–44.

Gal, S. and Kligman, G. (2000), *The Politics of Gender After Socialism* (Princeton, NJ: Princeton University Press).

Gregory, C. (2006), 'Among the Dockhands: Another Look at Working-Class Male Culture', *Men and Masculinities* 9:2, 252–60.

Heinen, J. (1997), 'Social and Political Citizenship in Eastern Europe', *Theory and Society* 26:4, 577–97.

Home Office, Department for Work and Pensions, HM Revenue & Customs and Communities and Local Government (2007), *Accession Monitoring Report March 2004–May 2007.* <http://www.ind.homeoffice.gov.uk/6353/aboutus/AccessionMonitoringReport11.pdf>, accessed 19 March 2008.

HPSC (2005), 'Building London, Saving Lives: Improving Health and Safety in Construction', *Health and Public Services Committee* <http://www.london.gov.uk/assembly/reports/health/construction.rtf>, accessed 23 April 2008.

IFF (2003), 'Workforce Mobility and Skills in the Construction Sector in London and the South East', Research Report prepared for Construction Skills, ECITB, SEEDA and DTI, London <www.seeda.co.uk/publications/learning_skills_&_workforce/docs/Workforce_Mobility_Oct_03.doc>, accessed 21 July 2008.

Iglicka, K. (2001), 'Migration Movements from and into Poland in the Light of East-West European Migration', *International Migration* 39:1, 3–32.

Jordan, B. (2002), 'Migrant Polish Workers in London: Mobility, Labour Markets and the Prospects for Democratic Development'. Paper presented at 'Beyond Transition: Development Perspectives and Dilemmas', Warsaw <http://www.surrey.ac.uk/Arts/CRONEM/Bill-Jordan-Polish-migration.pdf>, accessed 13 July 2008.

Kenny, P. (1999), 'The Gender of Resistance in Communist Poland', *American Historical Review* 104:2, 399–425.

Kligman, G. (1996), 'Women and the Negotiation of Identity in Post-Communist Eastern Europe', in Identities in Transition: Eastern Europe and Russia After the Collapse of Communism, University of California International and Area Studies Digital Collection 93, 68–91 <http://repositories.cdlib.org/uciaspubs/research/93/6>, accessed 15 July 2008.

Mac an Ghaill, M. (ed.) (1996), *Understanding Masculinities* (Buckingham: Open University Press).

Mac an Ghaill, M. (2000), 'The Irish in Britain: The Invisibility of Ethnicity and Anti-Irish Racism', *Journal of Ethnic and Migration Studies* 26:1, 137–47.

McDowell, L. (2002), 'Masculine Discourses and Dissonances: Strutting "Lads", Protest Masculinity, and Domestic Respectability', *Environment and Planning D: Society and Space* 20:1, 97–119.

McDowell, L. (2003), *Redundant Masculinities? Employment Change and White Working Class Youth* (Oxford: Blackwell).

Nast, H. and Pile, S. (eds) (1998), *Places Through the Body* (London: Routledge).

Nye, R. (2005), 'Locating Masculinity: Some Recent Work on Men', *Signs: Journal of Women in Culture and Society* 30:3, 1937–1962.

Paap, K. (2006), *Working Construction: Why White Working-Class Men Put Themselves – and the Labor Movement – in Harm's Way* (Ithaca: ILR Press).

Rukszto, K. (1997), 'Making her into a "Woman": The Creation of Citizen-Entrepreneur in Capitalist Poland', *Women's Studies International Forum* 20:1, 103–12.

Smith, A., Stenning, A., Rochovská, A. and Świątek, D. (2008), 'The Emergence of a Working Poor: Labour Markets, Neoliberalisation and Diverse Economies in Post-Socialist Cities', *Antipode: A Radical Journal of Geography* 40:2, 283–311.

Spencer, S., Ruhs, M., Anderson, B. and Rogaly, B. (2007), *Migrants' Lives Beyond the Workplace: The Experiences of Central and East Europeans in the UK* (York: Joseph Rowntree Foundation).

Van Hoven, B. and Horschelmann, K. (eds) (2005), *Spaces of Masculinities* (London: Routledge).

Watson, P. (1993), 'The Rise of Masculinism in Eastern Europe', *New Left Review* I/198, 71–82.

Watson, P. (2000), 'Re-Thinking Transition: Globalism, Gender and Class', *International Feminist Journal of Politics* 2:2, 185–213.

Chapter 10

The Material Worlds of Recent Polish Migrants: Transnationalism, Food, Shops and Home

Marta Rabikowska and Kathy Burrell

This chapter will discuss the roles of consumption and material culture in rooting the lives of recent Polish migrants in London and the Midlands. As will be shown, consumption is a central and highly visible component of A8 migration. Since 2004, there has been a marked increase in entrepreneurial activities across the UK by new migrants. By investing savings or arranging business loans, thousands of new businesses have emerged. Though these businesses are diverse – wood and metal manufacturing, construction industry, private schooling, nurseries and language schools – the biggest expansion of all has been in the grocery sector.

It should not come as a surprise that the need for Polish food has dominated business activities among and aimed at the new immigrants. The obvious connection between food, home and ethnicity has been researched extensively within many fields, especially anthropology, geography, psycho-social studies, feminist studies, art, and of course the sociology of food. While the simplified association 'we are what we eat' links food and identity on cultural, psychological and somatic levels, the 'we are where we eat' (Bell and Valentine 1997) approach anchors consumption in space. In the case of immigrants displaced from their homeland environment, the material space of consumption may also serve as an 'ethnic marker', balancing the lack of formal belonging to the host community and making a home attachment more visible and more meaningful. Historically, food has always been central in maintaining ethnic identity away from the original homeland, and an important means of asserting a presence on the new landscape through market stalls, shops and restaurants (see Gabaccia 2000; Diner 2001; Kershen 2002; Panayi 2008).

The importance of food for migrant experiences and identities exemplifies a much wider connection between consumption and material culture and social, cultural, economic and even political processes. Just as Miller (1998) explains how social relationships are embedded and reflected in everyday material practices, so Bridge and Smith (2003: 258) underline the significance of focusing on commodities to explore the 'reciprocal relations between the "cultural" and the "economic"'. The particular resonance of consumption and material culture for investigating migration is also now well established. Blunt's (2007) recent appraisal of the cultural geographies of migration illustrates the wealth of research being carried out in this area. Not only has the 'mobilities turn' in the social sciences (see Urry 2007) led to the spaces and experiences of travel becoming more materially contextualized, but the material transfigurations of transnationalism and settlement – remittances, material exchange, home making – are now increasingly popular concerns for migration researchers.

This chapter seeks to add to these debates by bringing together two separate projects on the materiality of recent Polish migration. Firstly it draws on in-depth interviews undertaken by Burrell with ten post accession migrants across the Midlands region, as part a larger historical study also considering Polish migration to the area during and immediately after socialism. Material culture and consumption were not the exclusive focus of the research, but the importance of these issues became very clear during the course of the interviews. Carrying significant objects and food back and forth between Poland and England, and the ability to buy Polish food in the Midlands, were key discussion points in most of the conversations. These interviews were carried out in English, predominantly with young highly skilled migrants working in a range of sectors including administration, veterinary medicine, education and hospitality. While not necessarily representative of those migrants with fewer skills and without English language proficiency, the stories of these respondents do illuminate the migration experiences of young people who felt compelled to leave Poland, frustrated that their skills and abilities were not being rewarded at home, and who are now building new lives across Britain.

Secondly, Rabikowska's research focuses specifically on different types of shops selling Polish food in London – an in-depth ethnographic study incorporating twenty interviews with Polish immigrants living in London, and eight with shop owners, undertaken between January 2006 and December 2007. The shop owners agreed to be interviewed on the site of their businesses and the twenty customers were chosen at random during their shopping routine in the same establishment. Each owner/manager was asked to give a tour around the shop and to talk about the supply of Polish goods. The clients, who were met inside the shops, were asked questions designed to discover the reasons why they chose to buy in a given shop. Rabikowska also did some shopping in each shop and took notes on its decor, layout, place settings, atmosphere and the behavior of the clients.

The findings of this research offer invaluable insights into the shopping habits of recent migrants and highlight the importance of Polish goods and food to their everyday practices in London and the Midlands. Taken together, these projects underline the extent to which consumption and material culture are pivotal in experiences of migration and settlement generally, but also how they reflect the 'roots' and shape the 'routes' of recent Polish migrants specifically.

Mobile Homes and Migrants' Material Worlds

In her study of Filipina migrants in Hong Kong, Lisa Law (2001: 277) argues that 'the absence of familiar material culture, and its subtle evocations of home, is surely one of the most profound dislocations of transnational migration'. As is widely recognized, much of the experience of the aftermath of migration is concerned with, in varying guises and intensities, reconnecting with some of the material contexts of pre-migration life and entering into the complex process of making a new home away from it. The concept of home being mobile, and something that can be recreated again at different times and in different places, is now readily acknowledged (see Miller 2001; Tolia-Kelly 2004; Walsh 2006). Finding and making the domestic component of these homes can be done in many ways, but material culture and consumption are usually at the heart of the process; as Reimer and Leslie (2004) argue, home identities, as well as individual identities, are created through consumption. While the different scales of home and homemaking practices are recognized (see Blunt and Dowling 2006), housing accommodation, whether shared with other immigrants or not, arguably offers the most immediate and easily manipulated space, and so can be used to create places which reflect experiences and identities. These places are furnished in part with things brought from the pre-migration home.

The migration stories collected with recent Polish migrants in the Midlands demonstrated the significance of material culture and consumption throughout the different stages of migration; preparation, travelling, and ultimately living in a new place (see also Burrell 2008). Several respondents spoke about what they had brought to the UK, narrating a mixture of practicality and emotion in their packing strategies. Elzbieta, for example, recounted what she transported with her on her initial journey:

> Firstly, I used to take with me food, tinned meat, fish, crisp bread, instant soups, everything which didn't go off quickly, all sorts of toiletries, pens, papers, envelopes and things which might be necessary, a thread and a needle, painkillers and other basic medicines, matches and torch, mug, spoon and knife etc. The reason was quite simple, I had some money but I felt quite insecure that it would be enough. Moreover, I didn't want to spend it on silly things I could've taken from home.[1]

Carrying useful things to save unnecessary expense once in the UK is an undeniably prudent strategy, but one which has deeper significance. By taking so many everyday things, Elzbieta was ensuring that, consciously or subconsciously, her subsequent daily practices in her new domestic environment would incorporate a wide range of familiar objects, and would offer an element of continuity with her

---

1   Interview with Elzbieta (5 May 2006, follow up email correspondence November 2006, July 2007), migrated to Wolverhampton in 2006 aged 32.

life before. Walsh (2006: 133) has found something similar with British expatriates in Dubai – the functionality of key objects from home, in this case kitchen utensils, can obscure their emotional meaning to everybody but the owner.

Other respondents spoke about bringing more obviously or visually significant objects with them on their first journey to the UK. Again, the importance of particular objects for connecting migrants to both home and past has been widely researched (see Parkin 1999; Tolia-Kelly 2004; Attan 2006; Walsh 2006). Adriana narrated her choice to bring both everyday and special things with her:

> I brought things from home, not exactly Polish, some African. We are quite homely people so we bought cutlery because we like it, and I did bring some pictures. Some things to put on the wall that my sister gave me from her trip to Tunisia. The other things, I would take other things but you can take only 15kg of luggage. But when my boyfriend went for a holiday he wanted to take the lampshades. We brought some mugs.[2]

As before, ordinary objects which feature heavily in everyday routines are chosen to accompany the migration, but the significance of bringing something which is given by a relative is also made clear. As Money (2007: 367–8) illustrates in her research into people's living rooms, and as Miller (1998) argues extensively, certain items act as markers of other people. By bringing specific items from her sister, Adriana can try to keep a physical connection with her; conversely, however, the wall hangings could also remind her of the distance between them.

The disclosure of bringing particular things from Poland to the UK is important. Polish migration after 2004 is frequently characterized as temporary, sometimes even portrayed as long-distance commuting, and the mobility of the population is highly stressed. Even if this is true for many of the migrants, there is also clearly a rooting process taking place at the same time. Whether the migration is considered to be temporary or permanent, tangible, material markers are brought into the UK to aid the practical and emotional strain of moving to and living in a new country. The spaces the migrants inhabit in the UK are being transformed into homes.

The Importance of Food

Of all the items brought to the UK from Poland, products relating to food were discussed the most widely, and perhaps the most enthusiastically. Much of the transnational ferrying of goods between the two countries revolved around food, and when asked what people missed most about living in Poland, food, after family and friends, was the answer most frequently given. Pawel spoke about how negatively his diet has changed since living in Leicester:

---

2   Interview with Adriana (24 November 2005), migrated to Birmingham in 2005 aged 31.

I've gained twenty five kilos since I came here, that's three, four stones. Because of the English food I think, and now I'm trying to lose it. No offence, but your bread, the bread is really like a sponge for me. Polish bread is different, after two days you can't eat Polish bread, it's not very good, it's really hard. Here when you buy bread after two days you can still eat it because it is like a sponge. That is the main difference actually with food. I'm not eating bread here.[3]

Missing familiar food is physiologically and emotionally challenging. As Marek commented; 'I miss the Polish cuisine, I mean my mother's cuisine. I have to cook myself and it is not the same'.[4]

Two interesting points in particular emerged from the discussion of Polish food. The first is the rapid change in provision of Polish goods in the UK since 2004, and particularly after 2006. When most of the respondents embarked on their initial migrations, they did not expect to find much Polish food at all when they arrived. Thus food was an important component of the packing for that first journey, and precious suitcase space was given over to processed food which would last a little while in the UK. Similarly, food was central to the subsequent trips made back home and suitcases would be brought back bursting with food products, with those travelling by airplane often exceeding Ryanair's 15 kg weight limit (see Burrell 2008). The proliferation of shops selling Polish goods appears to be changing this practice, however. Now that Polish food is readily available across the UK, only certain types of food are brought back from Poland – homemade dishes. A hierarchy of food has become apparent; UK shops selling Polish food can supply important products, but the most meaningful food is that made by family. Elzbieta spoke about bringing food back which has been prepared by her parents, and Magdalena, a recent migrant in Derby, made similar comments:

I packed some food, because now there are loads of Polish shops but I didn't realize it was like this, loads of Polish shops. Sausages. My mum, of course, cooked me some bigos, a dish made from cabbage and meat, and of course pierogi, dumplings. And I also bought some sweets and chocolates. It has turned out I shouldn't have, I shouldn't do this because I can buy all these things here, so now I don't do this. Only traditional Polish dishes which my mum cooks, this is what I normally bring here.[5]

This home cooked food, like the special objects chosen to accompany migration, reflects wider familial relationships. Resembling the Greek students who are sent and bring back copious amounts of food from home (Petridou 2001), these relatively young recent Polish migrants rely on homemade food to sustain an

---

3   Interview with Pawel (9 March 2007), migrated to Leicester in 2006 aged 21.
4   Interview with Marek (21 December 2005), migrated to Derby in 2005 aged 24.
5   Interview with Magdalena (16 February 2008), migrated to Derby in 2006 aged 26.

emotional closeness with their parents, and mothers especially, still in Poland. Arleta, also in Derby, discussed these issues at length:

> My luggage is full of homemade food, I should say meat dishes and sausages. We don't buy readymade stuff as it is easily available in Derby now, and even our corner shop run by Pakistani couple offers Polish food … Polish food and drinks are easily available in Derby now. The number of shops in Normanton offering Polish food is rising each month, it nicely reflects the influence Polish immigrants have on the local economy. The variety of products is sometimes overwhelming. We go to the Normanton shops usually once, sometimes twice a month. Polish beer and vodka are available in the most of bars and pubs in the city centre, which I find quite amazing as well. As I mentioned before, even our corner shop provides Polish food selection. The owners of the shop are so kind, they ask us what we need or want and they try to supply items requested. We usually buy sausages there, much better quality and taste better than local ones. We buy readymade meals like bigos and flaczki, some spices, dairy like Polish sour cream, full fat white cheese, our favourite mayonnaise. Those products are not available from English supermarkets and shops.[6]

The second point is that, although these shops may not be able to fill the loss of home cooked food, they of course allow the migrants to cook and consume their own Polish food in the UK, again allowing them to transform their immediate spaces into places of familiar rituals, smells and tastes. And while these shops aid the feeling of being at home for the migrants in their domestic settings, they simultaneously carve out Polish corners in local landscapes across the country. The Normanton area of Derby is an instructive example; along one road about a mile long there are more than ten different types of shop selling varying quantities of Polish goods, jostling alongside other products catering predominantly for the diverse local population. Leicester too has witnessed an intense proliferation of outlets selling Polish products since 2006. The same has happened across the whole country; 'Polishness' – or at least versions of Polishness – is now a visible and embedded part of the UK's public, commercial space. As Wang and Lo (2007: 186) argue regarding Chinese shops in Canada, ethnic shops are a 'focal point connecting the host society and the home country'. Similar to the UK's South Asian cinemas that Puwar (2007) draws attention to, they act as both private and public spaces, markers and sustainers of ethnic identity inwardly and outwardly. What is particularly important about these shops too is that they bring the Polish consumers into contact with other ethnic minority groups. As the last interview extract demonstrates, shopping for Polish goods involves talking to Pakistani shopkeepers, and in the case of Normanton especially, visiting, or even just walking past a wide array of ethnic minority businesses.

---

6   Interview with Arleta (10 December 2005, follow up email correspondence June and July 2007) who migrated to Derby in 2005 aged 29.

There are historical precedents of visible Polish consumption in Britain; the post-war refugee population also made its mark on local townscapes. Earlier research into Polish settlement in Leicester (see Burrell 2006) found that at one point there were so many shops in the city selling Polish products such as bread, butter and sausages – four or five distinctly Polish shops – that there were not enough Polish people to sustain them all. Even at the peak of Polish community life, owners relied heavily on the custom of Jewish and other European immigrant groups. As the population aged and decreased most of the shops closed, leaving only a market stall and one or two delicatessens selling key products. Despite this heritage, however, the speed at which the new availability of Polish products has emerged is, historically, staggering. Of course it reflects a new economic context of globalization, but it also bears testament to the size of this migration movement. The geographic reach of these shops selling Polish goods is also highly significant; Polish migration can be witnessed physically in bodies, but also materially through goods, across the whole country. Ultimately, these recent developments demonstrate the mutability of ethnicity and public space (see for example Li 2005). How long these shops continue to sell Polish products for will depend on how permanent this migration proves to be, but at the moment at least they have constituted another layer of Britain's commercial ethnic diversity. The next section will examine the experience of shopping for Polish products, using London as a case-study, in more depth.

Case-study: Shopping for Polish Food in London

Before 2004 there were just a few food stores in London that specialized in Polish food. They were mainly located in areas traditionally associated with Polish migration after the Second World War such as Hammersmith and Ealing, and were aimed at these post-war era customers and their families born in the UK. However, in central parts of London there were also many examples of expensive and elegant delicatessens supplying 'continental' groceries, where Polish sausage, vodka and chocolate sit next to French, Italian, Spanish, and German delicacies. Such shops tended to target middle class customers with disposable incomes who did not necessarily seek an ethnic affiliation with the site or the food itself, but were instead interested in the good quality and originality of the products, regardless of their origin. Therefore such shops were not perceived as symbolic sites in a nostalgic or ethnic sense, but rather as cultural sites highlighting a certain health-orientated lifestyle of their customers.

This link between middle class healthy lifestyles and Polish delicacies has changed dramatically since the influx of Polish immigrants after 2004. The number of shops selling Polish products increased visibly during the first year after Poland's accession. It began with the introduction of small supplies to existing shops selling to other migrant groups, mainly South Asian and in some cases Russian, which first recognized the demand for a new kind of product across inner

Table 10.1   Number and location of respondents using different shops

Shop Type	Location in London	Number of Respondents
A	North	5
A	East	4
B	South East	6
B	North East	5
C	South East	4
C	South West	6
D	South East	5
D	North East	6

and outer London. In a couple of months Polish entrepreneurialism, first spreading into tiny retail spaces (often of suspicious providence) such as market stalls, truck decks or door-to door sales, changed the landscape of the national food sector. In response to growing demand and keen competition, the chain giants, like ASDA (350 Polish lines in 85 stores, *Grocer* 25 August 2007), Tesco and Sainsbury's (32 lines in 11 stores, *Financial Times* 8 November 2006), and even upmarket stores such as Selfridges and Harvey Nichols, also launched new lines with specialized Polish products whose selection was 'based on research carried out directly with the community itself' (*Financial Times* 8 November 2006).

Based on participatory observation started in 2001, the different sites selling Polish products today can be categorized according to their most representative stock as follows:

A   South Asian shop – sells Polish products in addition to their main stock
B   Eastern European shop – sells a variety of Polish and other national products but has a strong emphasis on goods from the owner's country
C   Polish shop – specializes only in Polish products and is run by a Polish family
D   Chain shop – allocates space to Polish products among other ethnic groceries

The research was undertaken with respondents in two shops of each category, located in different areas of London, as Table 10.1 illustrates.

Each of these categories was researched in depth through interviews with customers and owners, and in addition another four 'type C' shops were chosen for participatory observation and the visual analysis of the sites' designs and product layouts. Classic international delicatessens have not been considered in this research as they precede the Polish expansion in the retail market in 2004.

Constructing Home Through Polish Shops

The internal spaces of shops selling Polish products hold symbolic meanings for their customers; this research has found that this meaning is complex and often quite ambiguous. On the one hand, such a shop can help promote a feeling of belonging, recreate a feeling of home, empower its customers as citizens and mark ownership of territory. In particular, exclusively Polish shops (type C) to some extent serve as platforms for communication and social exchange among customers. As several respondents commented, 'it feels like the heart of Polish life'. However, participant observation and conversations with shop owners revealed that interpersonal contact with other Poles on the shops' sites is not in fact as intense as Polish customers claim when speaking directly about this issue. This optimistic perception can be termed a 'modulated desire for home', influenced by the desire to use the shop in this manner. Using the shop as a forum for exchanging small adverts and job offers is quite popular among customers, but using it as a meeting point for more meaningful social exchange is something which is more of an aspiration than a reality. When doing their shopping, Polish customers do not get involved in conversations with each other and even tend to avoid eye contact with others, as if trying to separate themselves from any informal communication. They reply warmly to the staff and exchange all the characteristic phrases of politeness in their native jargon, full of abbreviations and idioms, yet when asked about any personal contacts with other Poles found through the shop, they deny having met anybody in this way and proudly unfold a list of contacts made elsewhere, especially among non-Polish communities.

Nevertheless, the shops' customers do express their delight in having a Polish shop in the area and emphasize its role for both the wider community and their own comfort. More than any social function, it is the atmosphere of home which is valued most highly, alongside the authenticity of the food imported from Poland. Customers even come for their daily groceries from further afield in London where Polish shops are not available, and where type A, B and D shops are not regarded as 'Polish enough' and lack in 'the homeliness of design and friendly attitude from the staff'. It can be concluded that on a public level Polish customers take the representational role of Polish shops for granted, but they do not perceive them as influential in terms of networking or social gain. They agree that the shops represent Poland and Polish tastes, and in that sense they directly relate to the customers themselves, but they do not tend to be involved in the making of that representation on a personal level and do not go to the shops in order to 'make friends'.

This feeling of home stems from the shop's position as a place where products, language, people and characteristically Polish design all merge to create an experience which resonates very intimately. The association of the shop with home, though, is also affected by this *need* to have this 'heart of Polish life', whose symbolic attributes are shifted onto the shop's site. Even when the migrants are resistant to social connectivity within the location, buying products in a Polish shop rearticulates a connection with the home country. The most mundane practice of choosing groceries becomes a statement, a material gesture acknowledging Polish origin and reinstating the meaning of home. A very obvious double signification of home has been recognized in customers' attitudes: home as a country and home as a personal space. When making an effort to locate Polish shops in their area and consuming products which remind them of the past, of their childhood, of ceremonial meals and eating and drinking as part of a social group, immigrants find a point of reference in a new reality. The selection of the same traditional products, such as flaki, bigos, barszcz z uszkami, kaszanka, sledzie, fasolka po bretonsku reinforces a memory of homely meals, even though these products are not necessarily part of the everyday diet of Poles. When consumed at home they must be prepared by hand, so such products in a can or a jar would rarely receive the approval of the family, and they are often the topic of national jokes and are generally scorned. Nevertheless, their reappearance on the shelves, even in shops A, B and D, creates a sense of home which cannot be found elsewhere in a foreign environment.

According to Terkenly (1995), recalling a historical study by Hobsbawm (1991), to recognize home one needs to first encounter a 'nonhome' – a place and condition which contrasts with what was familiar before immigration. The home which is missed by immigrants exists only under the condition of exile and needs constant confrontation with a 'nonhome' over which they have little control. Practising home through consuming original food enables them to regain some stability and orientation in a host culture, or, as Bentley (1998) has shown through the example of Mexican immigrants in America, it can be a means of affirming resistance to outside influences. For example, among the respondents the most common complaints about 'outside' culinary influences were those concerning English cuisine, regarded as unhealthy and over-processed, although other ethnic foodstuffs were not often held in high esteem either. Regular consumption of Polish foodstuffs not only evokes the safety of a home structure (country and personal space), but translates a new environment into home through routine shopping and habitual cooking, eating and drinking (again see Terkenly 1995: 326). Polish (type C) shops in particular, signifying group identity and offering familiar design and layout, allow customers to incorporate aspects of a Polish lifestyle into their daily routine and thus reinforce their emotional and physical connections with home.

Shop Preferences: Using Non-Polish Shops

Importantly, the strength of this kind of 'identity investment' varies in the other types of shops (A, B and D). In the first months after EU accession, type A and B shops, offering cheap Polish food, were the most popular sites in London and were often called 'Polish shops' by local customers, recognizing Polish identity in the otherwise foreign surroundings. Eastern European stores (type B), however, seem to be preferred to South Asian newsagents and Cash and Carry shops where the products are not displayed in a sufficiently distinct way and so do not inspire the same sense of recognition and representation. This preference also appears reciprocal; it was observed that non-Polish Eastern European customers tend to choose Polish shops (C) over type A shops if they do not have their own national food store in the neighbourhood. Furthermore, while the layout and the range of Polish products is similar in shops A and B (although with type B often offering smaller selections than type A), the Eastern European connection is much more visible in B where customers speak to each other in their national languages, 'sounding more like home'. Eastern European shops tend to reflect the language and background of the owner, and this dominates the adverts, groceries and the press titles available there, but this 'favouritism' also works to promote the authenticity of the shop and its stock.

Although Poles can hardly understand Lithuanian or Estonian, and their knowledge of Russian and Ukrainian is restricted to those who remember communist drills from school, their attraction to Eastern European ethnic products is rooted in the shared belief in staple 'homely food', devoid of 'toxic preservatives' or 'artificial shapes or colours – far from nature'. In spite of being served in English in type B shops, and being among a plethora of other ethnic foodstuffs, Polish customers still 'buy the homely atmosphere' embedded in some similar products and the familiar behaviour of people. As Marzena commented, 'Buying a loaf of Polish bread which lies next to the Lithuanian bread takes me closer to home, although the Lithuanian bread is dark and I have never tried it'.[7] Similarly, Beata chooses type B shops for 'the common appreciation of sauerkraut, sausage, herring, and borsch' which other ethnic groups do not have, 'especially Asians who do not know how to display certain kinds of sausage together, but they try to learn from us – clients'.[8]

Many South Asian shop owners have certainly tried to recreate this familiarity in their shops. As the previous example from Derby also demonstrated, asking Polish customers for advice about the choice of products and their purpose has become a usual practice which customers appreciate. Yet relying on the suppliers who specialize in ethnic food does not always meet the expectations of the customers, and may even cause confusion. An analysis of a brochure from 2007, delivered among shop owners in London by the global company EXSA Foods Ltd ('the leading suppliers of ethnic grocery products'), indicated that the understanding of ethnic differences among these specialists is rather limited. This brochure was discussed during an interview with Janak, an Indian shop owner (shop type A) in South-East London, who asked for advice in choosing products for a Polish section located on the lower shelves of the middle aisle of his shop. To a Polish eye this section had not been very well presented, with a sense of randomness and inaccuracy in the arrangement of products. For example, instant soups and soup spices were stacked on two different shelves, whereas drinking juice and beetroot juice used in soup were placed together. In fact, it was not easy to recognize the

---

7   Interview with Marzena (3 May 2007), migrated to London in 2005 aged 28.
8   Interview with Beata (10 January 2007), migrated to London in 2006 aged 33.

Figure 10.1   South Asian shop – type A

Polish zone; there were very few markers which would emphasize its presence among other products whose origins were not Polish at all. The brochure, which the owner used as his guide for the products' selection, reflected a similar lack of attention and, on certain pages, basic research. In a section entitled 'Polish Puddings and Meat Products' there were pictures of homemade cakes printed next to mushroom dumplings (pierogi), also alongside a whole range of halal pâtés of Turkish origin. The Polish soup section included mayonnaise and Turkish chilli sauces, in spite of the fact that chilli is avoided as a spice in Poland. By placing different ethnic products together, EXSA Foods are almost certainly unaware of the minor mistakes in their promotion strategy. Unintentionally they do two things: promote a feeling of local authenticity, appreciated by the individual immigrants who are able to recognize their own national products, and encourage the identification with global consumption which favours amalgamation of products and absorption of difference.

Mixing representative products from all ethnic groups living in the area in one shop, however, does not allow for much distinction between them. Figures 10.1 and 10.2 reflect this incoherence in the shops classified here as type A – South Asian. After a one season trial with Polish products, Janak observed that his old clients started leaving to go to other, more specialized, shops in the same street. His final decision was to close the Polish line and concentrate on Indian, Pakistani and Bangladeshi

Figure 10.2   South Asian shop – type A

groceries which were traditionally associated with his shop and drew customers from the whole region. Those South Asian shops which can afford a regular supply of Polish products, especially fresh Polish bread and meats, have to work harder to encourage customers by applying Polish names in shop windows, promoting sales on portable boards on the pavements and offering free Polish magazines printed in London, and most of all offering fresh food daily even if it does not sell entirely.

Being aware of the seasonal significance of certain food is also important when selling Polish food. During the Christmas period of 2007, for example, there was an abundant supply of carp across the country, probably the first time ever for South Asian shops in the UK. Even the big chains (D) decided to include carp in their festive offers which increased sales of 50 per cent in the fish section (*Guardian* 26 November 2007). Nevertheless, shopping in exclusively Polish shops is still regarded as 'more homely' than in type A, B or D shops, which are often criticized for the unreliability of their Polish selections: according to Viola 'If they have carp, they don't have cabbage, if they have cabbage, they don't have dried mushroom and we end up going to a Polish shop anyway'.[9] Lithuanian and Ukrainian shops are closest to Polish tastes and shopping habits, but even they do not receive as positive feedback as the Polish shop.

---

9   Interview with Viola (22 August 2007), migrated to London in 2004 aged 41.

Figure 10.3 Polish shop – type C

Nostalgia and Shop Design

Exclusively Polish shops have one very important advantage over the other sites – their design and product presentation. Crucially, customers can appreciate clusters of products displayed according to their traditional use, their different roles in a meal's composition, or in a current festivity. Baking powder, for example, is placed next to the foil baking formats for sugar bunnies to be made at home for Easter; candies labelled 'Krystynki' are put in a central position in March for the occasion of the Krystyna name day, one of the most popular female names in Poland; while herring and ham are situated next to the potato salad to mirror the most typical settings of a Polish table. These shop spaces are able to reflect the changing calendar of Poland, and the intricacies of the daily diet there. Furthermore, the décor of the Polish shop is designed to remind the customer of home through provoking traditional images of sturdiness and rustic warmth. Most of these shops use wooden shelves, often imitating oak or pine, frosted lights and willow baskets for bread or special offers. In Figure 10.3, there is a rack of wooden shelves in the middle and a coffee area in the corner which serves homemade cakes, especially Polish cheese cake and poppy cake, and where customers can order sandwiches made from fresh products in the shop and read the Polish press published in London. When asked why they chose this kind of décor, one shop owner replied:

> We want Poles to feel like at home and appreciate the difference from other shops where they use plastic and neon lights throughout. We want to offer our customers authenticity and good quality. Maybe our shops are a bit more expensive because of that but our customers know that they can only get the best here.

The fact that such an affected bucolic design in grocery shops is not a popular choice now in Poland itself seems to escape the attention of both the owners and the customers. Polish shoppers in London appear to engage willingly with mythical symbols of authenticity which in Poland are reserved for souvenir kiosks in Kraków, Warsaw and other tourist cities – shops which sell historical figurines, folklore accessories and expensive food items like jams, pickled mushrooms or herbal liqueurs, but which are, at the same time, stylized as peasant inns, conjuring images of restaurants with open fires, barrels of freshly pickled cabbage, gherkins and home baked bread spread with lard. This can be seen in Figure 10.3, where there is a Cracovian doll ('Krakowianka') in a traditional costume, sitting on the counter with her face turned to the customers, and a collection of the Russian nested dolls ('Matryoshka') on the upper shelf. Neither of them is for sale, although the clients ask for them almost every time when they visit the shop for the first time. This 'authentic' rural style was popularized during communism through the cooperative retail sector 'Cepelia', representing traditional Polish handcraft. However, in this case, mythical authenticity embraces the Russian folklore too despite the difference between the two nations, but neither the customers nor the shopkeeper regard that difference as meaningful or problematic. The symbolization of national identity draws upon the Eastern European, which is home related, as opposite to the Western, perceived as foreign. Although a stylized reference to the Polish traditional folklore was clearly part of communist propaganda aimed at restoring a sense of value among the lowest classes, Cepelia appeared to have gained respect and affection among Poles, to an extent transcending communist ideology. An appealing myth of collective Polish identity, or even more general Slavonic identity, was thus imposed on national industry and culture and was celebrated through folklore imagery and traditions across nationally regulated events, community festivals and commercial activities. Regardless of its ideological arbitrariness, this myth still intimates a sense of home and, as Bentley (1998) found in the US, may serve as a counterforce balancing the dominance of the multicultural host culture. One Polish shop owner expressed her desire to embed a picture of a white eagle – the Polish national emblem – in her local marketing campaign and to have it painted on the shop window, so 'everyone would know that we celebrate our Polish identity here'.

Being the 'Other': Ethnicity, Class and Settlement

Notably different to the nostalgically designed Polish shops are the anonymous chain shops (D) such as Asda, Tesco, Sainsbury's and others, which try very hard to respond to the demands of Polish migrants. Their stock is perceived by Polish customers as welcomingly universalist on the one hand, but unhelpfully separatist on the other. According to Beata, buying in big supermarkets lets customers 'intermingle with the crowd and forget about differences between people', and the lack of direct confrontation with others, especially staff 'who do not look into your basket', secures privacy and hides accents. As Mirek claimed, 'One can feel normal in a supermarket, everything looks like at home and nobody talks to you'.[10] While the effort to import Polish products is appreciated and the competitive prices sought, it is the ethnic differentiation that the shops display that is the real issue – it is praised for convenience, but it also arouses suspicion and uneasiness. It was noted, for example, that buying Polish food in chain stores does not promote any sense of belonging, and that in these shops the characteristics of Polish taste and lifestyle are lost in the synergy of different cultures, all placed under the common heading 'ethnic foods', fencing this aisle from others. It seems that the Polish customers often feel embarrassed when forced to scour the ethnic sector in the store where many 'outsiders' are grouped together in the search for their national products. In a similar vein, negative responses were also recorded about Polish products being compartmentalized in the South Asian shops, stocked on just two lower shelves or in one fridge freezer. Here though, the issue was not deemed to be about ethnicity specifically. In the eyes of the Polish consumers, the foreign signification of the Asian shop in the host community qualifies the site as 'equal' and blurs the political boundary between Polish and other. As Darek noticed: 'Everybody in this shop is foreign and we all speak broken English, I feel more accepted here than in English shops, and I can always approach the owner and order what I like for the next time'.[11]

Feeling 'equal' in shops A and B, therefore, relates to being foreign in the UK. For some Poles, though, this overt positioning as foreign feels uncomfortable and is rejected; they do not wish to be linked with ethnic shops and prefer to 'disappear into the crowd' devoid of definitive ethnic markers. Instead, 'English' for them signifies both whiteness and the wider society, mainly represented through the chain supermarkets but also in local retail shops run by English owners. Purchasing in such shops articulates the adaptation and confidence of immigrants who, for different reasons, try to avoid affiliation with a collective Polish identity. One of these reasons may be class, although this is rather difficult to prove; these Polish immigrants represent all classes, all doing similar jobs in the UK (there are famous cases of nurses working as cleaners, higher education lecturers being shop assistants), hence selecting them according to typical class parameters (A, B,

---

10   Interview with Mirek (10 June 2007), migrated to London in 2005 aged 38.
11   Interview with Darek (12 January 2007), migrated to London in 2004 aged 40.

C, D) is as yet impossible. Eating habits, of course, also reflect class background (Bourdieu 1984), and this is an area of this research which needs to be investigated further.

If class in a traditional sense has proved too nebulous to pin down so far in this research, a stronger argument can be made pertaining to the skills and education of the Polish immigrants, and their importance as tools facilitating adaptation and settlement. For Poles who speak English and work in office environments, the shift to settlement is often followed by a decreasing number of Polish contacts and increasing consumption of non-Polish products. Such a change in social behaviour among immigrants has been termed as a shift from a collective to an elective (Alba 1990; Portes and Rumbaut 1996) or symbolic (Gans 1979) identity, mostly characteristic of second and third generations for whom ties with co-ethnics are not so meaningful anymore. Although in this study it is the first generation of the post-2004 wave of immigration which has been scrutinized, it can be observed from this one sample at least that fewer Poles are tending to maintain ties with Polish networks, and more are trying to move away from a collective formation of Polishness, a process which has been defined as 'segmented assimilation' (Portes and Zhou 1993; Zhou 1997). Other socio-psychological and sociological studies of networking among Polish immigrants in the UK have also noted this desire for social distance from other Poles, and even go further, suggesting that there is growing resentment among fellow Poles, and that this prevents them from staying in homogenous communities and leads them to choose non-Polish groups of friends, and particularly English employers, who carry a higher status in society (Garapich 2007).

This notion of 'segmented assimilation', however, is not straightforward. For example, while 60 per cent of customers in the study stressed their intentional isolation from other Polish groups, they still maintained a commitment to a Polish lifestyle, meaningfully underpinned by the consumption of Polish food. The socio-economic choices which are made are therefore not necessarily reflected in choices concerning consumption, and particularly the decision to select Polish foodstuffs over non-Polish products, especially those regarded as the most basic elements of diet such as bread, meat, butter, flour, milk and juice which 'cannot be replaced with anything foreign'. Similarly, the all important family celebrations and religious rituals (Catholic baptisms, first communions, weddings) require a Polish way of consumption of which the immigrants are proud. Most of the products bought in Polish shops (C) were to be either consumed at home as part of an everyday diet (cottage cheese, yogurts, smoked sardines, ham, smoked sausage, herring, black pudding, beer, juice, oat porridge, grain) or as the most important ingredients for a Polish party (especially homemade cakes, lean meats and alcoholic spirits). In fact, as was unanimously acknowledged by all the interviewees, it was felt that food needed for meals and festive parties should be authentic and any replacements are not readily approved, even if produced by Polish-orientated companies in the UK. Certain products, like herring, carp, mushroom and meat dumplings, pork bread-crumbed escallops, boiled cabbage, gherkins and grain were defined as the most typical Polish foodstuffs and more meaningful than others for reinstating the sense of belonging and authenticity. As Turgeon and Pastinelli (2002) have observed, groups sharing a collective identity tend to associate their common origin with one symbolic product to enact their own self-definitions and to distinguish themselves from others; for example, clams in Massachusetts, pasties in Michigan, crawfish in Louisiana, or maple syrup in Quebec. Bigos and carp during Christmas were agreed to be those meals which express Polish ethnic identity in the most compelling and distinct way. More importantly, these meals are now cooked by those Poles who used to disregard them at home, with their new location in multicultural London transforming their ethnic significance.

Polish shops do not only sell food, but also provide a wide range of medicines and herbs. These constitute an important part of everyday lifestyles in Poland, but in the UK they also serve as an essential means of self-arranged health care, avoiding the need to engage with the NHS, which is generally regarded as 'too anonymous and detached from the patient'. Taken together, food, medicines, Polish newspapers, magazines and DVDs, and in some cases an adjacent café bar, all contribute to the representation of an external collective identity. Of course, each migrant accesses and uses these facilities and products differently, creating dialectical interplays between the internal and external processes of identity making (see Jenkins 1996). Internally, members of the groups try to differentiate themselves from each other, but externally they transfer this identification onto an objectified collective identity recognized by outsiders. As an example of this, it was noted several times by customers with administration or education jobs, often accompanied by non-Polish friends, that they needed Polish food (and sometimes music) for office parties to impress their non-Polish colleagues or as part of multicultural festivities. Although they did not use the shop's site for personal networking, for them Polish products were still symbolic of a group identity.

This study has demonstrated how powerfully these different venues selling Polish goods reflect and support ethnic identity for the migrants in London. When Polish food is overtly defined as 'other' and labelled as 'ethnic food' in separated aisles of the supermarket, recent Polish migrants generally feel discouraged from participating in this segregation of consumption. This resistance to being pigeon-holed as other, however, still competes with the feeling of pride at being recognized in the host community at all. As further interviews have shown, Poles feel more confident and empowered as citizens if they can find a point of reference with Polish identity, such as Polish food, the Polish press, Polish restaurants and the Polish cultural institutes. On a collective level, the attitude of the customers is tempered by the need to have a positive shared representation in London regardless of individual engagements and even the self-denial of Polish ties. In this sense, Polish shops represent Polishness better than any other entrepreneurial practice by Polish immigrants. As the customers acknowledged, it 'brings something to the community', to the English environment, rather than the Polish population. Being a business owner in particular magnifies the confidence of entrepreneurial Poles and facilitates their integration in the local community. All of the interviewed owners emphasized the fact that they have a growing number of English customers, as if this is a test of their social and economic success: 'they come for Polish sausage, homemade cake, juices, and other natural foodstuffs which they can't find elsewhere'. This pride in the shop's uniqueness is characteristic of Polish customers too, although many refrain from personal involvement in the social networking opportunities potentially available on the site. Depending on the customer's status in the host culture, they can opt for the collective relationship with the shop, underpinned by the idea of a common identity, or they can simply use the shop to sustain a symbolic relationship with their home country. For both groups, however, it is the concept of authenticity – found in the rustic imagery, décor and products in the shops – which is valued most highly.

Conclusions

This chapter has highlighted just how meaningful consumption is to the experiences of recent migrants in the UK. Two particular findings stand out; the significance of the shops as social spaces, and the importance of food to Polish migrants in Britain.

Firstly, this chapter has demonstrated how complex these shops are as identity markers. Different kinds of shops clearly perform different functions, but they all provide the means to resonate with the migrants on distinct levels. Externally they work as an outward symbol of presence in Britain; even those shops which are not exclusively Polish carry Polish signage and advertisements, visible to all who walk by. The internal sites of the shops also have a powerful emotional relevance to the migrants who visit. Polish shops especially offer a familiarity of products and style, and keep the migrants temporally in touch with Poland by following 'real time' seasonally adjusted offers and displays. Perhaps most interesting of all, the various shops also act as sites for social interaction among Polish customers. Here though, the London case-study has mirrored the findings of other research into social networks among recent Polish migrants (see Ryan et al. this volume; Garapich 2007). Participant observation and in-depth interviews have revealed a reluctance to use the shops as places of meaningful social interaction, and have highlighted instead the tendency to take advantage of what the shops offer to enhance social and cultural lives outside of them, rather than a willingness to invest in the shop spaces themselves. It is almost possible to see these shops as sites of anxiety for some – the desire to avoid eye contact and to remain as anonymous as possible. A picture is painted of a fractured group then, a series of individuals uncomfortable with being too closely associated with a more collective Polish identity. This is perhaps overstating the trend; the Polish shops especially do clearly act as important social places, even if just for the opportunity to access the information about work and accommodation displayed in the windows, and speak in Polish to the shopkeeper. The spaces of the Eastern European and South Asian shops are also immensely socially significant for positioning the migrants in their new multicultural contexts. These shops carry products from all over the world, introducing the migrants to foodstuffs that they would probably not otherwise come across. Most importantly, in cities such as Leicester, Derby, Birmingham and London, the shops act as forums of contact with other ethnic groups – an interaction that may not happen in other areas of the migrants' lives such as accommodation, employment and leisure activities.

Ultimately, though, this chapter has shown that it is the food itself which is so important to the migrants; the emotional value of being able to find Polish food is clear in both studies. The Polish products which are particularly meaningful, however, are quite specific. They have to be authentic and appropriately displayed, requiring specialized knowledge of consumption from both the seller and buyer. The shops in Britain cannot replace the most important food sources – homemade food brought back from Poland is still depicted as the most emotionally significant, imbued with the dynamics of close relationships. What they do is supplement these food networks, marking the start of a long process of transferring the homemade, intimate qualities of Polish food to Britain. This research keeps returning to the concept of home, and this is where the Polish shops especially have proved to be so influential. These shops have provided new outlets which offer the possibility of finding an element of home away from Poland, and which, unlike the transnational mechanisms of carrying food back and forth, are firmly located in Britain. They perhaps will not be a determining factor in whether the most recent wave of Polish migrants settle or return, but they have surely made it easier for them to stay.

References

Alba, R. (1990), *Ethnic Identity: The Transformation of White America* (New Haven, CT: Yale University Press).

'Asda Pushes Halal and Polish Ranges' (2007), *Grocer*, 25 August.

Attan, C. (2006), 'Hidden Objects in the World of Cultural Migrants: Significant Objects used by European Migrants to Layer Thoughts and Memories', in Burrell and Panayi (eds).

Bell, D. and Valentine, G. (1997), *Consuming Geographies: We Are Where we Eat* (London: Routledge).

Bentley, A. (1998), 'From Culinary Other to Mainstream America: Meanings and Uses of Southwestem Cuisine', *Southern Folklore* 55:3, 238–52.

Blunt, A. (2007), 'Cultural geographies of Migration: Mobility, Transnationality and Diaspora', *Progress in Human Geography* 31:5, 684–94.

Blunt, A. and Dowling, R. (2006), *Home* (London: Routledge).

Bourdieu, P. (1984), *Distinction: A Social Critique of the Judgement of Taste* (London: Routledge).

Bridge, G. and Smith, A. (2003), 'Guest Editorial: Intimate Encounters: Culture – Economy – Commodity', *Environment and Planning D: Society and Space* 21:3, 257–68.

Burrell, K. (2006), *Moving Lives: Narratives of Nation and Migration among Europeans in Post-war Britain* (Aldershot: Ashgate).

Burrell, K. (2008), 'Materialising the Border: Spaces of Mobility and Material Culture in Migration from Post-Socialist Poland', *Mobilities* 3:3, 331–51.

Burrell, K. and Panayi, P. (eds) (2006), *Histories and Memories: Migrants and their History in Britain* (London: I.B. Tauris).

'Carp Sales Rise to Serve Polish Festive Tastes' (2007), *The Guardian*, 26 November.

Diner, H. (2001), *Hungering for America: Italian, Irish and Jewish Foodways in the Age of Migration* (Cambridge, MA: Harvard University Press).

Gabaccia, D. (2000), *We are What We Eat: Ethnic Food and the Making of Americans* (Cambridge, MA: Harvard University Press).

Gans, H. (1979), 'Symbolic Ethnicity: The Future of Ethnic Groups and Cultures in America', *Ethnic and Racial Studies* 2:1, 1–18.

Garapich, M. (2007), 'Discursive Hostility and Shame – An Exploration into the Everyday Negotiation of Ethnicity among Polish Migrants in London'. Paper presented at 'Three Years On: EU Accession and East European Migration to the UK and Ireland' Symposium, De Montfort University, Leicester, 20–21 April 2007.

Hobsbawn, E. (1991), 'Exile: A Keynote Address. Home: A Place in the World', *Social Research* 58, 65–8.

Jenkins, R. (1996), *Social Identity* (London: Routledge).

Kershen, A. (ed.) (2002), *Food in the Migrant Experience* (Aldershot: Ashgate).

Law, L. (2001), 'Home Cooking: Filipino Women and Geographies of the Senses in Hong Kong', *Ecumene/Cultural Geographies* 8:3, 264–83.

Li, W. (2005), 'Beyond Chinatown, Beyond Enclave: Reconceptualizing Contemporary Chinese Settlements in the United States', *GeoJournal* 64:1, 31–40.

Miller, D. (1998), *A Theory of Shopping* (Cambridge: Polity Press).

Miller, D. (2001), 'Behind Closed Doors', in Miller, D. (ed.).

Miller, D. (ed.) (2001), *Home Possessions: Material Culture behind Closed Doors* (Oxford: Berg).

Money, A. (2007), 'Material Culture and the Living Room: The Appropriation and Use of Goods in Everyday Life', *Journal of Consumer Culture* 7:3, 355–77.

Panayi, P. (2008), *Spicing up Britain: The Multicultural History of British Food* (London: Reaktion).

Parkin, D. (1999), 'Mementoes as Transitional Objects in Human Displacement', *Journal of Material Culture* 4:3, 303–20.

Petridou, A. (2001), 'The Taste of Home', in Daniel Miller (ed.).

Portes, A. and Rumbaut, R. (1996), *Immigrant America: A Portrait* (Berkeley, CA: University of California Press).

Portes, A. and Zhou, M. (1993), 'The New Second Generation: Segmented Assimilation and its Variants', *Annals of the American Academy of Political and Social Science* 530, 74–97.

Puwar, N. (2007), 'Social Cinema Scenes', *Space and Culture* 10:2, 253–70.

Reimer, S. and Leslie, D. (2004), 'Identity, Consumption, and the Home', *Home Cultures* 1:2, 187–208.

'Supermarkets Cater for Polish Pound' (2006), *Financial Times*, 8 November.

Terkenly, S. (1995), 'Home as a Region', *Geographical Review* 85:3, 324–34.

Tolia-Kelly, D. (2004), 'Locating Processes of Identification: Studying the Precipitates of Re-memory through Artefacts in the British Asian home', *Transactions of the Institute of British Geographers* 29:3, 319–24.

Turgeon. L. and Pastinelli, M. (2002), '"Eat the World": Postcolonial Encounters in Quebec City's Ethnic Restaurants', *The Journal of American Folklore*, 115:456, 247–68.

Urry, J. (2007), *Mobilties* (Cambridge, Polity Press).

Walsh, K. (2006), 'British Expatriate Belongings: Mobile Homes and Transnationalism', *Home Cultures* 3:2, 123–44.

Wang, L. and Lo, L. (2007), 'Global Connectivity, Local Consumption, and Chinese Immigrant Experience', *GeoJournal* 68: 2–3, 183–94.

Zhou, M. (1997), 'Segmented Assimilation: Issues, Controversies, and Recent Research on the New Second Generation', *International Migration Review* 31:4, 975–1009.

Conclusion

Polish Migration to the UK After 2004

Kathy Burrell

There are several themes which have emerged from these different chapters on post-accession Polish migration, and four can be singled out as particularly pertinent for understanding the experiences of Polish migrants on the UK, why so many have migrated and what the future holds for this movement.

Poland as a Sending Country

Firstly, most of the chapters point to the fundamental importance of conditions and contexts in Poland for framing contemporary migratory trends. Economic dynamics have been pivotal in pushing people to move away from Poland, and even though many other factors have been at play – crucially the role of the UK in opening its labour market – the chapters paint a picture of Poland as a country which is still experiencing sufficient economic difficulties to make emigration an attractive option for a significant proportion of the population, and young people especially. Svašek's chapter, for example, highlights the importance of economic push factors in the stories that the migrants wanted to tell the local Belfast population. While issues such as high unemployment in key regions are obviously at the heart of this, these chapters allow for a more nuanced understanding of how economic conditions have fuelled this migration. Elrick and Brinkmeier, for example, demonstrate how reliance on low paid agricultural work in rural areas has had such a detrimental effect on livelihoods that it has led to a high level of dependency on pension incomes as a means of financial support for family units. White also illustrates how migration is often a fundamental part of a family's livelihood strategy – an integral mechanism for sustaining incomes and living standards. Leaving can be pushed as much by issues such as not being able to afford a child's bus ticket to school, as it is by unemployment specifically.

The impact of these underlying economic matters runs very deep. White, again, shows the importance of other considerations in family migration, citing wider concerns about children's quality of life – facilities and leisure opportunities – as an influential factor in deciding to move a whole family abroad. The insecurity of available work is also an important issue. In their chapter, Galasińska and Kozłowska demonstrate how damaging aspects of working life in Poland have been for the confidence of their respondents and their belief that they could ever lead a 'normal life' there. The perceived continuation of corruption throughout the economy, and lack of transparency in hiring and firing decisions in particular, appear to be almost as influential as unemployment in pushing people to look abroad for work – at least those without the requisite connections to find the work they want at home.

Many of the chapters have also pointed to just how important it is to place this current migration in its historical context. Poland has a long tradition of emigration; social networks supporting outward migration to a range of destinations are well established and there is a cultural awareness of emigration as a part of Polish history, even if, as Mazierska shows, this is a history which has not been showcased positively in film. During Poland's socialist era, when movement was so heavily politicized, outward migration still flowed, and to some extent current trends can be seen as a continuation and intensification of the migratory patterns established in the 1980s. For a selection of chapters tasked with analysing post-2004 movements, it is striking just how many discuss this historical background.

Poland's recent history is also highly relevant to this migration in other ways too. Galasińska and Kozłowska illustrate how powerful the mindsets of the socialist and post-socialist eras continue to be, demonstrated here by the narratives of recent migrants who are eager to show that they do not desire ostentatious wealth, but are merely striving for a just life and a job which pays them enough to live comfortably. The important notion of a generational identity is discussed here too – the shared experience of socialist to post-socialist transformation among young people in Poland. Datta's chapter also indicates the importance of the socialist era as a social reference point for many migrants. For those who experienced them first hand, the social and cultural norms of the socialist period offer an important bonding opportunity for migrants in their new environment – a common understanding of the past that can be accessed to strengthen social ties in the present. While other post-socialist countries have similar histories, the specificities of Poland's socialist and post-socialist pasts are carried forward in the memories and perceptions of the recent migrants, helping to mark out a shared ethnicity once in the UK.

Migrants' Vulnerability in the UK

A second theme which runs through many of the chapters is the potential vulnerability of these new migrants once they have arrived in the UK. Although this specific migration is often characterized as being comprised of highly skilled and highly mobile young people, well placed to configure their lives across international borders with relative ease, many of the chapters uncover different stories behind this image. Ryan et al., in their chapter, have demonstrated this very effectively with their examples of people who arrived before 2004 without any existing networks to draw upon in London. The mother and daughter who responded to an advertisement for cleaners in a shop window, going back to the unknown man's house with him, offer an important reminder that migration is still a risky business for a great many migrants. Even though EU accession has potentially improved the living and working conditions of Polish migrants, many are still susceptible to exploitation, homelessness and unemployment. Svašek's chapter on Belfast also demonstrates that these recent migrants are vulnerable in other ways too. Although the migrants in her case-study seemed keen to play up the positive links they have made in their new Northern Irish environment, the backdrop of this research acts as a reminder of the dangers that migrants can face in their destinations; the 'Shared History' project this chapter studies was partly conceived as a way of overcoming local hostility to new immigrants. Siara's chapter also hints at a different, less straightforward vulnerability, this time surrounding gender identities and how Polish masculinities especially are perceived by some Polish men to be under threat in the UK. However this is viewed, migration has clearly been socially and culturally unsettling for many migrants.

The 'brain waste' that Fihel and Kaczmarczyk have warned against – the situation of so many highly skilled young migrants working in unskilled employment – is another important indicator that migration has been a difficult experience for a significant number of newcomers. Although this is a well established migration trend, and something particularly pertinent for refugee movements, the failure of a large proportion of the young A8 migrants to develop their skills within the UK economy needs to be taken seriously. Interestingly, it is these issues of vulnerability and skills waste that have inspired much of the more recent filmmaking on emigration in Poland. As Mazierska shows, the cultural discourse of migration in Polish cinema appears to accentuate these difficulties, although the various warnings against migrating have not discouraged people from leaving for the mythical promise of the 'West'.

This vulnerability seems more marked when it is set in the wider context of the social pressures that migration brings. Several chapters illustrate the expectations and optimism that the migrants had for their new lives before they left, and the disapproval that migrants generally have to face at home, either for leaving at all, or for not being sufficiently successful in their migration projects. Measured against these yardsticks, the problems encountered in the UK must be all the more difficult.

Migrants' Positionality in the UK

A further theme has also emerged regarding the lives that the migrants are living in the UK: their ethnic positioning in their new environments. Several chapters have considered how the Polish migrants fit in with the specific ethnic dynamics of their places of settlement, with Svašek's chapter on Belfast illustrating the importance of geography in this matter particularly well. Datta's work on Polish builders draws attention to the performance and maintenance of ethnic boundaries between the migrants and the white British builders they work with, confirming that whiteness is not in itself enough to transcend constructions of ethnic difference. Rabikowska and Burrell also demonstrate the important role that local shops play as sites of multi-ethnic interaction in the everyday lives of the new migrants, facilitating, albeit limited, inter-ethnic communications that may not happen otherwise. By buying from and shopping alongside other local populations – South Asian, Turkish, Russian or other East European – the new migrants can become familiar with the wider population of their immediate areas. Siara's chapter focuses on this matter directly, showing how ethnicity has been highly significant in the discussions that new migrants have been having about their migration experiences. The findings on this issue are instructive. There is no doubt that the diversity of the UK population – very different from Poland which, barring small numbers of minority groups, is still relatively ethnically homogenous – has been surprising for many new migrants, and while there is hostility towards the notion of ethnic diversity among some new migrants, others are very comfortable with this, carving out different inter-ethnic relationships and acquaintances.

At the same time, the chapters have shown that there has been just as much negotiation going on 'within' the Polish population as there has with those outside of it. A key issue in several of the chapters was the level of tension between Polish migrants, and the social distancing that takes place by some Poles from others. Rabikowska and Burrell show this with the somewhat lukewarm embrace of Polish shops as places of social interaction, and Ryan et al. consider this in some depth, highlighting the persistence of the idea that 'Poles abroad don't help each other', and demonstrating particularly the difficulties which have arisen between the post-war population and the recent arrivals. Class is clearly an important fault-line in this new migration, although this should not be surprising. Being Polish on its own, even with this shared history, is not enough to cement bonds with other Polish people – other factors have to come into play too. Gender is another important negotiation point, as Siara shows, highlighting some of the culture clashes among the new migrants on issues of morality, sexuality and gender roles.

Timings

Finally, one of the strongest themes to emerge from these chapters has been the multi-scalar issue of timing – the historical significance of 2004, but also the matter of length of stay for the different migrants. Many of the contributions show the temporal importance of EU accession, with this date marking key changes in migration patterns away from Poland. It seems safe to argue now that May 2004 has been a truly historic moment for Polish-UK migration flows. While there are definite continuities – especially as many Poles had already come to the UK before 2004 – and other key points in time can also be considered just as significant for wider European movements (January and December 2007 especially), the impact that EU accession has had on Polish and UK population dynamics has been immense.

2004, furthermore, has not only led to an increase in the scale of migration; it also appears to have signalled a change in the type of migration which is taking place. While some of the chapters suggest that the prevailing discourses of migration, in the most recent films and in migrant narratives, still seem to depict an image of open-ended flexible mobility, rather than a more fixed permanent emigration, other chapters indicate that this post-accession migration *is* displaying signs of being temporally different from previous movements from Poland and from migration to other countries in Europe. As part of what Elrick and Brinkmeier describe as a formalized and visible migration movement, there is strong potential for a large proportion of these migrants to stay – to settle in the UK and only go back to Poland periodically for visits. This issue of settlement is extremely difficult to gauge; at what point is it possible to describe migrants as settled, and in this era of fast communications and low cost travel is settlement still even a realistic endgame of migration? These chapters, however, show that the signs of settlement are there. Not all migrants are young and single, looking to return after a year or so. As White and Ryan et al. illustrate in their chapters, families especially become closely integrated into their local areas, and have a real need to invest in their UK situations as much as possible, economically, socially and emotionally. Rabikowska and Burrell show that the ability to buy Polish goods helps migrants to feel at home in the UK, and Ryan et al. also illustrate the wealth of networks that the migrants can access once they have arrived, helping to embed them more easily in their new environments.

It is important to remember, however, that this migration is still in its infancy. Some of these signs of settlement could still be reversed. With an economic slowdown affecting the UK economy, the employment prospects for Polish migrants could be reduced substantially, especially for those working in the construction, retail and hospitality sectors. As sterling weakens, a strengthening złoty may also tempt more people back. If a large proportion of migrants return, their markers on the UK landscape will lessen; there will be fewer shops, less press coverage, fewer local 'shared history' projects. The economic climate could have an enormous impact on the transnational mobility of these migrants too; if any of the low cost airlines which fly between Poland and the UK collapse, or at least withdraw from some of these routes, many migrants may find themselves having to reassess their migration plans, no longer able to rely on cheap and quick travel between the two countries, and without flights to and from their closest regional airports. This issue is clearly not yet resolved, although the evidence does suggest that at least some of these migrants will stay.

A Brief Agenda for Future Research

While a substantial amount of research has now been undertaken on this migration, there is enormous scope for future work. Perhaps the most pressing need is for more research on a local scale within the UK, assessing the different dynamics of different locales. How have those towns and villages unused to international migration reacted to this influx? How have they changed as a result? The issue of hostility also needs to be addressed more closely. How have these Polish, and other A8 migrants, been received across the country? How relevant is their 'whiteness' in this context? Finally, there is potential for more research engaging with different social and cultural aspects of this migration and migrants' lives. What can be learnt about church attendance and religious ties, for example? What about homosexuality – have recent attitudes and policies towards homosexuality fuelled the emigration of gay Poles? What about relations between different A8 and East European workers – how significant is nationality? And what about age and older migrants? According to the Home Office, seven per cent of registered A8 workers are over 44 (Home Office 2008). Research into the UK's A8 immigration has many more questions to address.

Reference

Home Office UK Border Agency, Department for Work and Pensions, HM Revenue and Customs and Communities and Local Government (2008), *Accession Monitoring Report May 2004–March 2008*. <http://www.ukba.homeoffice. gov.uk/sitecontent/documents/aboutus/reports/accession_monitoring_report/ report15/may04mar08.pdf?view=Binary>, accessed 3 June 2008.

Index